TRIBAL
DEVELOPMENT
IN INDIA

Thank you for choosing a SAGE product!
If you have any comment, observation or feedback,
I would like to personally hear from you.

Please write to me at **contactceo@sagepub.in**

Vivek Mehra, Managing Director and CEO, SAGE India.

TRIBAL
DEVELOPMENT
IN INDIA

Challenges and Prospects in Tribal Education

Edited by
R. R. PATIL

Los Angeles | London | New Delhi
Singapore | Washington DC | Melbourne

First published in 2020 by

 SAGE Publications India Pvt Ltd
B1/I-1 Mohan Cooperative Industrial Area
Mathura Road, New Delhi 110 044, India
www.sagepub.in

SAGE Publications Inc
2455 Teller Road
Thousand Oaks, California 91320, USA

SAGE Publications Ltd
1 Oliver's Yard, 55 City Road
London EC1Y 1SP, United Kingdom

SAGE Publications Asia-Pacific Pte Ltd
18 Cross Street #10-10/11/12
China Square Central
Singapore 048423

Published by Vivek Mehra for SAGE Publications India Pvt Ltd and typeset in 10.5/13 pt Bembo by AG Infographics, Delhi.

Library of Congress Cataloging-in-Publication Data

Name: Patil, R. R., editor.
Title: Tribal development in India : challenges and prospects in tribal education / edited by R.R. Patil.
Description: New Delhi, India; Thousand Oaks, California : SAGE Publishing, 2020. | Includes bibliographical references and index.
Identifiers: LCCN 2020018752 | ISBN 9789353884277 (hardback) | ISBN 9789353884284 (epub) | ISBN 9789353884291 (ebook)
Subjects: LCSH: India—Scheduled tribes—Education. | Ashram schools—India. | Educational sociology—India.
Classification: LCC LC4097.I4 T735 2020 | DDC 370.954—dc23
LC record available at https://lccn.loc.gov/2020018752

ISBN: 978-93-5388-427-7 (HB)

SAGE Team: Abhijit Baroi, Shipra Pant, Madhurima Thapa and Rajinder Kaur

Contents

Part I. Issues of Tribal Education in India

Part II. Innovation and Best Practices in Tribal Education

Part III. Rethinking Policy and Planning for Tribal Education

List of Figures

List of Tables

List of Abbreviations

ADB	Asian Development Bank
ATCs	Additional Tribal Commissioners
ATLC	Academy of Tribal Languages and Culture
BIE	Bureau of Indian Education
CSR	Corporate social responsibility
DBT	Direct Benefit Transfer
DFID	Department for International Development
DISE	District Information System for Education
DRD	Division of Research and Development
EMRS	Eklavya Model Residential School
FGD	Focus group discussion
GER	Gross enrolment ratio
GHS	Girls high schools
GRs	Government resolutions
HM	Headmistress
HSA	Higher secondary school assistants
HSC	Higher secondary certificate
IAS	Indian Administrative Service
ICDS	Integrated Child Development Scheme
ICT	Information and communications technology
IGMMRS	Indira Gandhi Memorial Model Residential School
ISO	International Organization for Standardization
ITDA	Integrated Tribal Development Agency
JMI	Jamia Millia Islamia
KGBV	Kasturba Gandhi Balika Vidyalaya
MADA	Modified Area Development Approach
MDM	Midday meal
MGLI	Mahatma Gandhi Labour Institute
MHRD	Ministry Human Resource Development
MIS	Management information system

MoTA	Ministry of Tribal Affairs
MRS	Model residential school
NAS	National Achievement Survey
NCERT	National Council of Educational Research and Training
NCF	National Curriculum Framework
NGO	Non-governmental organization
NIEPA	National Institute of Educational Planning and Administration
NPE	National Policy on Education
PIL	Public interest litigation
POA	Programme of Action
PTG	Primitive Tribal Group
PVTGs	Particularly Vulnerable Tribal Groups
PWD	Public Works Department
RTE	Right to Education
SC	Scheduled Castes
SDM	Sub-divisional magistrate
SS	Superintendent of school
SSA	Sarva Shiksha Abhiyan
SSD	ST & SC Development
SSLC	Secondary school leaving certificate
ST	Scheduled Tribes
TDD	Tribal Development Department
TISS	Tata Institute of Social Sciences
TRTI	Tribal Research and Training Institute
TSP	Tribal sub-plan
U-DISE	Unified District Information System for Education
UEE	Universal elementary education
UNDP	United Nations Development Programme
UNICEF	United Nations Children's Fund
UTs	Union territories

Foreword

Professor R. R. Patil's edited book titled *Tribal Development in India: Challenges and Prospects in Tribal Education* is a timely and much-needed contribution to the field of education in general and of tribal people in particular. The book brings together a good and valuable collection of chapters on the conditions of ashram schools and larger issues of education of tribal people in various parts of India. The chapters included in the book bring insightful ideas combined with analytical rigour and good scholarship.

The studies on tribes hold geographical isolation, cultural differences and exploitative practices as key to low human development and educational backwardness of the tribal population in India. The poor access to school and communication facilities, poverty and lack of awareness among parents about the importance of education are cited as other factors leading to their poor educational status.

In order to minimize exclusion and marginalization of the Scheduled Tribes (STs) in general and their integration into the mainstream formal education in particular, the Government of India has taken up various measures. These include legislations, policies, schemes and programmes. To provide better access to formal schooling system, the Ministry of Tribal Affairs under the central scheme of 'Establishment of Ashram Schools in Tribal Sub-Plan Areas' expanded the system of ashram schools for the ST students in remote and tribal areas in 1990–1991. The ministry also introduced a scheme of 'Eklavya' Model Residential Schools for the ST students in 1998 to provide quality middle and high-level education to the ST students in remote areas.

However, despite such efforts by the government, the educational backwardness of the tribal population remains a major problem in India. As per the estimate in 2016, the tribal communities' gross enrolment ratio (GER) in elementary education stood at 104.0 which was higher than the national average of 96.9. However, the GER at secondary education fell to 72.2 and furthermore to 38.8 at senior secondary as compared to the national average GER of 78.5 and 54.2, respectively. This shows that the school dropout rate is very high after Class 10.

The literature on education of tribes shows that very limited data are available at the national level on the number of tribal ashram schools/residential schools in India. And so is the case with the condition of these schools and their contribution to the educational development of tribal children. In short, there is little information and understanding on the overall outcome of ashram school scheme in India. These and other related facts are neither available at the state nor at the national level.

It is important to note that the ashram schools in India have been in news for varied wrong reasons such as mismanagement of government funds, lack of administration, poor quality of infrastructure, overcrowding of children, lack of toilet facilities, unhygienic living condition, poor quality of mid-day meal, lack of safety and security, sexual harassment of tribal girl students and death of tribal students due to various reasons. This state of affair of ashram schools has posed a new challenge to the government in the implementation of ashram school scheme in the tribal areas.

Such state of ashram schools has been troubling educators and government officials. The collection of chapters in the book attempts to address these and other related issues required to bring changes within the ashram schooling system and evolve comprehensive policy framework for educating tribal children in India. Although ashram schooling system has been able to create a minuscule middle class from amid tribal population, it has not benefitted a large number of tribal population due to its systematic issues and challenges. What adds value to the book is the fact that there is no national-level study on education of tribes in India in general and ashram schooling system in particular.

The book holds out huge promise for those interested in elevating educational status of tribals in India. It provides significant information as also crucial insights about issues of governance in tribal education. These will be extremely valuable to governments' efforts to improve the educational status of tribal population in India for social justice and inclusive growth.

Virginius Xaxa
Former Deputy Director,
Tata Institute of Social Sciences,
Guwahati Campus, Assam, India

Acknowledgements

The compilation of various chapters for this book was a time-consuming and tedious process. It is needless to mention that this difficult task was made relatively easier by the help I received from a number of individuals. I would also like to convey my sincere gratitude to Professor M. M. Salunkhe, Vice-Chancellor, Bharati Vidyapeeth Deemed University, Pune; Mr A. P. Siddiqui, Registrar, Jamia Millia Islamia, New Delhi; and Dr B. T. Lawani, Associate Professor (Retired) for all their support and encouragement to organize a seminar at Bharati Vidyapeeth Deemed University, Pune. My sincere thanks are also due to all the contributors of this book, namely Alkha Dileep, Bibekananda Nayak, Bipin Jojo, Buveneswari Suriyan, Chipemmi Awung Shang, D. K. Panmand, Dhaneswar Bhoi, Gomati Bodra Hembrom, Mrityunjay K. Singh, Muhammed Shafi C. T., Naresh Kumar, Noorjahan Kannanjeri, P. C. Jena, Pradyumna Bag, R. Vasundhara Mohan, Rajashri Tikhe, S. N. Tripathy, Saumya Deol, Saurabh Katiyar, Sonal Shivagunde and Vetukuri P. S. Raju for their revised and timely submission of chapters for the publication. I would like to convey my special thanks to Abhijit Baroi of SAGE for the constant support he extended during the publication of this book. Finally, the usual disclaimer applies.

Introduction

R. R. Patil

The tribal population is one of the most marginalized groups in India. Majority of them live under chronic poverty and are facing acute food insecurity. In comparison to any other social group, tribals' representation is very low in Human Development Index and high in Human Poverty Index of the country. The studies have shown that tribals lag behind in all developmental spheres, that is, social, economic, educational and political. The tribal population is numerically small in numbers but represents enormous diversity in respect of size, language, identity, colour, physical features, etc. They are largely away from the mainstream society but spread over large areas of the country. India is home to single largest tribal population in the world. Here, more than 20 states and 2 union territories (UTs) have the highest concentration of Scheduled Tribe (ST) population. There are 834 tribal communities that form 8.6 per cent, that is, 103 million of total population in India (Census of India 2011). It has a higher decadal population growth rate of 23.66 per cent from Census 2001 to Census 2011, as compared to the decadal growth rate of 17.69 per cent for the entire population. Total 89.97 per cent of the ST population resides in rural areas and 10.3 per cent lives in urban areas. The sex ratio is more balanced at 990 females per 1,000 males as against 940 females per 1,000 males for the entire population (Census of India 2011).

As per available data, it has been observed that more than half of the ST population is concentrated in Central India in states such as Madhya Pradesh (14.69%), Maharashtra (10.08%), Odisha (9.2%), Rajasthan (8.86%), Gujarat (8.55%), Jharkhand (8.29%), Chhattisgarh (7.5%) and Andhra Pradesh (5.7%). The areas with distinct ST population in the northeast are Assam (3.72%), Meghalaya (2.45%), Nagaland (1.64%), Tripura (1.12%), Mizoram (0.99%), Arunachal Pradesh (0.91%), Manipur (0.87%) and Sikkim (0.20%). All these states also have an ST population that is higher than the country's average (8.61%). Two states of Punjab and Haryana and three UTs of Delhi, Puducherry and Chandigarh have no ST population as no STs are notified.

It is also observed that more than two-thirds (67.17%) of the ST population of the country is concentrated only in the seven states of Madhya Pradesh, Maharashtra, Odisha, Gujarat, Rajasthan, Jharkhand and Chhattisgarh. Among states, Mizoram (94.43%) has the highest proportion of STs in its population, and Uttar Pradesh (0.57%) has the lowest population. Among UTs, Lakshadweep (94.8%) has the highest proportion of STs and Daman and Diu (6.32%) has the lowest proportion (Statistics Division, Ministry of Tribal Affairs, 2013).

The literacy rate for the ST population is 58.96 per cent as against the literacy rate of 72.99 per cent for the entire population, which shows a gap of 14.03 percentage points (Census of India 2011). The Constitution of India, through Article 46, mandates the protection of the educational and economic interests of the weaker sections of the society, including STs, and their protection from social injustice and all forms of exploitation. To cater to their educational needs, tribal ashram schools and Eklavya Model Residential Schools (EMRSs) have been established in tribal areas to improve both accessibility and quality of education for STs.

ASHRAM SCHOOL PROGRAMME FOR TRIBAL EDUCATION: GENESIS, DESIGN AND IMPLEMENTATION IN INDIA

The schooling system in India follows various patterns such as ashram and non-ashram, residential and non-residential and day boarding or day scholar, and the learning environment among these schools are different. Residential schools are meant for those schools where children are living within the hostel care system by providing facilities related to their learning and development besides food, nutrition and medical care. However, schools not able to provide such facilities for children are called non-residential schools or day care schools where students come only for the purpose of learning.

Residential school system is a complex process for tribal children to transit out of residential care for living outside the family care for the upliftment of physical, mental and educational development. India is a home for such children all over the world where almost 12.44 million are parentless, mostly living a life under residential care school system. The opportunities provided by the residential care school system is formal instruction, curricular and extra co-curricular activities which offer a chance to connect with other students for working under one roof. The students living in the residential care school system are being socialized by providing formal instructions of knowledge and a good relationship between students and teachers which motivates them for paying attention to their studies. The residential school system is a means for developing good sense of humour, good habits, personality and moral values through exchanging of ideas which would be a basis for improving good leadership qualities among tribal children.

Basically, the concept of ashram schools is drawn from the traditional Indian values of schooling in *Gurukulas,* where the guru or the teacher and the pupils lived together with close interaction. It was based on the Gandhian philosophy of basic education and assisted the students in the development of a complete personality and in enhancing their potential and capabilities. Thakkar Bapa, social reformer and Gandhian, was deeply moved by the condition of tribals when he went for famine relief efforts in the areas of Dohad and Zalod in Gujarat. For the upliftment of the tribals and under the inspiration of Mahatma Gandhi, he initiated educational activities for the tribal children under the name of ashram schools in western India, presently known as Gujarat and Maharashtra. The first tribal ashram school was set-up in a tribal village known as Mirakhedi in the 1920s. These ashram schools were residential in nature and motivated tribal children towards education and improvement of social status. So historically, tribal ashram schools were found in pre-independence India and Thakkar Bapa and some Christian missionaries had started residential schools exclusively for civilizing tribes and educational development of tribals in India. Moreover, apart from the *gurukula* schooling system, the genesis of residential schools/ashram schools also lies in the colonial rule. As part of larger civilization agenda, the British government had recommended and established residential schools for tribal education and integration of tribals in pre-independence India (Start Committee, 1928; Symington Committee, 1938; Wandrekar Committee, 1947).

After independence, during the First Five-Year Plan, an attempt was undertaken by the Government of India to establish ashram schools in tribal areas. However, it was during the Third Five-Year Plan onwards that the momentum in opening ashram schools picked up. Its establishment was conceptualized as a direct intervention to address the socio-economic and geographical inequities of the tribal population through education (Mishra and Dhir 2005).

The centrally sponsored scheme of Establishment of ashram schools in Tribal Sub-Plan Areas, operational in tribal sub-plan (TSP) states/ UT administration, relates to the construction of ashram schools for the primary, middle, secondary and senior secondary stages of education, including the upgradation of existing ashram schools. Its objective is to increase education among the STs through the provision of education with residential facilities in an environment conducive to learning. Under the scheme, 100 per cent funding assistance is provided for the establishment of ashram schools, that is, school buildings, hostels, kitchens and staff quarters for girls in TSP areas. In addition, 100 per cent funding for establishment of ashram schools for boys in only the TSP areas of the Naxal-affected districts identified by the Ministry of Home Affairs from time to time is provided. All other ashram schools for boys in TSP states are funded on a 50:50 basis. One hundred per cent funding is provided to UTs. Financial assistance is also given on a 50:50 basis for other non-recurring items of expenditure, that is, purchase of equipment, furniture and furnishing, purchase of few sets of books for a small library for use of inmates of hostel, etc. The ashram schools should be completed within a period of two years from the date of release of the central assistance. For the extension of existing ashram schools, a period of the construction of 12 months is granted (Ministry of Tribal Affairs, 2008).

The scheme is in operation since 1990–1991. Presently, as part of the rationalization of schemes by the Ministry of Tribal Affairs (MoTA), the scheme for ashram schools has been subsumed under the schemes of Special Central Assistance to Tribal Sub-Scheme and Grants under Article 275(1) of the Constitution from 2018–2019, with the rationale that a substantive part of these schemes is expended on promotion of education among tribals including the construction of hostels and schools (Ministry of Tribal Affairs, 2019). As on 9 August 2017, funds were provided by the MoTA for the construction of 1,205 ashram schools across the country for creation of about 115,500 seats. Besides, 3,272 ashram schools were also opened by various state governments (Ministry of Tribal Affairs 2019).

The government has implemented several programmes and schemes under different constitutional provisions to promote education among tribals. In order to improve educational status of the tribals, the Government of India has introduced innovative schemes for the promotion of education among STs through the establishment of ashram schools in the TSP areas in India. The ashram school programme has been implemented by the Government of India since 1975 to promote education among tribal children to uplift their educational status and mainstream them into the society. The establishment of ashram schools in TSP areas is one of the initiatives to provide free education among tribals with residential facilities. The tribal children are studying in ashram schools (residential schools) care system and are being educated by providing residential facilities and formal schooling to promote education among them. But at the same time, the ashram schooling system also addresses tribal poverty and hunger in the country apart from bringing them together to avail formal schooling facilities and acquiring formal education for tribals' educational development.

At present, more than 4,000 ashram schools are functioning in the TSP areas of India. These schools are one of the important means to promote education among tribals. Although exact data are not available related to ashram schools' contribution in educational development of tribals in India, the trends in key indicators over the last few years indicate gradual improvement in terms of improved access to school, increased enrolment rate, reduced dropout rate and higher transition rate among STs. Similarly, the learning outcomes, measured through National Achievement Survey (NAS) by National Council of Educational Research and Training (NCERT) also indicate improvement in the educational achievement levels of the STs in India. Similarly, it has been observed that because of ashram schools, the upward social mobility became possible among tribals and a new middle class has emerged among them. This new middle class is largely working in the service sector, academics, politics and non-governmental organization (NGO) sector of India. They are the representative of backward tribals and torchbearer of contemporary tribal rights movement. However, despite positive contribution of ashram schools, the gap in educational indicators between the STs and general population still exists at the national level. It also reflects that the educational status of STs is still very low in India, and there is much to be done at both policy and implementation levels for improving the educational status of STs in general and school education of STs in particular.

Regarding school education, currently, a total of 251,309,665 students are enrolled from Class 1 to Class 12 in 1,535,610 schools across the country. Among these, 32,632 (3.03%) schools are managed by the Department of Tribal/Social Welfare, and 4,815,284 ST students (19% of total enrolment) are enrolled across different schooling systems, and 48 per cent among them are females. Exact data are not available regarding the total number of ashram schools and enrolment. The trends in key indicators over the last few years reflect gradual improvement in terms of improved access, increased enrolment, reduced dropout rate and higher transition rate among the STs. The learning outcomes, measured through NAS by the NCERT, also indicate improvement in achievement levels of the STs. However, the gap in indicators between the STs and national average reflects that there is much to be done at both policy and implementation levels for improving school education of the STs, with a special focus on ashram schools.

ASHRAM SCHOOLS IN INDIA: VARIATIONS IN IMPLEMENTATION AND KEY ISSUES

The nature and implementation of ashram schools programme in India varies from state to state. The MoTA guideline provides flexibility to the state governments to adopt suitable operational mechanism leading to the state-to-state variations in the model of implementation of the ashram school programme in India. For instance, in the states such as Maharashtra, Rajasthan, Jharkhand and northeastern states, the ashram school programme is directly implemented by the Tribal Development Department (TDD) of the state. However, some schools are also run and managed through voluntary organizations/NGOs under the scheme 'Grant-in-aid to Voluntary and Other Organizations' for running ashram schools. In Gujarat, Odisha, Andhra Pradesh, Telangana and Karnataka, autonomous societies/bodies have been formed by the TDD of respective states to run the ashram school programme. These societies manage ashram schools, EMRS and hostels. Further, it undertakes curricular and co-curricular activities, teachers' training, staff development activities and overall monitoring and supervision of ashram schools. In addition to the aforementioned two models, Gujarat state also has its own unique public–private partnership model (PPP) for running the ashram schools or sponsoring specific activities such as meals, teachers' training, and distribution of books and uniforms across the school. Madhya Pradesh, Chhattisgarh and West Bengal have adopted a mixed model, wherein the schools are established and funded by the TDD, but the overall management and administration is entrusted to the Department of School Education.

The studies on 'Ashram Schools Scheme' in India reveal that promoting education among the STs through the ashram school scheme is neither aligned with aims and objectives of ashram schools nor to the needs of ST learners. The literature on ashram schools has found that there are major gaps in the implementation of ashram schools in India. These gaps in the implementation of ashram schools due to several systemic as well as circumstantial factors have been contributing to malfunctioning and ineffectiveness of ashram schools. It is essential to understand these gaps and issues of ashram schools from policy, design, planning, funding, management, administration, implementation, monitoring and evaluation perspective for effective service delivery for the STs' education in India.

Overview of literature on ashram schools reveals that there are multidimensional issues of ashram schools in India. These issues of ashram schools are more particularly related to lack of infrastructural facilities, poor condition of classrooms, lack of desks, leakage and seepage on walls, lack of bedding, unavailability/ill-maintained toilets and bathrooms that leads to open defecation, and it further leads to snake and scorpion bites, issues of safety and security of ST girl students, issues of molestation and sexual harassment of ST girl students, recurrent incidents of death, poor health and nutritional condition, low quality and inadequate quantity of food, serving food in unhygienic condition due to lack of dining space, lack of nutritious meals leading to malnutrition, anaemia among ST students, prevalence of communicable diseases, alien curriculum, lack of multilingual education, lack of vocational education, lack of sports facilities and sports promotion, lack of co-curricular activities, lack of qualified teachers, low motivation and high absenteeism among teachers, low quality of education, lack of science and computer laboratory, high dropout and low scholastic performance of ST students, corruption, mismanagement and lack of governance, weak monitoring mechanism, lack of single integrated policy for governance and management of ashram schools, etc. (Bagai and Nundy 2009; Sharma and Sujatha 1983). Thus, the overall condition of ashram schools shows several gaps and lacunae. These gaps and limitations have posed a serious challenge to the implementation of the ashram school scheme in India.

It is in this context that the present book on *Tribal Development in India: Challenges and Prospects in Tribal Education* has been designed and chapters have been invited on various themes. The chapters in this book cover various aspects related to the status of ashram schools and tribal educational development in India. Similarly, the book covers the various aspects and themes related to the status of tribal education in India. There are 19 chapters in this book divided into 3 major parts, namely 'Issues of Tribal Education in India', 'Innovation and Best Practices in Tribal Education' and 'Rethinking Policy and Planning for Tribal Education'.

PART I. ISSUES OF TRIBAL EDUCATION IN INDIA

This part majorly illustrates multidimensional issues of tribal education in India. It consists of 9 chapters representing issues of tribal education in India with special reference to tribal ashram schools. Here, the contributors have highlighted issues of tribal education and ashram schools from different perspectives and described the state of tribal education in India. Chapter 1, 'Sociological Analysis of Educational Experiences of Adivasi Children', by Gomati Bodra Hembrom highlights that education is considered to be the most potent instrument of social transformation and means of national development. It helps to achieve individual well-being, economic independence and empowerment. Any economy, whether it is developing or developed, can flourish only when human resources have been developed to the fullest extent. But despite substantial progress in literacy and education in the post-independence period, and the numerous programmes that have been launched by the government for the expansion of basic educational facilities among tribals, the overall picture remains bleak due to numerous obstacles. Till today, the accessibility and affordability of education for a big proportion of the tribal population have remained a major issue. This chapter attempts to understand and situate unequal schooling and the lack of cultural capital among the tribals due to poverty and exploitation by the dominant mainstream community, which leads to the reproduction of disadvantage and educational stratification. Schooling as a discourse is not a monolithic construct. Pierre Bourdieu will be the principle theoretical anchor in this endeavour. It also looks at the crisis involving residential schools or *ashramshalas* for the tribals. Finally, this chapter also seeks to assess the role of the state in defining an educational policy for tribals, which failed miserably to combat the problem of illiteracy and ensuring better learning outcomes in central and eastern India. It is based on secondary data derived on the basis of a review of various sources and case studies.

Chapter 2, 'Ethnocentrism in Education: Effects of Hidden Curriculum on Tribal Students', by Pradyumna Bag highlights that studies show that geographical isolation, cultural differences and defective integration with the formal education system are major factors behind educational backwardness among the tribals in India. Poor access to school, meagre infrastructure and shoddy management further weaken their opportunity to access quality education. The present education system wilfully oversees the difficulties encountered by the tribal children, especially in residential schools which add on to their poor educational performance. Prejudice and discrimination are inbuilt in the educational system that breaks the already delicate morale of the tribal students resulting in low enrolment and high dropout rates. Tribal culture, ecology and economy find no place in the curriculum; in fact, the pedagogic practice abhors tribal culture, language and their life world. Irrelevant and inappropriate curriculum, low level of motivation, untrained and substandard teachers and the personal idiosyncrasies of the upper-caste, middle-class teachers contribute to their low scholastic performances. However, poor academic performance and low educational attainment have been invariably attributed to individual students or the community rather than deficiencies in the education system. In addition to the formal curriculum, educational institutions impart the principle of ethical values, beliefs and attitudes informally, which is known as hidden curriculum. Ashram schools blithely ignored the unpleasant consequences of the hidden curriculum and make no attempt to acknowledge it, let alone address its unintended consequences. The study attempts to examine the impact of the hidden curriculum on scholastic performance. It also explores how these implicit curricular practices encourage cultural assimilation and how it influences their self-worth and motivation.

Chapter 3, 'Status of Tribal Ashram Schools in Maharashtra', by Bipin Jojo highlights that the Government of India has taken a number of steps to not only strengthen the social, economic and political life but also develop the educational status of the STs. The National Policy on Education (NPE), which was envisaged in 1986, and the Programme of Action (POA), as modified in 1992, provide a remarkable way for the development of tribal education. The provisions of NPE (POA) 1992 have incorporated special provisions for the STs to give priority in opening primary schools, especially in tribal areas and the construction of school buildings to be undertaken in those areas. On the grounds of sociocultural milieu, the NPE 1992 focuses that the curricula and instructional materials would be made in tribal languages at the initial stages which could be switched over to the regional language in a later stage. The NPE has space for educated and promising ST youths who can be encouraged and trained to take up teaching in tribal areas. This policy has also instructed to open residential schools and ashram schools on a large scale. Several commissions were set up to evaluate the condition of education and its quality. These commissions provided different strategies for the tribals to access education at the school level. Emphasis was given to open schools and residential schools for the tribal children through the ashram school scheme. Quantitative expansion of education was, in time, achieved in numbers by opening more ashram schools, establishing hostels, etc. Due attention was paid for the qualitative improvement of tribal education by providing remedial coaching, counselling and guidance in vocations. However, all the provisions have proved insufficient in addressing the needs of tribals, and running of ashram schools in tribal areas is in serious jeopardy. Most of the children are struggling to access schools, and those who do manage to gain access fail to get quality education.

Chapter 4, 'Language as Instrument of Exclusion and Inclusion in Tribal Educational Development', by Saumya Deol and R. R. Patil highlights that language is a potential instrument of integration and inclusion in society, being linked to the appropriation of cultural capital in the society. The state, in order to assimilate all into the larger dominant society, imposes dominant knowledge on deprived and indigenous tribal people. The agenda of imposition of dominant knowledge is basically to bring under fold the population or tribal group which are not part of the mainstream society, which should result in imbibing cultural values of the dominant society through mainstream language. Majority of the tribal ashram schools, run by the government, are using mainstream language as the medium of instruction. However, some of the tribal ashram schools have been experimenting with the medium of instruction for their students, with states such as Maharashtra and Odisha undertaking translation of standard study material into local languages of the tribals, though this practice is not a pan-India phenomenon for tribal education development. It is in this context that the chapter studies the different components and characteristics of language and different theories which support the particular aspect of language relating to imparting knowledge in local language. Similarly, the chapter also studies the medium of instruction in ashram schools and how it plays a role in social exclusion and inclusion. The chapter is based on secondary literature and highlights the findings of the study and suggests appropriate and relevant measures to make the tribal ashram schools more inclusionary from the policy perspective.

Chapter 5, 'Living Conditions, Learning Status and Educational Performance of Tribal Students', by Dhaneswar Bhoi highlights that the idea of ashram schools was initiated by the Government of India with the recommendation of Dhebar Committee in 1962. The focus of the ashram school scheme was on concentrating on the sparingly populated interior backward areas where the normal schools are not available. This scheme is to provide residential schools for the STs including Primitive Tribal Groups (PTGs) in an environment conducive to learning to increase the literacy rate among the tribal students and to bring them at par with non-tribal population of the country (Joshi 1980; Mishra and Dhir 2005). The provision of ashram schools started in 1972 as part of the national scheme, but this scheme has been in operation in Maharashtra since 1952. It was initially implemented through voluntary organizations and was later taken over by the state government in 1972–1973 where the students get boarding and lodging facilities to promote education among the STs. The local children attend the school as day scholars. The aim of the ashram schools was envisaged as a direct intervention to tackle the socio-economic and geographical inequalities of tribal population and providing educational opportunity to them. Later, the ashram schools aimed to reduce the absenteeism, wastage and stagnation of education at the primary level.

Chapter 6, 'Insights on High Dropout Rates among Katkari Tribal Children in Maharashtra', by S. N. Tripathy highlights that the total ST population in the country, according to the Census 2011, was 8.6 per cent of the total population of the country. The states of Madhya Pradesh, Chhattisgarh, Maharashtra, Odisha, Jharkhand and Gujarat have more than half of the total tribal population of our country. In recent years, there has been a tremendous increase in the rate of distress migration among the STs, which has an adverse effect on their socio-economic and educational well-being. Presented in two sections, the chapter briefly evaluates a macro picture of Katkari tribe of Raigad (Maharashtra) in Section 1 and examines the problems encountered in the attainment of education by Katkari children in the *ashramshalas* because of distress migration, at the micro level in Section 2. Based on both primary and secondary sources of data, the chapter suggests that the migrant tribal children who are out of school need to be included in the schooling system and be treated equally with all other children.

Chapter 7, 'Education of Scheduled Tribes in Residential Schools in Manipur', by Chipemmi Awung Shang and R. R. Patil highlights that education plays a significant role in the overall development of tribal communities. Education among tribals is given utmost priority. In order to enhance education among tribal children, the MoTA and Ministry of Human Resource Development had introduced special educational schemes and residential facilities such as ashram schools, EMRSs, Kasturba Gandhi Balika Vidyalaya and Jawahar Navodaya Vidyalayas, and various vocational training centres were opened in remote tribal areas. Apart from the government-run residential schools, many NGOs, missionary organizations and private agencies also run the residential schools for educational improvement of ST children. The chapter examines the current status of residential schools run by the government, NGOs and Christian missionary organizations in the northeast region with special reference to Ukhrul and Churachandpur districts of Manipur. In its methodology, descriptive research design is used to describe the present status of residential schools as accurately as possible. Simple random sampling is applied to select the sample in the selected area. The sample size consists of 14 residential schools from two tribal-inhabited districts of Manipur, and interview schedule was conducted with all the selected residential schools' principals. The findings discuss in detail the existing status of residential/boarding schools including infrastructural facilities, administration and staff management, teaching and learning pattern, curriculum, extracurricular activities and tribal sub-group representation comprising of age, gender enrolment and dropout rates. In addition, the study enlightens the best practices of residential/boarding schools. Furthermore, it explains various issues and challenges of residential schools located in selected districts and thus draw some recommendation for optimum benefit for ST children studying in these residential schools.

Chapter 8, 'Status and Functioning of Tribal Ashram Schools', by Prakash Chandra Jena highlights that the Indian society is a complex mix of diverse cultures, people, beliefs and languages. These complexity and richness give the Indian society a unique appearance of a very vibrant and colourful cultural country. The Constitution of India assigns special status to the STs, and realizing that the STs are one of the most deprived and marginalized groups with respect to education, a host of programmes and measures have been initiated by the Government of India since independence. NEP, 1986, and POA, 1992, recognized the heterogeneity and diversity of the tribal areas, besides underlining the importance of instruction through the mother tongue and the need for preparing teaching–learning materials in the tribal languages, upgradation of some tribal ashram schools and establishment of more tribal ashram schools in TSP areas. Therefore, there is a need to study the existing status and functioning of tribal ashram schools in the light of the educational development of the STs in India.

Chapter 9, 'Educating Tribal Children: Issues', by R. Vasundhara Mohan highlights that India is home to the single largest tribal population in the world. The 834 tribal communities form 8.6 per cent, that is, 103 million of the total population (Census of India 2011). The ST population represents one of the most marginalized, economically impoverished and educationally backward groups in India. For ameliorating the situation of the STs, education, among others, is the key driving factor. Issues and prospects of their education are embedded in the larger socio–economic, pscyho–social and cultural factors and hence cannot be analysed in isolation. As a result, although policy initiatives and programmes, including setting up of ashram schools in tribal habitations, have been undertaken since 1956, the overall educational development has lagged behind when compared to the mainstream population. The ashram school programme, implemented since 1975, has significantly contributed to this positive trend in literacy level among the STs since these were the only schools accessible to the tribal population until the 1990s (8.53% in 1961 to 58.96% in 2011, as per Census of India 2011). Access to other schools increased after the universalization of primary and elementary education was achieved post 2001. Among these, 32,632 (3.03%) schools are managed by Department of Tribal/Social Welfare, and 4,815,284

ST students (19% of total enrolment) are enrolled across different schooling systems, and 48 per cent among them are females. Exact data are not available regarding the total number of ashram school and enrolment (UIDSE 2017). The trends in key indicators over the last few years reflect gradual improvement in terms of improved access, increased enrolment, reduced dropout rate and higher transition rate among the STs. The learning outcomes, measured through NAS by the NCERT, also indicate improvement in achievement levels of the STs. However, the gap in indicators between the STs and national average reflects that there is much to be done at both policy and implementation levels for improving school education of the STs.

PART II. INNOVATION AND BEST PRACTICES IN TRIBAL EDUCATION

In this part, total four chapters are representing innovations and best practices in tribal education. The chapters mainly highlight unique practices of ashram schools such as balancing indigenous and modern knowledge, codebook for quality management, centralized kitchen for meals distribution and effective management of service delivery for tribal education. Chapter 10, 'Balancing Indigenous Culture and Formal Education: Ashram Schools in Kerala', by Noorjahan Kannanjeri and Alkha Dileep highlights that Wayanad district of Kerala has the highest number of tribes (45.41%, 136,062) and is thus known as the homeland of various tribal communities in Kerala (Census of India 2001). The tribes were the original inhabitants of the Wayanad region. The literacy rate of the district has increased to 89.32 per cent in 2011 from 85.25 per cent in 2001, where male literacy remains on the higher side compared to that of females. The ST population of the district is 151,443, which represents 31.24 per cent of the total ST population (Census of India 2011). Although government and other non-profit organizations have been taking a lot of efforts to promote and develop the educational status of tribes, the situation is changing very slowly. ashram schools also aim at the empowerment of tribal students through education by preserving their tribal culture. Wayanad has two ashram schools run by government and a few run by private trusts and NGOs. But how far these ashram schools are able to achieve the objectives of empowering the tribal students by maintaining their indigenous culture is a matter of question. This is an attempt to study the ashram schools run by the government to explore how the system is contributing to improving the educational status of tribal students as well as preserving their culture. This is a qualitative study in which the case study method is the chief research strategy. The study observed that ashram schools are the major factor in increasing the literacy rate of the tribal students as any other residential school, but it is not achieving other major objectives including building a healthy relationship between teachers and students, imparting formal education by preserving their culture, training them in vocational skills, etc.

Chapter 11, 'Ashram School Codebook: Framework for Qualitative Management', by Rajashri Tikhe and Buveneswari Suriyan highlights that ashram schools in India have a long history since the pre-independence period. They were initially started by Gandhian disciples like Thakkar Bapa with the objective of imparting formal education along with craft-oriented vocational education to help children lead self-reliant, self-sufficient lives in future. In the decade of 1953–64, state governments provided support to 12 ashram schools started by private trusts. Total 40 government ashram schools were started in 1972–1973. Initially, these schools were in the jurisdiction of the Education Department of the State Government. In 1975–1976, they came under the administration of the Social Welfare Department, followed by the TDD taking the charge, as it came into existence in 1984. Initially, codes of Secondary Schools of Education Department were followed for administering the residential tribal ashram schools. In 1995, considering the different nature of residential schools, especially started for children of the STs, the need for independent guidelines or codebook was identified by the TDD. The committee for drafting guidelines was formed in 1995, which comprised of officers from TDD and representatives of private-aided ashram school. The draft submitted by this committee was issued on 14 September 2001 as *Ashram School Codebook*. The need for revising this draft was again felt in 2003 because of the gaps observed in the draft as well as the changed policies of the government. The committee to revise the *Ashram School Codebook* was formed in 2003. The committee was chaired by the commissioner, TDD, and it mainly consisted of the authorities in Education

Department, namely Director (Primary and Secondary) Education, Director, MSCERT, Director, MPSP, along with the representatives of private-aided ashram school. The revised codebook came into action in 2006–2007. At present, the same version of the codebook (2005) is being used in tribal residential ashram schools.

Chapter 12, 'Centralized Kitchen: Providing Nutritious and Hygienic Meals to Tribal Students', by Saurabh Katiyar highlights that ashram schools were set up in the state of Maharashtra to reduce the inequity of tribal population and reduce the gap between tribal and other populations, and it was identified that education plays a big role in bridging this gap. Ashram schools were set up in Maharashtra with this objective, and under its code, ashram schools must have a residential facility, provision of nutritious meals, school dress, books, bedding, potable drinking water, toilets and other education materials, which are provided free of cost to the students. Centralized kitchens were established with the vision of providing nutritious and hygienic food to the school while being able to manage operations from a single point of control, including receiving, storage, preparation, delivery and maintenance of material that is required for the feeding operation. One of the biggest advantages of centralized kitchens has been its ability to provide hygienically prepared standardized high-quality food.

Chapter 13, 'Indira Gandhi Memorial Model Residential School (IGMMRS) in Malappuram, Kerala: A Case Study', by Muhammed Shafi C. T. and R. R. Patil highlights that out of the total 25 EMRSs in Kerala, IGMMRS in Malappuram district plays an inexplicable role in the pursuit of educational upliftment of Cholanaikkar and Kattunaikkar, which are Particularly Vulnerable Tribal Groups (PVTGs) in Kerala. This chapter examines the role of IGMMRS in educational upliftment of Cholanaikkar and Kattunaikkar students in the state and the changes thereof in the tribes. A case study research method is adopted for this chapter. As the secondary source is very less, the study primarily relies on survey and interview of headmistress (HM), superintendent of school (SS) and representatives of students. Some newspaper reports are used as a secondary source. Being a senior secondary school, IGMMRS provides education, food, clothes, books and other study materials along with accommodation, free of cost to all students admitted there from

Classes 1 to 12. The school is run in its own building and has separate hostel buildings for boys and girls. All classrooms are well furnished with good furniture and teaching–learning materials on par with private schools. Some classrooms are equipped with state–of–the–art facilities such as a projector and computer. The entire school premises are under CCTV surveillance, observable from office rooms of HM and SS. The school looks after the health requirements of students who are encouraged to utilize their evenings in sports activities of their will. The study will be helpful to understand the loopholes in the project, if any, and can provide details of a successful ashram school as a model to be replicated in other states. To enhance the standard of school and make the students more competitive, qualified and sincere, teachers should be appointed and up–to–date amenities should be made available at par with private institutes.

PART III. RETHINKING POLICY AND PLANNING FOR TRIBAL EDUCATION

This part mainly emphasizes on the nature of policy and planning for tribal education and suggested measures to bring out reform and reformulate policy for tribal education in India. There are total six chapters in this part that mainly highlight policy redesign and reform in tribal education, micro-planning for ashram schools and innovative methods for financing tribal education.

Chapter 14, 'Revisiting Policies and Need for Reform in Tribal Education', by Sonal Shivagunde highlights that the establishment of residential ashram schools across the country through TSP in 1990–1991 was a landmark step for providing access to education for tribals. Efforts for safeguarding their right to education through policies and regulations were made from time to time since independence, to create an enabling environment for accelerating their development. The Constitution of India; recommendations of Kothari Commission, 1964; NPE, 1986; POA, 1992; NCF, 2005; National Tribal Policy, 2006; Draft NEP, 2016, etc., have special provisions and clauses regarding education of tribals at school and higher education. Effective implementation of these policies was expected to gradually facilitate mainstreaming of the ST students, empowering them to avail deserving opportunities for development. However, literature review and evaluation studies conducted in various states indicate that the education delivery at ashram schools is neither conforming to the policy recommendations and not up to the mark.

It is in this context, author emphasizes, that there is a need to revisit the policies and regulations for school education with special reference to education of tribals and the socio-economic transition of tribal communities. The ashram school guideline itself is very generic, with state governments mandated to refine it further. Except for three states, the guidelines have not been strengthened. The RTE Act, 2009, does not incorporate specific provisions for residential schools. DISE, the single largest database for schools in India, does not capture variables related to ashram schools. There is a lack of clarity about regulatory mechanisms for taking corrective actions in the case of anomalies at school level. Hence, reforms are pertinent to address these critical gaps and ensure delivery of quality education for the tribal learners, without which the development of 104 million (Census of India 2011) tribals in India is at stake.

Chapter 15, 'Rethinking Policy Design and Reforms for Tribal Education in India', by Naresh Kumar highlights that the tribal population has always remained at the margins of the mainstream society. Recent decades have witnessed initiatives from the government to bring them into the fold of the development processes. Most of the development initiatives have remained controversial as they supposedly disturbed tribals' relation with nature. One of the major concerns which the policymakers are addressing is their educational development, and this has remained staggered. The chapter takes a relook into the status of tribal education in India with a socio-anthropological perspective to argue that development initiatives have seriously undermined the essence of their culture and therefore failed to address the core issues of tribal education. Tribal being the marginalized group undergo huge dropout, especially the tribal girls. Their underperformance in the educational field results in different marginalities. Governments from time to time have acknowledged the poor educational performance of tribals. Apart from mainstream schooling, alternative school provisions have facilitated their educational growth. For example, programmes such as Eklavya and Ashram schools, which are running in a few states, have remained limitedly successful as against the policy objectives. Even the promotion of tribal non-residential schools has failed to perform. The chapter strongly urges that the policy initiatives have undermined the socio-anthropological perspectives for planning the education of tribal children. There is a need to look into their development through sociological perspectives rather than purely development steered by economic agenda.

Chapter 16, 'Inclusive Education Policy for Tribal Ashram Schools in Odisha', by Bibekananda Nayak highlights that education is a powerful instrument for the development of society and community in particular. In all societies, it is an accepted fact that educational achievement and economic success are closely interlinked. When we consider the progress of the tribes, in particular, education becomes an effective medium of growth and empowerment. The tribes are deprived of the accessibility to the modern education system because of ethnocentric attitude towards habitat and government negligence. Tribal residential schools or ashram schools have been relevant in uplifting tribal education. These schools are governed under the Tribal Welfare Department. Therefore, it is necessary to impart the most appropriate tribal education specifically designed to suit the demands, aspirations and capabilities of the tribes. The educational policies, provision and programmes concerning the tribal population must be enforced properly. The issues such as illiteracy, enrolment, girls' education, diet, social exclusion, teacher and student ratio and the inclusion of tribes in the modern education system need to be prioritized.

Chapter 17, 'Ashram Schools and Education of Tribal Children in India: A Policy Perspective', by Mrityunjay K. Singh highlights that ashram schools were started to bring about the educational development of the tribal children in line with the Nehruvian Panchsheel policy which emphasized the development of the tribals along their original genius. In the evolution of tribal schools in India, Mahatma Gandhi played a key role and his Nai Taleem emphasized indigenous models in imparting education which made productive work at the centre of decolonized education. This chapter is based on a review of various research papers on ashram schools in India. The methodology adopted is both a survey of secondary literature and primary data from fieldwork in Jharkhand. The study finds that the literacy rate of tribal continues to be low in the country, and this is because still, the medium of instruction is not in their mother tongue. Ashram schools removed Adivasi children from the environment of their homes and communities, preventing them from learning the hundreds of traditional knowledge and skills that formed the basis of self-sufficient, largely subsistence economies. These schools suffer from a lack of proper infrastructure as well as quality teachers and teaching. Some of the key recommendations are that ashram schools should not remove tribal children from their culture and the indigenous models need to be developed to teach tribal children in their mother tongue using more and more oral traditions. The education needs to be sensitive to the culture of tribals, and pedagogy needs to incorporate a tribal way of life in primary education and appoint teachers from tribal communities to remove the cultural gap between the teacher and the student. Ashram schools must promote respect for the local traditions of the tribals which enhances their self-esteem and empowers them.

Chapter 18, 'Government Ashram School: Micro-planning', by D. K. Panmand highlights that the scheme called 'Ashram Shala Group' started in 1972–1973. There are 502 government ashramshalas under TDD. In these ashramshalas, 206,163 tribal students are taking education in which 105,558 are boys and 105,605 are girls. The scheme was started according to the local conditions. Initially, 20 ashram schools had been started, and there was an increase in the number of ashram schools, step by step, and now there are 552 ashram schools. Due to fewer numbers of students and due to some other reasons, some ashram schools have been merged, and now there are as many as 502 government ashram schools that are in operation. Due to continued education services provided to the tribals, today there are a lot of highly educated people in the tribal family. Their former outlook has changed. Therefore, running an ashram school in a traditional way is not acceptable. The author emphasizes that the adoption of modern educational technology in government ashram schools is mandatory to make ashram schools suitable for the demand of the contemporary society. TDD has the potential for innovation, but there is a need for just words, inspiration, policy, execution and persistence. Thus, to make government ashram schools more advanced and sustainable than the other formal schools, it is very necessary to prepare a micro-planning plan for each ashram school.

Chapter 19, 'Financing Tribal Education in India', by Vetukuri P.S. Raju highlights that education is the pre-eminent device for socio-economic, political and cultural transformation. At all times, societies from different social backgrounds have been interested to undergo the avenues of knowledge. Tribal education and its liberating power were needed much more by the Indian society due to geographical disad-vantage, redundant age-old customs, 'superstitions' and rustic traditions of the past. Tribal education in independent India progressed at a low pace and was unable to reach the target of fulfilling universality. The trials of making Indian tribes literate seems to be an uphill task, as trib-als representing the socially challenged sections—landless agricultural labourers and unlettered masses—could not send their children to schools due to lack of awareness and access. The state has organized a wide range of self-evolved strategies and transforming mechanisms for reaching the unreached tribal children largely to bring issues of tribal education into public discourse through a number of innovative programmes attempting and making a crucial paradigm shift from sub-alternity to social respectability. This chapter focuses on the financing of an innovative scheme offered to the tribal children belonging to the underprivileged sections of the society by the Government of India—centrally sponsored scheme of Establishment of ashram schools under Sub-Plan States/UTs—for the construction of ashram schools for the primary, middle, secondary and senior secondary stages of education as well as upgradation of existing ashram schools for ST boys and girls. The chapter systematically analyses the financing pattern of ashram schools since 1990–1991. It also highlights the interstate disparities in effective utilization of available funds under the scheme, and its impact and impression on the school life of tribal children in the school educa-tion, leading into making some impressive hallmarks in the education of tribes in India.

The chapters in this book call attention to the urgent need to recon-sider the approaches towards tribal development in general and tribal education in particular. The book unfolds that though government has taken initiatives in a planned manner for the development of the STs in India, at the implementation level, schemes and programmes pertaining to tribal development suffer from administrative and governance issues and thus make government intervention ineffective. Specifically talking about the ashram school scheme, if made free from systematic and circumstantial issues, it can contribute a lot for tribal development in India. However, the role and contribution of government, policymakers, administrators, voluntary organizations, tribal parents and local community are equally essential for effective implementation and sustenance of the ashram school scheme in India.

REFERENCES

Bagai, S., and N. Nundy. 2009. *Tribal Education: A Fine Balance*. Mumbai: Dasra.

Census of India. 2001. *District Total Tribal Population*. Available at https://mahades.maharashtra.gov.in/files/report/CensusReport.pdf

————. 2011. *PCA Maharashtra 2011*. Available at http://pibmumbai.gov.in/English/PDF/E2013_PR798.PDF

Joshi, S. D. 1980. 'Educational Problems of Scheduled Castes and Scheduled Tribes of Baroda District'. In *Third Survey of Research in Education*, edited by M. B. Buch, 143–144. New Delhi: NCERT.

Ministry of Tribal Affairs, 2008. *Centrally Sponsored Scheme of Establishment of Ashram Schools In Tribal Sub-Plan Areas*. Government of India. Available at https://tribal.nic.in/writereaddata/Schemes/AshramSchoolGuideline.pdf (accessed on April, 2008).

————. 2019. 'Guidelines for Programme/Activities under Special Central Assistance to Tribal Sub Scheme during 2019-20 and onwards'. Government of India. (Retrieved from https://tribal.nic.in/DivisionsFiles/sg/Guidelinesof SCA-TSS17092019.pdf)

Mishra, B. C., and A. Dhir. 2005. *Ashram School in India: Problems and Prospects*. New Delhi: Discovery Publishing House.

Sharma, G. D., and K. Sujatha. 1983. *Educating Tribals—An In-depth Analysis of Ashram Schools*. New Delhi: NIEPA.

UDISE. 2017. *Secondary Dashboard: Unified District Information System for Education*. National Institute of Education Planning and Administration. New Delhi (Retrieved from http://udise.schooleduinfo.in/dashboard/Secondary#/)

PART I

Issues of Tribal Education in India

Chapter 1

Sociological Analysis of Educational Experiences of Adivasi Children

Gomati Bodra Hembrom

Education is considered to be the most potent instrument of social transformation and means of national development. It helps to achieve individual well-being, economic independence and empowerment. Any economy, whether it is lower-middle income or high-income countries, can flourish only when human resources have been developed to the fullest extent. But despite substantial progress in literacy and education in post-independence period as well as numerous programmes being launched by the Indian government for the expansion of basic educational facilities among tribals, the overall picture remains bleak due to numerous obstacles. Till today, the accessibility and affordability of education for a big proportion of tribal population have remained a major issue. This chapter attempts to understand and situate unequal schooling, lack of cultural capital among the tribals due to poverty and exploitation by the dominant mainstream community, which leads to reproduction of disadvantage and educational stratification. Schooling as a discourse is not a monolithic construct. Pierre Bourdieu will be the principle theoretical anchor in this endeavour. It also looks at the crisis involving residential schools or *ashramshalas* for tribals. Finally, this chapter also seeks to assess the role of state in defining an educational policy for tribals, which failed miserably to combat the problem of illiteracy, and ensuring better learning outcomes in central and eastern India. The present chapter is based on secondary data derived on the basis of review of various sources and case studies.

Inequality in education is the major concern in Indian society, jeopardizing any effort at universalizing education, as large sections of the society including the Adivasis remain disadvantaged and marginalized. It is the reflection of the structural inequalities embedded in Indian social system. The structural inequalities have implications for discriminatory education as they determine access to valued resources. The social hierarchy creates its own layers in the educational system with the Adivasis and Dalits at the margins. The skewed educational opportunities clearly mark the crisis in education system.

On the other hand, education is one of the basic vehicles of social mobility. Here, by education, we are referring to the formal education and the system that tries to universalize the education. Dr B. R. Ambedkar considered education as the agent of breaking the caste hierarchies and domination. Likewise, education plays a crucial role in imparting knowledge to the marginalized people that makes them aware of their rights and opportunities. The political consciousness and the aspiration for power come through education and thus lies the importance of education.

UNEQUAL SCHOOLING AND TRIBES IN INDIA

The persistence of tremendous inequalities in education access, pretension, performance and outcome between an oppressed section such as the Dalits and the Adivasis, and rest of society has laid bare the huge gap between the promise and reality of state-sponsored education. To understand the operation of the education system in an unequal and hierarchal society, it must be located in the larger context of the structure and ideologies of power and domination, and of the political economy. Dominant ideology and interest which in contemporary India are predominantly routed in caste, class and patriarchy which have got articulated through the state and largely determine the course of educational development, change and expansion in India. They have impinged upon the structure, content and process of education in socially significant ways making it a complex political and ideological mediator. The caste and class ideology and structural processes have a close relationship with the educational structure of schooling in post-independence India. The dominant cultural, social and economic values, both Brahminical and capitalist of the ruling classes, are deeply embedded in the hierarchal design of the institution, making it most significant source of inequality the various ramification to this dominance and mechanism through which educational stratification serves these dominant and influential caste, class and political influence and serves the interest of the oppressed. Both external and internal structural features and internal hegemonic processes act as mediator of hierarchy and inequality. Apart from sustaining, consolidating and perpetuating the historical condition of educational advantage and disadvantage, educational policy and practice has led to new division and hierarchy that breed new difficulties. The social historic roots of modern educational structure lie in the colonial period but it reflected the power and educational needs of the colonizers. It was the sole powerful model on the educational scenario having affectively destroyed the indigenous system. The British evolved a new educational system that seems to rest on the traditional social order. The issue of which social, political forces, with what ideology that shape the post-independence system has not received much attention in the post-independence period of political discourse that was mainly dominated by national development, nation building and nationalism, but education came to be identified as a master instrument of change and development. The development agenda cast in Western liberal ideology was that of Nehruvian modernity and Nehru called for the resolutionization of education to fulfil it. The dominant characteristic of the national paradigm were: massive industrialization growth of science and technology in the service of an industrial civilization, the creation of a scientific and rational temper and instilling the values of the secularism, liberty, equal opportunity and justice. Its chief proponents were the new social elites. The metropolitan, Western educated upper and middle classes, the intelligence predominantly all upper caste that had benefitted from the colonial system. They were the architects of the new national educational system. All these symbolize the ideological roots of modern educational system.

There is a clear-cut hierarchal stratification of the educational structure. All existing schools can be broadly classified into four-tiered pyramidal hierarchy. This hierarchal school system ranges from the exclusive, elitist public school that caters to the top of the social hierarchy to the impoverished rural school that caters exclusively to the bottom, namely the overwhelmingly poor Scheduled Caste/Scheduled Tribe (SC/ST) section. The internal structure and the culture of the colonial model of schooling have remained unchanged. Whole-day school, unconducive time span of vacation and compulsory attendance have served as deterrent factors in household dependent on children for domestic work or other productive work to supplement household earning. The fundamentally economic situations, life aims and social circumstances of different strata households have been given due cognizance in selection of structure. Culturally, in education, the norms of attendance, discipline, homework, tests and exams, cognitively ethnocentric demands of concentration, comprehension, relating to mastering what is being taught are all problematic. The crucial factor of the content of education, the curriculum itself, a tool of cultural dominance and hegemony has an alienating and intimidating impact. Overall, the education structure has been particularly ill-suited to develop the vast reservoir of the rural sector. The few years of primary education are useful to gain the label as educated, however, it is not adequate for meaningful learning or preparation for gainful employment. For the children who succeed beyond the primary level, absence of middle or higher school in the vicinity puts limit to their motivation and aspiration. Public educational facilities at this level remain highly restricted till today. Vocational training which could be of some use to them has remained a grossly neglected area.

According to Geeta Nambissan (2000a), the National Curriculum Framework (NCF) for school education has reiterated the need to provide for equal opportunity to all, not only in access but in the conditions of successes. It specifically raises the concern of educational deprivation of communities such as the SCs (Dalits) and STs (Adivasis). The NCF is of interest because the quality of schooling is an important factor in the educational backwardness of poor and marginalized groups. Both the large magnitude of discontinuation from school, particularly in the early years of schooling when poor children are usually too young to work, and the citing of 'lack of interest in education' as a significant reason for dropout from school has drawn attention to the curriculum and pedagogic practices that shape the educational experiences of children. Curricular and pedagogic concerns in the NCF, however, fail to be adequately informed by an understanding of the specific context of educational deprivation, particularly where the economically and socially vulnerable communities such as the Dalits and the Adivasis are concerned. For instance, it is important to recognize that these communities were historically deprived of education because of the isolation, exploitation and stereotypes of 'cultural backwardness' of the Adivasis. That these factors may continue to be relevant to the educational experiences of these communities today has largely been ignored.

Special constitutional provisions, policies and programmes in post-independence India were directed towards the economic and educational development of the Adivasis. However, the situation of these communities today is one of economic marginalization, social vulnerability and educational backwardness. A significant proportion of the population belonging to these communities lives below the poverty line in rural India. Literacy levels in these communities are extremely low and the Adivasis are increasingly witnessing the breakdown of their traditional economic and social institutions as well as the marginalization of their cultures. For these communities, poverty (and the phenomenon of children's work) is still a major deterrent to enrolment of their children in schools. The educational experiences of Adivasi children are influenced by the larger context of social marginalization of these communities. On the other hand, curriculum, language of educational transaction and the hidden curriculum of teacher attitudes are all related to unequal schooling. The NCF pronouncements regarding equal opportunity in education disregard the concrete educational realities that children from these communities actually encounter in schools. On the other hand, the assumption by the NCF that non-formal and alternate structures of schooling will meet the educational needs of these children suggests that they are unlikely to be assured of 'equality of access or conditions of success'.

The question arises that what kind of learning conditions Adivasi children, often first-generation learners, first encounter as they enter school. Schooling in the relatively backward villages and remote Adivasi regions is generally characterized by poor physical infrastructure, lack of basic amenities, as well as less than the adequate number of teachers. Dilapidated buildings, leaking roofs and mud floors appear quite common in schools and provide a depressing atmosphere for children. Teaching aids, apart from the blackboard (or what usually passes for a blackboard), are relatively absent. The conditions of the schools can be quite appalling as seen in Sainath's reference to a school in an Adivasi village in Odisha 'now being used to stock tendu leaves and corn'. Teacher absenteeism as well as non-functioning schools is also a feature of the more backward regions and, in particular, the Adivasi areas. A government report observes that a number of schools, especially in the tribal areas, had remained closed for certain periods of time and in a number of cases these schools had not functioned since the beginning of the academic year. Almost a decade later, Sainath finds a similar if not worse situation in the Adivasi villages in Odisha. This was mainly because 'A majority of these teachers do not stay in the village and belong to the dominant castes, displaying a distinctive negative attitude towards the education of tribal children. Teachers rarely relate to the knowledge base of children and their community' (Nambissan 2000a).

As members of Adivasi communities, children often find that their languages and cultures are other than that which is officially the 'standard' or considered 'mainstream' in schools. This has important implications for the educational experiences of children from these communities. Today, there is a considerable body of research that shows that the exclusion of minority tribal cultures from schools adversely affects the sense of self and identity of children, their motivation in school, as well as the very process of learning. In relation to language, special emphasis is placed on the importance of 'home languages' in primary education, not only as bridges between home and school but also in that they facilitate the development of conceptual and linguistic abilities of children, and hence the process of learning. However, despite policy pronouncements to the contrary, schools in the predominantly Adivasi areas mainly use the regional language as medium of instruction in schools, with the exception of Adivasi pockets in the north-east of the country. It is hence not surprising that non-comprehension is seen as an important reason for the poor performance of Adivasi children in schools.

In addition are derogatory attitudes to the languages of the Adivasis that stem from prevailing stereotypes of these communities as 'backward' and 'uncultured'. Nambissan (1994) suggests that the exclusion of tribal languages from school as well as negative teacher attitudes to what are usually referred to as 'tribal dialects' could be partly responsible for lack of interest of children in their studies, poor performance and ultimately dropout from schools. The NCF as well as other policy documents emphasize the need to incorporate the culture of the Adivasis into school curriculum, primarily to integrate Adivasi children into the school and reduce their alienation from the content of education. However, schools in predominantly Adivasi areas continue to follow the centrally prescribed curriculum that reflects 'mainstream culture'. Official curriculum barely acknowledges the existence of Adivasi communities, despite the fact that they form a significant proportion of the population especially at the district and local level in many states in the country. On the other hand, these communities, when represented in the textbook, are portrayed largely in subservient roles in accordance with what is perceived as their traditionally low position in the social hierarchy (Nambissan 1996, 2000a). Jharkhand government's decision to take up National Council of Educational Research and Training syllabus is also problematic as it will never take into account the geo-political, social and cultural significance of this region.

Classroom culture in the context of the hidden curriculum of social discrimination as reflected in teacher attitudes, classroom interaction and peer culture, teachers and school heads tend to relate the poor performance of Adivasi children to their social backgrounds: ethnic status, apathetic attitudes of parents, the fact that parents prefer to make children work, as well as their lack of ability and basic intelligence. Geeta Nambissan (2000b) suggests that for Adivasi children, classroom processes are likely to be pervaded by discriminatory attitudes and practices that stem from the position of these communities in the larger social structure. And how these processes deeply affect the educational experiences of children and deny them access to education of quality and learning with dignity. The exclusion of children's language and culture from the medium and content of school knowledge, as well as messages of inferiority that are conveyed to them through the hidden curriculum, are critical factors that are likely to adversely affect children's motivation to learn and their interest in their studies. Also, there is the lack of sensitivity of schools to the economic and social realities that children experience in their daily lives. The fact that schools have failed to provide adequate academic support to Adivasi children, a majority of whom come from non-literate and poorly educated homes, is also a factor that is usually ignored. On the other hand, the rapid expansion of 'para teacher schools' points to the possible institutionalization of inferior systems of education within the formal school system.

CULTURAL CAPITAL AND EDUCATION AMONG TRIBES IN INDIA

Pierre Bourdieu (1973) developed a distinctive cultural explanation for achievement and the role of education in society. Cultural capital theory is influenced by Marxism. Bourdieu argues that the education system is biased in favour of the culture of dominant social classes; it devalues the knowledge and skills of the working class. He refers to possession of the dominant culture as cultural capital because, via the educational system, it can be translated into wealth and power. Cultural capital is not evenly distributed throughout the class structure and this largely accounts for class differences in educational attainment. Students with upper class/caste backgrounds have a built-in advantage because they have been socialized into the dominant culture. Rajagopalachari (1955) stated that how religious scripts and epics play an important role in shaping values and ideas. According to him, 'Great minds have been formed and nourished and touched to heroic deeds by the Ramayana and Mahabharat. In most Indian homes, children formally learnt these immortal stories as they learnt their mother tongue at the mother's knee. Such traditions of learning are not there in tribal households'. Bourdieu claims that the success of all school education depends fundamentally on the education previously accomplished in the early years of life. Education in school merely builds on this basis; it does not start from the scratch but assumes prior skills and knowledge. Children from the dominant classes have internalized these skills and knowledge in the preschool years. According to Bourdieu, the major role of the educational system is cultural reproduction. This does not involve the transmission of the culture of society as a whole, but instead the reproduction of the culture of dominant classes. These groups have the power to impose meaning and to impose them as legitimate. They are able to define their own culture as worthy of being sought and possessed, and to establish it as the basis for knowledge in the educational system. Traditionally, tribals were skilled cultivators and forest dwellers. They have good knowledge about the medicinal herbs in the forest. For example, only 15 years back, the Birhors of Hazaribagh (Jharkhand) were the principle suppliers of herbal medicines, but now their main occupation is begging. They are totally addicted to *gutka* (tobacco) and speak mainly Hindi and sing Hindi cinema songs. Tribals have rich cultural traditions of art, dance, music, handicrafts, etc., but the educational policy has been unable to treat them as a part of the mainstream education system. Moreover, there is a crisis in the tribal society due to the historical processes of marginalization that the traditional educational centres like youth dormitories have lost their significance which led to a lacuna. The Adivasis have little influence in the power dynamics and power struggle in polity and economy, which have its resultant influence on teaching–learning process. At the same time, the agents of school, such as teachers, are influenced by the structure and identity of the actors such as parents and teachers. The tribes don't have representation in the school governing committees and the dominant voice of the non-tribal group directly results in the poor participation and performance of tribal students. So there is a need of inclusion of the tribals in the control and decision-making process of school functioning which can benefit the tribal kids from the schooling process.

SOCIAL REPRODUCTION OF DISADVANTAGE AMONG TRIBES

Anthropologist Tarak Chandra Das in his presidential address of Indian Science Congress in 1941 criticized the colonial educational policy stating, 'Education is perhaps rightly claimed as the panacea of all evils that befall mankind. But people differ in its definition, and naturally it has different types. There is one kind of education which uplifts an individual morally and intellectually and makes him/her fit for the struggle for existence. There is another kind of education which is intended for the exploitation of the so-called educated. There is a third type of education which the enthusiast in their zeal for ameliorating

the condition of the poor and the ill-fated impose upon them without considering their necessity or capacity. We have neither time nor
inclination to discuss this point here but suffice it to say that much
labour and public money have been squandered in imparting education which neither suits the people nor helps them to put a morsel of
food into their mouth'. He gives the examples of two tribal schools in
the north-east in which they teach Meithei and little bit of arithmetic,
which the students managed to forget within a few months after their
departure from the school. According to him, it is difficult to understand how high school education will help Manipuri agriculture or
textile industry. The employments at the disposal of the state are very
limited and the students who pass out of these schools every year will
increase the number of unemployed as they no longer think of going
back to their fields. During the first few years, they will be idolized by
the community but this will soon pass away when they will be looked
upon as parasites and it is not impossible that they will be a source
of trouble to the state. The adoption of the mass education system
has represented a shift from mass exclusion to mass inclusion which
is incredibly weak and highly discriminatory. And tribal children are
being made victims of this highly unjust, alienating and dehumanizing
system. Educational deprivation, failure and low achievement for the
oppressed sections are thus inbuilt in the system. Therefore, there is
a continued effective exclusion or the achievement of low levels of
education, which do not necessarily reflect learning. This achievement
level is an overall poor qualification in the labour market. With levels of
learning officially declared to be a minimum level for the disadvantaged,
there is a further dilution in their learning. In contrast, the privileged
are scaling newer heights of elitism in education. The situation of
disadvantaged thus will not only persist, but there will be an increase
in the relative gap between advantaged and disadvantaged in terms of
both quantity and quality of education. The inevitable, therefore, has
happened, low education levels have not been much consequent in
raising the status of the oppressed and with growing jobs ceiling, the
pool of educated employed is expanding rapidly. R. Guha (2007) in
his analysis of Naxalite problem in tribal areas clearly states that the
teenage tribal boys who have joined Salwa Judum for much the same
reason as other boys have previously joined the Naxalites. Educated

just enough to harbour certain disenchantment for labouring in field and forest, but not enough to be absorbed with honour in the modern economy. This clearly reflects the tragedy of tribal education. On the positive side, education for those who have been able to secure it has fetched dignity and self-respect. The achievement has been of immense symbolic value in itself. It has led to class-based social stratification among the tribals. On the other hand, the psychological, intellectual and cultural consequences are damaging. At the psychological level, unequal schooling and failure marks put on these children create a range of negative impacts such as low self-esteem, low motivation, a low aspiration which in turn serves to instil fear and dislike for schooling. Education backwardness dominates reality but contrary to the general assumption and belief, it is backwardness kept alive by the system itself. It would be futile to expect otherwise that a hierarchal system would function as a harbinger of equal opportunity.

RESIDENTIAL SCHOOLS—CRISIS OR SOLUTIONS

Tribal residential schools in India are known as *ashramshalas*. These schools represent an innovation and are different from the general type of day primary schools (Zila Parishad, or district board schools) seen in rural India. In ashram schools, tribal pupils are provided free boarding facilities, together with free school uniforms, textbooks and other learning materials. These schools are expected to impart elementary education in areas which are remote and sparsely populated and where, on account of the geographical spread of the numerous hamlets, single-teacher schools cannot be established. ashram schools were also originally conceived with a view to providing training in vocational trades and in agricultural and animal husbandry skills, thus promoting the integrated development of a complex of villages. Ashram schools are being established under the direct control of the government in the Ministry of Education and Social Welfare, through the agency of the Directorate of Tribal Welfare, created in 1972. The tribal welfare officer is appointed in each district of a state to look after eight school complexes in the district. Since the overall cost of maintenance is higher in ashram schools than in general schools, ashram schools cannot be expected to reach the target coverage of tribal children in any state as a whole.

Madhu Singh Wetzlaugk (1984) in her study examined contradictory goals, embodied in bureaucratic discourse of an educational programme, specifically geared towards the integrated development of tribal communities in India. The bureaucratic discourse expressed in the formal rules of the school's organizational structure, prescribes, for example, the official size of classrooms, the number of day scholars, the nature of their selection, the ratio of boys and girls, the selection of villages to be served by the school, etc. For policymakers, such rules ideally serve to ensure the proper functioning of ashram schools, that is, through admitting pupils according to the prescribed ratio between boys and girls, for the stated objectives relating education with area development. Even though schooling is seen both as a basic element and instrument of development, there has been no agreement on developmental goals. Very often, growth is equated with development. Growth is a simple quantitative term, whereas to achieve development one has to change the structure so as to raise productive capacity. In the case of ashram schools, this aspect of development is totally absent. The policy of integrated development was even more problematic as the nature of the linkage between the various units—educational curricula and rural development—was not specified. Neither was there a framework provided for translating an educational programme geared to agricultural development into a pedagogical practice. The possibility of framing a new curriculum will need an understanding that the rural world in its present form is the product of historical processes resulting in specific economic and social conditions of the peasants' existence. The peasants' attitudes and interpretations are a direct response to the objective conditions of their existence: their position within the social and economic division of labour will determine, in the last instance, their support to the official policy and ideology of schools. Authority relations in schools also act as constraining factors towards the crystallization of a curriculum oriented towards development goals as envisaged by planners. The divergent origins and orientations of the pupils, their families and teachers versus those of official policymakers assign a study, such as this, a general relevance for understanding the hindrances in using an educational innovation as a vehicle for change, without considering simultaneous changes in the distribution of power and factors of production.

Residential schooling contributed to a new form of subjectivities that compound a simple reading of resistance to state power and also offered certain possibilities to those on the margin (Bloch 2005). The colonial perspective of residential schooling for indigenous people had a civilizing agenda as well as a hegemonic aim. Institutions such as residential schools act as a form of productive power within the historical context of the Indian states' efforts to transform tribal communities through the creation of new forms of citizenship subjectivities. The Adivasi population represented backwardness that the Indian state power sought to civilize.

In tribal areas, most families send their children to a nearby town for education. Hiring a room next to a relatively well-established educational institution is a common practice. The relatively better-off families send their wards to residential schools (set up by either the government or the missionaries or other private schools). There are other well-known advantages of a residential school: inculcating sense of discipline among the students, greater emphasis on co-curricular and extracurricular activities and weaning away students from the practice of private tutors. The residential schools would also ensure a critical mass of teachers for ensuring specialization among the teaching faculty in the sciences, social sciences, psychology and economics, etc. Residential schools are already being set up under various government schemes/programmes. Some prominent examples are Eklavya schools set up by the Ministry of Tribal Affairs in tribal areas, and Navodaya Vidyalayas set up at the rate of one per district. All these schools, with some rare exceptions, are immensely popular and have done well in providing quality education to students from inaccessible areas. What is required, perhaps, is to institutionalize this practice by setting up more such schools (Jindal 2015). Of late, ashram schools have been in news for the wrong reasons such as child abuse, rape of tribal girls and the suppression of tribal culture and language and corruption. Over the past century, the provision of residential schooling for many Adivasi communities in eastern and central India was the only practical way of gaining access to formal education. Many tribal villages were too small to have their own fully equipped schools and many of the parents were out to work on farms, forest or as labourers. The overall culture, such as socializing in weekly markets, taking alcohol and participating in cook fights, in the rural areas doesn't help in promoting formal education. But on the other hand, residential schooling also erodes the language and cultural specificity such as music, art, dance and craft. The tribal children do not have a sense of belonging to their villages and they feel displaced. Hence, there is a differing vision.

CONCLUSION

The formal schooling system in India has suffered because it has been ignored by the government. The students are shifting from government schools to private schools, as the latter are considered superior to the former in terms of equality. With increasing privatization and commercialization of education, social inequities are further accentuated by educational inequalities. One may contend that education has become a party to the prevailing social inequalities. Recent changes in the education sector have confirmed the state's abdication of its responsibility to make education of good quality accessible to all children. The inadequate provisions for tackling inequality in the education system (in the form of non-formal education, para teachers, etc.) expose the weakness of the policies and dilute the commitment of the authorities. Although the 86th constitutional amendment has created legal space for better educational opportunities, the state's commitment should be backed by adequate resources. Inequity in education, conceived as the main agenda during the independence struggle, has been sidelined. The education policies are myopic and fail to locate the education of children in their socio-economic contexts. There is a need for adopting a holistic approach. Access, participation and quality are interrelated and should be treated in an integrated manner.

REFERENCES

Bloch, Alexia. 2005. 'Longing for the Kollektiv: Gender, Power and Residential Schools in Central Siberia'. *Cultural Anthropology* 20 (4): 534–569.

Bourdieu, Pierre. 1973. 'Cultural Reproduction and Social Reproduction'. In *Knowledge, Education and Cultural Change*, edited by R. Brown, 71–112. London: Tavistock.

Guha, R. 2007. 'Adivasis, Naxalites and Indian Democracy'. *Economic & Political Weekly* 42 (32): 3305–3312.

Jindal, Ashutosh. 2015. 'Access to Education in Tribal Areas—Rethinking the Traditional Approach'. *Economic & Political Weekly* 50 (41): 24–25.

Nambissan, G. 1994. 'Language and Schooling of Tribal Children: Issues Related to Medium of Instruction'. *Economic & Political Weekly* 29 (42): 2747–2754.

———. 1996. 'Equity in Education? Schooling of Dalit Children in India'. *Economic & Political Weekly* 31 (16/17): 1011–1024.

———. 2000a. *Dealing with Deprivation*. Available at Seminar.www.indiaseminar.com (accessed on 2 April 2020).

———. 2000b. 'Identity, Exclusion and the Education of Tribal Communities'. In *The Gender Gap in Basic Education*, edited by Rekha Wazir, 175–224. New Delhi: SAGE Publications.

Rajagopalachari, C. 1955. *Mahabharata*. New Delhi: Bhavan Book University.

Wetzlaugk, M. S. 1984. 'Official Discourse, Pedagogic Practice and Tribal Communities: A Case Study in Contradiction'. *British Journal of Sociology of Education* 5 (3): 227–245.

Chapter 2

Ethnocentrism in Education
Effects of Hidden Curriculum on Tribal Students

Pradyumna Bag

INTRODUCTION

Socio-economic backwardness of the tribals has been attributed to their imperfect integration with the wider society. Living in isolation has resulted in socio-economic exclusion and political marginalization of the communities. Realizing their relative disadvantage, the successive governments in the post-independence period have initiated a series of measures to address their backwardness. Special policies were formulated in addition to general welfare and development programmes to bridge the development gap. Over the years, the government has realized that one of the important reasons for their backwardness is their inadequate educational attainment. Education, especially the literacy mission with three Rs—reading, writing and arithmetic, facilitate individuals to overcome various socio-economic barriers faced by the tribals. In addition to general educational policy, special initiatives were taken to address the unique disadvantage the tribals encounter in getting an education. Sluggish literacy growth and the dwindling gap in literacy rate within the tribal groups have drawn the policymakers to the concept of ashram schools. During the third plan period, ashram schools were started in all Scheduled Areas across India especially customized to advance the educational backwardness of the tribals. Hostels were constructed to facilitate boarding and lodging for tribal students in the Scheduled Areas. These provisions have been added up with the provisions of the tribal sub-plan areas by Ministry of Tribal Affairs since 1990–1991. These special measures were introduced to achieve targeted results in elementary education among the tribals. Ashram schools were opened in the remote parts of rural areas to meet the educational requirements of the dispersed settlement. These schools provide free boarding, textbooks and other study materials including uniforms to tribal children.

Schools are teaching beyond and above the formal curriculum which is otherwise known as 'hidden curriculum' (Jackson 1968). It is ingrained in pedagogical practice and informally imparts stereotypes, categories, values and perception. Culturally insensitive curriculum, untrained teachers and cultural and linguistic differences set hurdles in the scholastic performance of the pupils. The tribal children found themselves at odds under the prevalent pedagogical arrangement as it reduced their culture, language and world view to a quarantine zone. Their fragile identity and delicate morale in an alien environment habitually subjected to scrutiny and held in contempt.

Education is the key to all-round development which emerged as an important institution modern society to enhance human potential. The methods and processes of organizing teaching and learning impart important lessons about everyday life. In addition to the formal curriculum, the school imparts values, ethics and ideals which have been disseminated in the processes of classroom interactions. It does impart important values to perpetuate the existing social order. 'Society can survive only if there exists among its members a sufficient degree of homogeneity; education perpetuates and reinforces this homogeneity by fixing in the child from the beginning the essential similarities which collective life demands' (Durkheim 1956 cited in Giddens 1972). Education enriches the understanding of culture, norms and values of the society and nourishes the young mind with human faculty. In the given context, it acquires special meaning as the symbiotic relationship between them and their immediate environment. The tribals have received invaluable offerings from nature and have invented ingenious methods to survive the harshest and hostile environment with bare minimum resources. An education system which is devoid of reverence to culture, identity and dignity of social groups has no definite objective and perpetuates hegemonic ideas and normalizes subjugation of the subordinate groups. How applicable and relevant is the ashram school education for tribal children? Is the education system making itself relevant to these flagging learners or do these learners have to make themselves relevant to education?

The significance of educating indigenous children in the natural environment using indigenous languages, phrases and idioms is continually underlined in various UN documents on culture and education in the Permanent Forum on Indigenous Issues.

> It is observed that millions of children continued to be taught in languages they did not use or even understand. The participation of indigenous peoples in designing curricula was still limited, and education still fell short of eliminating prejudice and discrimination targeted at indigenous peoples. (UNESCO, 2003)

UNESCO recommended its member countries to integrate indigenous languages into national curricula and design materials sensitive to the cultural and educational needs of indigenous people. It also stressed that multilingual education should occur at all educational levels and that indigenous peoples be trained so that they could compete both nationally and internationally. Children were at a much higher risk of dropping out of school due to the discrimination, which could be addressed by teaching tribal culture and history in public schools to both tribal and non-tribal children. The tribal children were deprived of the opportunity to take pride in their indigenous background, which hindered their identity and dignity.

Ashram schools are residential schools set up to improve the educational status of children belonging to Scheduled Tribes (STs) as they lag far behind the general population in terms of literacy and educational attainment. Being a total institution, it departs from the basic social arrangement of the tribal society and the pupils are put together to lead a formally enclosed administered system. How does this system impact their overall experience in life, as they are governed by the strict regime of food, culture, language and disciple? To understand the overall impact of education on tribal children, the chapter attempts to highlight the pedagogical arrangement of ashram schools. The chapter investigates: How successful these schools are in facilitating cultural learning? How successful is the present model of education to improve the lives and livelihoods of the tribal children? How has the school helped the children to improve and implement their learning? How enabling is the school curriculum including the medium of instruction to improve their learning? Do the teachers apply 'normative neutrality' during classroom transaction?

SCHOOL CULTURE AND THE HIDDEN CURRICULUM

Teaching, learning, classroom interaction and knowledge constitute important parts of school culture. This pedagogic culture influences and alters the learning ability and the scholastic performance of the pupils. It also significantly impacts their sense of social self or identity as well as self-worth. Being imparted through multiple channels, the hidden curriculum impacts tribal children significantly about their culture, language, traditions and world view. Philip W. Jackson (1968) in his book *Life in Classroom* defined 'hidden curriculum' as the unwritten, unofficial and often unintended lessons, what otherwise Jackson called, the 'unofficial or implicit expectations'. Jackson defined: 'It is a concept used to describe the often unarticulated and unacknowledged things that students are taught in school' (Johnson 2000).

Peter McLaren (1998) expanded the work of Jackson by identifying the hidden curriculum as 'the unintended outcomes of the school-ing process'. These unintended outcomes are often unrecognized by those who teach in and administer the school. Although the function of hidden curriculum and its significance of social control remains unacknowledged, the impact is perhaps far more effective and has far-reaching consequences than on purpose teaching of academic content and skill, which ultimately legitimize the schooling.

> School are teaching more than they claim to teach, that they are doing it systematically, and doing it well. A pervasive hidden curriculum has been discovered in operation. The functions of this hidden curriculum

have been variously identified as the inculcation of values, political socialization, training in obedience and docility, the perpetuation of the traditional class structure-functions that may be characterized generally as social control. (Vallance 1973: 5)

Though it has a significant influence on pupils, it neither appears in the formal curriculum nor is acknowledged in the formal processes. It has been an integral part of the education system and informally imparts stereotypes, categories, value and reactions that affect behaviour and understanding. The hidden curriculum includes behaviour, attitude and perspectives that students learned in the school settings.

Since its inception, schools have been an institution for disciplining, controlling and making children meek and submissive. Students need an organized and disciplined environment to learn but the schools have gone far-off where the students are taught to be willing to oblige, accept and obey the authority without questioning anything were demanded of.

The functions of the hidden curriculum are performed openly, sometimes by the most mundane and venerable practices of the schools. If these practices constitute a hidden curriculum, it is hidden only in the sense that the function of social control goes unacknowledged in current rationales for public education. The schools' social control function has been hidden from the language of justification. Indeed, it has vanished from that language, for much that is today called a hidden function of the schools was previously held to be among the prime benefits of schooling. (Vallance 1973: 5)

Schools are instrumental in upholding, practising and perpetuating the middle class and upper caste values. This cultural diffusion through education prioritizes the dominant culture, making them appear the standard and the natural system. Some of these ideas and spirit are in contradiction with the students' individual or community values and ethics. To understand that, let us examine a few important ethical practices promoted in the school. For instance, individualism is preferred over collectivism and competition is prioritized over cooperation. As a result, instead of sharing the knowledge and learning cooperation and interdependence, students are secretive about knowledge and hide it from others to score better grades, achieve ranks and win reward.

One of the essential characteristics of the tribal society is cooperation, either during fishing, hunting–gathering or even in the field of
agriculture production, as these activities are often conducted with
cooperation. In sharing agriculture equipment or sharing knowledge
about how to tame animals or remove pests, the tribals have never been
secretive about it. Collectivism is inbuilt in the sociocultural processes
as the well-being of the collective is a moral consensus. The popular
African idea of *Ubuntu*, that is, 'I am because we are' is the essence of
being human; particularly it speaks about the fact that you can't exist as
a human being in isolation. However, opposed to this, one behaviour
the students learn in school is that competition is more important than
cooperation and the secret of success is to be secretive and individual-
istic rather than acting on the communal ground.

For many children, ashram schools instil an alienating experience.
Away from home at a tender age, these students have to adapt to
multiple difficulties. In the absence of parents and without parents
and teachers' intervention, these kids develop different social ills and
adjustment problems. The school lesson completely shambles the
students; the experience confuses them about their past and promises
a hope they barely can materialize. A substantial change in taste and
preference have been observed among the ashram school students. For
instance, Deena Sabar (name changed), a student in ashram school in
Class 7. Since the beginning, he did not like to go to ashram school.
Once, after shifting to school, he came home on Nuakhai (a local
festival celebrated to consume the first harvest) and when the time
came to go back, he kept hiding from his parents and ran away to
his maternal uncle's place and made every attempt to avoid going
there but eventually his parents managed to send him back to school.
Now, when he comes home, he wants to remain isolated and offers
no help to his parents on agriculture or other activities which is
often expected from a boy of his age. He developed hatred towards
a number of activities which are the source of his parent's livelihood;
especially, he absolutely detests agriculture. Instead of tribal gods and
goddesses, he is attracted to Hindu gods and goddesses. He conducts
different Hindu rituals and bathes twice or thrice a day for ritual
purification. He has become an introvert but when he talks, he only
talks about sports or religion. His parents are worried that there are

a number of things children of his age have mastered and he knows little about them.

TEACHERS AND THEIR PERSONAL IDIOSYNCRASIES

A teacher has been glorified by the phrase 'Friend, Philosopher and Guide' because he/she has to play all vital roles to introduce the young minds to this world. He/she uses scientific knowledge, reason and logic to unravel the mystery of the world and instil the values of humanity among his/her pupils. In India, traditionally teachers are revered as gods—*GururBrahma GururVishnu GururDevo Maheshwaraha Guru Saakshaat ParaBrahma Tasmai Sri Gurave Namaha* (guru is the creator [Brahma], guru is the preserver [Vishnu], guru deva is the destroyer [Maheshwara] guru is the absolute [singular] lord himself, salutations to that sri guru). In a nutshell, guru (teacher) is the source of knowledge and liberates pupils from their ignorance and sets them on the path of righteousness by destroying their ignorance.

But is the teacher really a 'friend, philosopher or guide' to tribal children in ashram school? The story of Eklavya goes like that a lower born expressed his deepest desire to learn archery from the greatest teacher Dronacharya but not only was his request turned down but he was also made to pay a heavy price for installing a clay idol of him for being inspired. It is important to underline the fact that teachers are not free from their biases and prejudices which they impart to the pupils in the course of various interactions. Why do teachers conduct themselves in the way they do? Do they subscribe to universal values or do they commit to the particularistic views? Being a modern institution, school is supposed to subscribe and nurture common values, cooperation, empathy, social awakening and social sensitiveness. But how successful is the ashram school system in putting into practice these ideas in their teaching–learning process?

Teaching–learning represent a miniature prototype interaction found in wider society. Each interacting party has its own identity and status while the *classroom interaction is on.* The *classroom* interaction flows from the simple fact that the *teacher occupies* an important role and exerts considerable influence over the students. With their subjective idiosyncrasy, they become instrumental in imparting hidden curriculum. The forces that influence their belief, ideology and expectation are far greater, varied and complex and with few exceptions, they are unable to offset the conservative influences which they received during their student days. As a result, 'Teachers are principal actors in the perpetuation of the hidden curriculum' (Giroux 1978: 149). The aforementioned story of Dronacharya epitomizes an ideal model of relations between an educator and a learner and how the values upheld by the teacher are revered and celebrated in the society regardless of their unreasonable and unfair consequences.

Experience from the field suggests that students perceive teaching in terms of individual personalities of teachers rather than a well thought out pedagogy. Classroom interactions are more teacher-centric, that is, the personal idiosyncrasies of the teacher considerably influence the students. The teacher imparts more than the formal curriculum and conveys his/her personal ideas and beliefs which matter to a great deal. With this, an interaction pattern emerges which is based on 'individual personalities rather than pedagogical principles' of the teacher (Lortie 1975 cited in Giroux 1978: 151). This is how the hidden curriculum maintains the time-honoured social inequalities and dominant values system. The institutional set-up and school practices are harmonized with the existing social structure which facilitates reproduction of itself. Either in the school assembly or on the wall around the school, the message about the goal and objective of education is presented to respect the dominant ideas.

SANCTIONS, REWARD AND EXPECTATION IN ASHRAM SCHOOLS

Studies show that inappropriate application of sanctions produces adverse consequences including for mental health and scholastic performance. In schools, elaborate sanctions are in place to govern pupils' conduct. The positive sanctions include grades, recognition, prizes, praise, privileges and anything else that can be assumed that students desire and aspire for; and the negative sanctions include verbal and physical abuse, sending a child out of class, asking them to go and dig field (vegetable) or clear the weeds and even humiliate them for their parent's occupations. While the formal sanctions are noticeable to common observers, the implicit sanction remains hidden beneath the veil of discipline, order, success and future prospects. In popular belief, those sanctions are usually employed to influence students' behaviour to encourage good behaviour and to discourage unwanted conduct, but it is seldom that the sanctions applied against the students are in agreement with the formal curriculum. Large parts of the sanctions are infused with the personal idiosyncrasies of the individual teacher.

In the local popular narrative, it is accepted that the teachers apply sanctions impartially without bias or prejudice. Experience from the field suggests that the teachers often use sanctions to encourage dominant values which they themselves hold dear. Instead of installing universal values, teachers end up rewarding and perpetuating performance and conduct which they think is desirable. Using his/her power and social location, the teacher legitimizes the prevalent dominant ideas in society. There is an important hidden curriculum operating behind allotment and distribution of grades. 'Grades in many instances become the ultimate instrument of discipline by which the teacher imposes his or her norms and beliefs upon students' (Bowles and Gintis cited in Giroux 1978: 151). It is worth noting here that how pedagogical practice and the use of symbolic power disciplined the child to conform to the ideology and values supportive of the existing socio-economic order. 'Whether handing out grades or gold stars, the teacher usually ends up doing more than evaluating cognitive performance. Praise and power have become sanctioning mechanisms used to sanction both academic and non-academic student behavior' (Giroux 1978: 149).

Bias and prejudice against the tribals are inbuilt in the social structure. Subrahmanian (2005) reported that in almost all government schools, teachers show severe forms of a stereotyping trend towards Dalit and Adivasi students' learning potential. The entire pedagogical attitude towards pupils of marginalized section suffers from a deficit future prospect. The teacher rationalizes the prejudice and develops deficient expectation from the tribal students. The low expectation is implicitly expressed through words, gesture and symbolic recognition. These deficient expectations and differential treatments have important consequences on the personal and academic performance of the students. Such prejudices considerably reduce the potential and stunt the pupils from actualizing their self. Instead, the poor academic performance is then often attributed to individual failure and lack of interest among the tribal children. 'While analyzing the poor response of Tribal children to formal schooling, scholars tend to emphasize the economic marginalization of these communities, their illiterate home environments, inadequate facilities for education and, culturally, the alien nature of school system' (Nambissan 1994: 2747). These factors do impact the educational success of the children but how supportive and sympathetic is the school pedagogy? Nambissan also found that upper caste teachers have low expectations from the students of marginalized groups. 'More importantly, despite active encouragement from impoverished family members, the apathetic treatment by teachers and school administrators largely shaped the learning experiences of these socially disadvantaged groups' (Nambissan 1996: 1011). Teachers link poverty and marginalized status of the pupils with their lack of enthusiasm and intelligence and marginalize them further in the classroom. While assessing, teachers consider students' socio-economic background as important factor in their academic achievement (Becker 1952).

Residential schools have institutionalized assimilation by stripping aboriginal people of their language, culture and connection with the family. The results for many have included a lifestyle of uncertain identity and the adoption of self-abusive behaviours, often associated with alcohol and violence, reflecting a pattern of coping sometimes referred to in First Nations as 'The Residential School Syndrome' (McKenzie and Morrissette 2003, cited in Partridge 2010: 34).

MARGINALIZATION OF TRIBAL CULTURES AND LANGUAGES

Identity and dignity are fundamental to human existence, as they represent the unique sociocultural practices of social groups. Groups are defined, identified and allocated a place in the hierarchy of society on the basis of the presence of desirable dominant traits. Social groups are constantly contesting to occupy an important position in the graded inequality of society. Proximity to dominant social groups and their cultural and institutional apparatuses elevate the position of a social group. The underdeveloped economy, imperfect integration with wider society and the distinctive sociocultural practices have become the reasons for reordering the sociocultural order of the tribal society. While the intended objective of ashram schools was to enhance the enrolment and to improve the educational attainment of the tribals, the schools are instrumental in cultural diffusion where the tribal sociocultural practices were subjected to alteration and change. Even though ashram schools are meant for the tribals, the language, culture and the way of the life of the tribals are yet to find a place in the curriculum. The centrally imposed curriculum and their outcomes are seldom subjected to public scrutiny.

Hierarchy and gradation are omnipresent in institutions of Indian society. The linguistic state perpetuates majoritarian ideas. It has been inhabited by multiple linguistic groups, some with few thousand speakers and some others with million speakers, but the language of the dominant community becomes the language of the state. In fact, the language of the upper caste and class becomes the language of the state, at least it is true for Odisha. The language spoken by numerous economically weaker groups, namely SCs, STs and OBCs, is reduced to the fringes and virtually forbidden in the educational institutions. Linguistic hierarchy reflects the power dynamics in the society where not only the dialects of the small groups were excluded from the state but also the speakers of these languages were located at the fringes the power corridor. The ideology of linguistic chauvinism has enabled the dominant community to have hegemonic influence over the subaltern. With the imaginary threat to *matrubhasha* (mother tongue), the dominant community consolidates their ideology which gradually percolates down to the subaltern groups. Replication of these ideas and ideologies through various means inculcates a false sense of pride among these groups who gradually consent to something which is against their own interests.

Before approaching the issue in hand, it is important to understand the socio-economic realities that are prevalent in rural Odisha. The following accounts are findings of one of the village studies the researcher undertook. The village was inhabited by seven communities—three intermediary castes (Gouda, Sahu, Mali), two SCs (Mahar and Dombs) and two tribal groups (Kandh and Sabar), who spoke five different dialects. Total 43 per cent of households belong to ST communities and together with SCs, they make 92 per cent of the village households.

Despite their overwhelming numerical strength, the languages of these communities were forbidden in the school. All interaction in the school was conducted on standard Odia language.

There are 62 tribal groups in the state of Odisha who constitute about 23 per cent of the state population. Barring few, all these tribal groups have their own dialect, and some of these tribal languages have more speakers than some of those mentioned in the Eighth Schedule of the Constitution. Not a single language of the vast tribal people in India had been accorded official status till 2004. Only after an extensive slumber, the government woke up to the issue and incorporated two languages namely, Santhali and Bodo. In fact, there are a number of tribal languages such as Gondi, Oraon/Kurukh that have more than a million speakers and more speakers than Sanskrit and Sindhi but have not yet been accorded any official status.

In order to protect and promote the tribal language and culture, the Government of Odisha conceived an institution called Academy of Tribal Dialects and Culture in 1979, and later on, in 2009, it was renamed as Academy of Tribal Languages and Culture (ATLC). A closer look at its website tells a few interesting facts about the functioning of the academy. Invariably, the heads of the institution belong to upper caste and it was evident enough from their social location that they could barely speak or understand the tribal language. In fact, the upper caste and the so-called mainstream culture view all constitutives of tribal identity with contempt. It raises important question about the ongoing attempt for integration of the tribals in the associative social processes. It speaks volumes about tribal development and empowerment, whereas out of 23 per cent of the state's population, a single suitable tribal person is not found to head the institution. The colourful ATLC website was overflowing with conspicuous photos of tribal girls, dancing, attired in folk costumes.

Dialects are strictly forbidden in the school settings and any deviation—intentional or unintentional—invites punishment. The school goers must be mindful while speaking in the school premises, as often when these first-generation school goers utter traditional words and terms, they get subjected to humiliation. While struggling to get along with the formal methods of learning, language creates additional hurdles in the leaning processes. Since the medium of instruction in school is standard Odia, the tribal children have to put up with this hard reality. Students encounter various degrees of difficulties depending on their proximity and the integration with the wider society. While students have difficulties in understanding Odia spoken by teachers from coastal Odisha, apparently, it is easy for them to understand the same language spoken by the local teachers. While researchers have highlighted that mother tongue or home language plays a significant role in early learning but the medium of instruction in ashram schools continues to be in the official language of the state and in English. Although the Constitution in 1956 recognized the need for primary education in mother tongue for linguistic minorities, today, education is still being imparted primarily in the 15 'official' languages and English (Nambissan 1994). The denial of schooling in the mother tongue is just one of the many forms of exclusion that the tribal children encounter in school settings, the others being culture, food habits and world view. The education system makes tribal culture, language and food habits irrelevant to the learners. It is fairly conclusive from the pedagogical attitude that the language, culture and the life-world of the tribals must be prescribed from the educational settings as it is in the wider society. Ethnocentrism is ingrained in the pedagogy and ashram schools are instrumental in cultural assimilations and legitimize the ideology behind civilizing the savage.

The ongoing processes of assimilation have stripped the tribals of their language and culture and have deprived them of the vital life skills in their immediate surroundings. But children in ashram schools miss out on these important life skills otherwise available to them in their home environment. Growing up in these natural surroundings, those children acquire knowledge about indigenous plants, herbs and the behaviour of all the flora and fauna. Furthermore, the composite systems of knowledge include stories, taboos, rituals and diseases, which are essential for an individual to be a full-fledged member of the society. The strict ashram school regime of food, culture and language indoctrinates them to the dominant culture and subsequently the pupils develop detestation against their own culture. The education system is frequently used as a tool to separate indigenous children from their families, traditions and languages, which helps the state to gain control over tribal peoples and their lands. 'Our children are stuck somewhere between a past they don't understand and a future that won't accept them and offers them nothing', said Bonniface Alimankinni from Tiwi Islands (reported in Survival International).[1] There has not been any concerted attempt for content integration. The meaning and significance of the tribal world are wilfully ignored in the curriculum making.

Under the ashram school regime, control and compliance remain concealed and operate under intensive control and surveillance. The school system seems to care little about the tragic disappearance of entire indigenous cultures, languages and other important social institutions. The tribal culture has fallen prey to government policies, emphasizing state language at the expense of indigenous languages. Ignoring those languages has severed ties between indigenous youth and their ancestors, damaging the confidence of the people. Lack of content integration endangers sociocultural and economic institutions of the tribal society as it conspicuously made local knowledge system obsolete.

CONCLUSION AND SUGGESTIONS

Among the public-funded schools, ashrams are at the bottom in terms of facilities and priority for imparting quality education. They are infamous for inferior infrastructure, untrained and insensitive teachers and the imposition of dominant culture upon them through the ethnocentric curriculum. Reports about issues of safety and security and extreme cases of sexual harassment and death of tribal girl students make headlines on occasion but seldom get the underlying reasons behind such ailing system examined. Prejudices against the tribals have pervaded into the education system and the school pedagogy constantly reminds the tribal pupils of their inferior status. Low literacy, low enrolment, high dropout, absenteeism, stagnation and low academic performance are some of the outcomes of such practices.

Social differences engender a strong sense of ethnocentrism among the teaching staff who often express pride, vanity and superiority about their own culture. To enhance and enrich multicultural learning,

---

[1] Survival international. n.d. *Schooling and Tribal Children*. Available at https://www.survivalinternational.org/about/schooling (accessed on 11 November 2018).

teachers must be sensitized about tribal ways of life. Teachers from students' own community instil a sense of comfort and confidence and the pupil find a role model to imitate. A growing body of research literature from the West shows that students from ethnic minority perform better when instructed by the teacher from their own community. 'Most results show that when black teachers teach black students, black students achieve more than when taught by white teachers,' writes Andy Porter in *Rethinking the Achievement Gap*.

Educationists, various tribal groups including rights activists, have been suggesting to the government to introduce the tribal languages at least at the primary level. However, many of our tribal groups do not have their own alphabets, letters and literature. Therefore, the first important step could be to devise appropriate scripts for the tribal language. Anthropologists and linguists have done that by using various signs, symbols and methods of verbal and non-verbal communication. The alphabet letter will facilitate to devise the primers and schoolbooks to ease and enrich the teaching–learning processes.

It is important to address the inbuilt deep prejudice and deficient thinking found among the teachers. It is not uncommon to hear a teacher's characterization of the students as poor first-generation students, and poor in language and communication. Deficit thinking diminishes the potential effectiveness of both teachers and students. The teacher operates on self-fulfilling prophecy that there are remote chances that these students will succeed, and they give up even before taking the first step. This self-fulfilling prophecy adversely diminishes teaching quality and outcomes. When a conscientious teacher teaches the tribal children, they dig at the root causes of low expectations and open doors of opportunity. Higher expectations can check the deficit thinking that festers in segregated schooling environments. Nip ethnocentrism in the bud by teaching equality to youngsters.

REFERENCES

Becker, H.S. 1952. 'Social Class Variations in the Teacher-Pupil Relationship: American Journal of Educational Sociology'. *American Sociological Association.* Vol, 25, 451–465. USA: Washington D.C.

Durkheim, Emile. 1956. *Education and Sociology*. New York, NY: The Free Press.

Giddens, A. 1972. 'Elites in the British Class Structure'. *The Sociological Review* 20 (3): 345–372.

Giroux, H. 1978. 'Developing Educational Programs: Overcoming the Hidden Curriculum'. *The Clearing House* 52 (4): 148–151.

Jackson, Phillip W. 1968. *Life in Classroom*. New York, NY: Rinehart and Winston.

Johnson, A. L. 2000. *The Blackwell Dictionary of Sociology*. Oxford: Blackwell.

McLaren, P. 1998. 'Revolutionary Pedagogy in Post-revolutionary Times: Rethinking the Political Economy of Critical Education'. *Educational Theory* 48 (4): 431–462. USA: University of Illinois.

Nambissan, G. 1994. 'Language and Schooling of Tribal Children: Issues Related to Medium of Instruction'. *Economic & Political Weekly* 29 (42): 2747–2754.

Partridge, C. 2010. 'Residential Schools: The Intergenerational Impacts on Aboriginal Peoples'. *Promising Practices in Mental Health: Emerging Paradigms for Aboriginal Social Work Practices* 7: 33–62.

Subrahmanian, R. 2005. 'Education, Exclusion and the Development State'. In *Education Regimes in Contemporary India*, edited by R. Chopra and P. Jeffrey, 62–82. New Delhi: SAGE Publications.

UNESCO. 2003. *Importance of Indigenous Education and Culture Highlighted, as Permanent Forum Continues Second Session*. Paris: UNESCO.

Vallance, E. 1973. 'Hiding the Hidden Curriculum: An Interpretation of the Language of Justification in Nineteenth-century Educational Reform'. *Curriculum Theory Network* 4 (1): 5–21. doi:10.2307/1179123.

Chapter 3

Status of Tribal Ashram Schools in Maharashtra

Bipin Jojo

The Government of India has taken a number of steps to strengthen not only the social, economic and political lives but also to develop the educational status of Scheduled Tribes (STs). The National Policy on Education (NPE) which was envisaged in 1986 and the Programme of Action (POA) as modified in 1992 provide a remarkable way for the development of tribal education. The provisions of NPE (POA) 1992 have incorporated special provisions for STs to give priority in opening primary schools especially in the tribal areas and construction of school buildings to be undertaken in those areas. On the grounds of sociocultural milieu, the NPE 1992 focuses that the curricula and instructional materials would be made in tribal languages at the initial stages, which could be switched over to the regional language at a later stage. The NPE has space for the educated and promising ST youths who can be encouraged and trained to take up teaching in tribal areas. This policy has also instructed to open residential schools and ashram schools on a large scale.

Several Commissions were set up to evaluate the condition of education and its quality like the Backward Classes Commission (GoI 1956), the Renuka Ray Committee (1959) and the Scheduled Areas and Scheduled Tribes Commission (GoI 1962). The Verrier Elwin committee report (1960) and the Dhebar Commission on Tribal (1962) highlighted the problems of primary education for the various tribes in the areas of medium of instruction, stagnation, getting the right teachers, etc. (Agrawal and Aggarwal 1991; Duary 2010; Jojo 2013; Mehta 2006). These commissions and committees provided different strategies for the tribal to access education at the school level. Emphasis was given to open schools and residential schools for the tribal children through the scheme of ashram schools. Quantitative expansion of education was, in time, achieved in numbers by opening more ashram schools, establishing hostels and so on. Due attention was paid for the qualitative improvement of tribal education by providing remedial coaching, counselling and guidance in vocations. However, all the provisions have proved to be insufficient in addressing the needs of the tribal, and the running of ashram schools in tribal areas is in serious jeopardy. Most of the children are struggling to access schools and those who do manage to gain access, fail to get quality education.

Starting from literacy to higher education, the STs are sharing a very negligible portion of Indian educational attainment despite having several policies and programmes. They are lagging behind other categories of population at different levels of education including literacy. Over the decades, one can see a positive change in the percentage of literacy among the tribal. The gap has been decreasing gradually. However, in the year 2011, the literacy rate for the tribal was 63.1 per cent and for the others it was 72.99 per cent. At the same time, the literacy for ST male was 71.70 per cent and for female 54.4 per cent, and for others it was 80.89 per cent and 64.64 per cent for male and female, respectively (Census of India 2011).

The educational policies and programmes are unable to encompass the complex social reality within a single framework and are, therefore, unable to bridge the gap between policy and practice. The suffering of tribal children was reflected in the literature and the gaps were visible through empirical evidence collected in the process of conducting this study.

The level of the socio–economic development and education varies considerably between the tribal and non–tribal population, between one tribe and another tribe and even among different sub-groups of the tribal groups. It is found that the smaller groups have high literacy rate than numerically larger tribal groups (TISS 2015). Due to these facts, the development schemes have to be devised in the light of sociocultural factors and economic needs of the tribal in each region and sometimes each community. The ashram school is an important determinant for the educational achievement of the tribal and so the policy planning and coordination for improving the condition of tribal education become very important.

EDUCATIONAL STATUS OF THE TRIBAL IN MAHARASHTRA

The state of Maharashtra has a literacy rate of 82.91 per cent which puts it at the 12th position among the top states in terms of literacy. However, the condition of literacy and education for the STs is not comparatively good. The STs are always lagging behind people of the other categories in terms of literacy and are at different educational levels. In the year 2011, the literacy for the STs was 65.73 per cent and 82.91 per cent was for all categories (Census of India 2011). There has been tremendous improvement in literacy in general and for STs in particular over the decades. However, despite special emphasis on education for STs, the literacy rate is much lower than others.

Statistics of School Education 2010–2011 and the Statistics of Higher & Technical Education 2009–2010 data on Gross Enrolment Ratio (GER) of the STs in Maharashtra shows that at primary level, the GER for STs is higher than any other category and signifies that more number of STs are repeated or remained in primary level as over/ under-age enrolment. The GER of STs is much lower than the other categories at secondary, higher secondary and higher level of education. It is just 49 per cent for STs against 73.7 per cent of all the categories at secondary education level and it is just 6.5 per cent for STs as compared to 21.4 per cent of all the categories at higher education level. Apart from this, as the level of education increases, the GER decreases for both the categories, however, the rate of decrease is more for the STs than the others. The same trend is seen across the gender groups for both the social categories. At the same time, the above reports also show that the dropout rate of STs is also higher than others in Maharashtra. There is a low enrolment of ST students and higher rate of dropout across the levels of education. As the dropout rate of STs has gone up from 21.1 per cent at primary level to 69.8 per cent at secondary level, it has gone up from 20.3 per cent to 38.2 per cent for other community students. Across gender groups, a similar trend is seen, but in case of STs it is more prominent (MHRD 2011; MHRD 2012).

Thus, the educational status of tribal is very low in Maharashtra like most of the other states. Tribal are struggling in their social, economic and educational life in the state and they are facing challenges in every sphere of life. One of the arguments is that efforts at imparting education in their mother tongue and at the same time familiarizing them with their regional language were subsequently disappointing and it was a difficult task for the teachers to teach every tribe's mother tongue in one classroom (von Furer-Haimendorf 1982). Similarly, Bhargava (1989) and Kamble (1992) also studied the educational facilities for weaker sections like STs/SCs. The educational policies and programmes are unable to encompass the complex social reality within a single framework and therefore, the gap between policy and practice remains unabridged.

The STs in Maharashtra are facing many problems in their social and economic spheres and especially in education even when there is a provision of several schemes and programmes for the development of STs in the state. Out of all the STs, some STs are more vulnerable than other STs in the state; the Katkaris are one among them. Socio-economic and cultural constrains make the STs, particularly the Katkari tribe, more vulnerable. They are unable to access education at different levels. The educational status of the Katkari population is very low. The majority of school-going aged children from this community are not attending school. Those who are attending, most of them are facing sociocultural constraints and discrimination at different Government schools and the ashram schools in Maharashtra. The opportunity cost of child labour, high dropouts, peer-group and neighbourhood effects, including different structural issues in Government primary schools, are the other factors which are hindering school enrolment and attendance of the Katkari tribe in Maharashtra. Among the students who are studying, their participation and attainment is drastically low as compared to the other STs and with the other category students. The lower level of participation and attainment affects their livelihood means and gives low result in the evaluations of educational attainment. The ascribed statuses of the Katkaris engaged them in the job-like wage labourer. They are unable to overcome their assumptions of the futility of education. They are unable to make link and utilize education to their immediate return or immediate survival concerns. There is also hardly any success story within their groups to achieve higher education goal and educational attainments contributing to upward mobility and improvements in their earning capacity (Mutatkar 2004, 2007). Similarly, in case of Pardhis, who are Denotified Tribes, formal education's structure and content have been very different from the Pardhis' indigenous knowledge and traditional patterns of its assimilation (Jha 2010). Kurup (2005) argued that the education of STs, especially for the girls, is obstructed with the help required by their parents in livelihood work. They take a weekly break from their school to meet their parents and remain there to help them with their work in the fields. It shows that even with so many difficulties, the tribal girls have great aspiration to study at higher level of education. Normally, schools in tribal hamlets offer education up to Class 4. Those who aspire to study beyond Class 4 face many difficulties (geographically) to reach the school. As a result, most of the children dropout of school or enrol in the nearest boarding school. Tribal and their children have great aspiration for education, but the geographical inaccessibility and the need for parental support become obstacles in their education.

BRIEF HISTORY OF ASHRAM SCHOOLS

Ashram schools have been the most important intervention of the Indian Government to promote the education amongst the tribal. The concept of ashram schools has been derived from the traditional Indian *gurukulas* and the Gandhian philosophy of basic education in which the teacher and the student live together and have close interaction with the purpose of helping the students in the development of complete personality and in sharpening their capacities (Patel 1984).

During the famines of 1919–1920 and 1921–1922, Thakkar Bapa and Indulal Yagnik, under the instructions of Mahatma Gandhi, worked in the famine-stricken areas of Dahod and Jhalod talukas of Gujarat. During the relief work, Thakkar Bapa was moved by the pitiable conditions of the tribal in this area, and he realized that the educational and welfare activities need to be a part of the programme and decided to settle and work in this area. Thakkar Bapa decided to prepare social workers locally from the community itself. A sought of ashram schools was run at Mirakhedi by one Sukhdevbhai. In 1922, Indulal Yagnik, with financial support from Gujarat Pradesh Congress Samiti, took up the responsibility of supervising this school. Later on, Thakkar Bapa took up this responsibility. Thus, due to the efforts of Indulal Yagnik and Thakkar Bapa, the first ashram school was established at Mirakhedi. The ashram school was a Residential School and was interested not only in education of the tribal children but also in their total development. This was perhaps the real beginning of tribal education in Panchamahals. Bhil Seva Mandal, an organization for the welfare of the tribal, was started in 1923 at Dahod. The Bhil Seva Mandal, with the help of some devoted and selfless workers extended its activities very rapidly. Within a few years of its inception, a number of ashram schools and hostels were started at various places in the district. Later on, Thakkar Bapa extended his activities and motivated special workers in Bihar, Madhya Pradesh, Rajasthan, Maharashtra and Odisha to work among the tribal. This resulted into the establishment of an all-India service organization, known as the Adimjati Sevak Sangh. This added a new dimension to the spread of education and welfare activities among tribal in India. Although, their principal aim is to ameliorate the conditions of tribal people, education of tribal children has remained an important part of their programme (Patel 1984).

After independence, the ashram schools retained their existence. The momentum in opening ashram schools increased from the Third-Five-Year Plan onwards. The establishment of ashram schools was envisaged as a direct intervention to tackle the socio-economic and geographic inequalities of the tribal population, particularly, sparsely populated areas, by providing educational opportunities.

The concept of the ashram schools combines both functional and literacy-based aspects of education, relieving the tribal parents from the burden of feeding and clothing their school-going children besides providing a congenial school environment. Consequently, ashram schools are expected to reduce the incidence of absenteeism, wastage and stagnation, and improve the standard of education at primary level. Further, it is also intended to reduce the burden on tribal parents by saving them from incurring expenditure on their children's education as these ashram schools provide free boarding and lodging facilities apart from supplying books, stationary, clothes (uniforms) and so on to the students. All these facilities have been provided to favourably motivate the tribal children and their parents towards education.

The idea of the ashram schools was initiated by the Government of India with the recommendation of Dhebbar Committee in 1962. The focus of the scheme of ashram schools was concentrating on the sparingly populated interior backward areas where the normal schools were not available. The aim of this scheme was to provide Residential Schools for STs including Primitive Tribal Groups in an environment conducive to learning to increase the literacy rate among the tribal students and to bring them at par with the non-tribal population of the country (Joshi 1980; Mishra and Dhir 2005).

ASHRAM SCHOOLS IN MAHARASHTRA

The provision of ashram schools started in 1972 as a part of the National Scheme but this scheme has been in operation in Maharashtra since the year 1952. It was initially implemented through voluntary organizations and was later taken over by the state Government in the year 1972–1973, where the students get boarding and lodging facilities, to promote education among the STs. The local children attend the school as day scholars. The aim of the ashram schools was envisaged as direct intervention to tackle the socio–economic and geographical inequalities of the tribal population and to provide educational opportunity to them. Later the ashram schools aimed to reduce the absenteeism, wastage and stagnation of education at the primary level.

Even after different specific policies, programmes and schemes, the educational status of STs is still low at different levels of education. Starting from their learning aids need to the Residential School facilities, several policies, programmes and schemes are trying to bring the STs at par with the other categories at different levels of education. Despite these efforts, the STs have still very low access to enrolment, retention and evaluation (pass out/successfully completion) at the national as well as state and union territories level.

However, there are many reports and studies like Goyal (2014) showing unpleasant conditions and experiences in these schools. The Standing Committee on Social Justice and Empowerment of 15th Lok Sabha submitted its report on the working of ashram schools in tribal areas on 18 February 2014. The committee pointed out that 793 children died in ashram schools in Maharashtra between 2001–2002 and 2012–2013 as a result of scorpion/snake bites and minor illnesses. Jojo (2011) identifies, with the officials of Tribal Development Department (TDD), Government of Maharashtra's finance, infrastructure, manpower and administration as the major roadblocks in the effective implementation of the scheme of ashram schools. This in turn has resulted in lack of achievement, enrolment, poor academic results, high dropout rate among the students and lack of gender equity. Chattopadhyay (2009) studied the situation of primary education in some tribal villages of a backward district of Maharashtra. Besides infrastructural improvements, the author strongly argued in favour of introducing tribal languages for basic education, provision of personnel for clerical works and proper maintenance of records, which reflects the reality of primary schooling. Economic uncertainty and financial hardship are the contributing factors for the age-old disinterest in education among the tribes.

The public interest litigation (PIL) filed in the Honourable Bombay High Court by the petitioners Mr Ravindra Umakant Talpe and others allege that proper arrangements have not been made in respect to basic public utilities which are provided in the *ashramshalas* all over Maharashtra. The Honourable Bombay High Court directed the state Government to make an assessment of the facilities available in the *ashramshalas* for the students by taking assistance of Tata Institute of Social Sciences and other similar organizations. The state of Maharashtra was directed to make teams either from Social Justice Department or Child Welfare Department along with members of the Non-Governmental Organisations which are doing work in these areas (refer CRPIL 69 of 2013 heard on 18 June 2014). As a result, Government Resolution (GR) was issued by the Government of Maharashtra in July 2014 to carry out a survey.

The designated teams in each district of Maharashtra surveyed the *ashramshalas* in the months of August and September 2014. This survey covered 1,076 schools covering 51.4 per cent (553) aided schools and 48.6 per cent (523) government-run ashram schools. A large number of tribal students (5,61,644 students for the academic year 2014–2015) were registered in these ashram schools of Maharashtra (TISS 2015). This chapter has addressed some of the critical issues based on the observations from this study and then recommends for the policy implications.

STATUS OF THE ASHRAM SCHOOLS IN MAHARASHTRA

It is important to examine the situation of the ashram schools against their objectives of social, economic and educational advancement of the inhabitants in scheduled and remote areas (Jojo 2011). The ashram schools have a significant impact on the educational achievements of the tribal populations. Even though the scheme is plagued by issues, it is important to reiterate the fact that many students have directly benefited from this scheme. The calculation of the unit cost per student for each year is stipulated in the Ashram School Master Plan. The unit cost consisting of all the variable expenses—salary, wages, travel expenses, office expenditure, rent and taxes, equipment, food expenditure, special provision service and other expenses—have been calculated and arrived at ₹9,567.79. This does not include the fixed cost like land and buildings (Jojo 2011).

However, it was observed that much is lacking where the education facilities for the tribal populations are concerned. Though 16 per cent (174) schools are very good, many of the other schools do not meet the infrastructural requirements like the amount of land (minimum 2 hectare), classroom space, learning environment with maps, charts, office for the Head Master, staff room, storage room, kitchen, dining room, sick room, lights and fans, and so on. Similarly, the living space and provisions like bedding/mattresses, poorly maintained rooms with broken doors and windows in many cases, are serious concerns. There are many school hostels in which the students have to go out for defecation and taking bath as there are unusable toilets and bathrooms or they are not available. The school and hostel surroundings are also not cleaned or not so clean. This can become the breeding ground for malaria and many other illnesses. These conditions lead to poor health and hygiene of the residents. The girl students are prone to poor reproductive healthcare with poor monitoring of menstrual cycle and provision for sanitary napkins. Though lunch is provided as per the norms, hardly any of the hostels provide breakfast, despite having the provision for it. This can affect the nutritional status of the students. The unhygienic living condition draws attention for improving the living condition and for proper healthcare services as many children have been dying mostly from illnesses.

Safety and security are also a concern as many of the schools are with no boundary wall and no security guards. Many of the wardens' posts are vacant and so some of the staff are given additional responsibility sometimes.

Without the basic living condition, one cannot expect the quality education to be delivered, though curriculum and pedagogy are other crucial elements in imparting education to the tribal communities. The poor condition of the ashram schools is an injustice to the young tribal boys and girls, violation of Right to Education, and disrespect to human dignity. The objective of the ashram schools is not met in true sense. Therefore, the Government has to take serious note of this status of ashram schools and take the corrective steps before the young tribal minds get frustrated and misplace their aspirations. Based on the observations of the status of the ashram schools in Maharashtra, the following recommendations are suggested at policy and implementation levels for the better condition of these schools.

RECOMMENDATIONS

The programme of ashram schools has to be effective, efficient, participatory and accountable. For that, the following steps need to be taken.

At Policy Level

1. *Convergences:* As the ashram schools have components of academic, land and buildings, water and sanitation, health, sports, food and electricity, the TDD has to interface with various other departments, namely, the Department of Education, Department of Sports, Department of Health, the PWD, Water Supply and

Sanitation Department, Forest and Revenue Department, Food and Civil Supplies Department and the Maharashtra State Electricity Board. These convergences are necessary for efficient implementation of the scheme and efficient utilization of the resources.

2. *Input-output-outcome analysis:* Most of the time the budget allocation and expenditure is emphasized in the public finance and governance systems. This process does not analyse the outcome or the impact of the public finance. Therefore, the input–output–outcome analysis must be done to ascertain the intended result of the ashram schools. A participatory and accountable process must be introduced through public verification exercises like social audit by the team of all the stakeholders like TDD, teachers, parents, students, local self-governance institutes, civil society organizations and external experts.

3. *Benchmarking:* The GR of 1999 known as 'Ashram Schools Code Book' has provisions for staffing pattern, library, laboratory, health and hygiene, school discipline, teaching, curricular and extracurricular activities, as well as extra coaching classes for better performance of the ashram schools in the state. These guidelines have been accepted as benchmarks for all the schools. The existing best practices are to be fixed within all the ashram schools in the state to set an achievable standard for all the other schools to follow and replicate.

At the Implementation Level

1. Structural audit must be carried out in every three years with reference to the Ashramshala Master Plan and/or Guidelines for School Infrastructure and Strengthening (Civil Works) Rashtriya Madhyamik Shiksha Abhiyan (2014).

2. The classroom should be separate from the sleeping room (dormitory). The classroom must have 'BaLA' (Building as a Learning Aid) in school premises as suggested in Sarva Shiksha Abhiyan. At the same time, the dormitories must be safe, clean and hygienic with ventilation, lights and fans, with cots/mattresses along with the cupboards. In addition, all other basic infrastructure in the school as well as in the hostel as per the Master Plan must be provided.

3. There must be safe drinking water available in the school as well as the hostel premises as per the guidelines.

4. There must be regular monitoring of the academic and infrastructural performance of all the schools by the High level Committee of educationists, community representatives/civil society organizations, teachers, parents, senior TDD officials. The responsible people must be made accountable for the negligence and non-confirmation to the guidelines according to the Master Plan. This monitoring should not only look at outputs but also assess the outcome/impact of the provision and facilities in the quality of life and performance of the students.

5. The vacant post must be filled up so that the students grow in the curricula as well as extracurricular aspects and develop holistically. Therefore, the ashram schools must be developed as centre of learning with vibrant and energetic atmosphere.

6. The health check must be strictly enforced in order to monitor the health and hygiene status of the students. The Health Card must be maintained with their health status for each student. There must be a district-level medical team with mobile medical van dedicated to the ashram schools for each of the 15 Scheduled Districts.

7. The hostel wardens/superintendents and caretakers must be trained on sensitivity towards the tribal children, first aid, care and management of the hostels; so that good care is taken of the tribal students as the hostels are away from their homes.

8. Since there are more than 5 per cent of ashram schools run by the voluntary organizations, the criteria for selecting a school for aid should be reviewed and the ongoing support must also be reviewed by the independent agencies so that they are made accountable and if any organization fails to run the school with the prescribed condition, their aid must be discontinued and the school could be merged with other nearby schools.

REFERENCES

Agrawal, S. P., S. Agrawal, and J. C. Agrawal. 1991. *Educational and Social Uplift of Backward Classes: At What Cost and How? Mandal Commission and After.* Vol. 26. Delhi: Concept Publishing Company.

Bhargava, S. 1989. *A Descriptive Analysis of Teachers Expectations in Secondary Schools.* Bhopal: Department of Psychology, Bhopal University.

Chattopadhyay, A., and V. Durdhawale. 2009. 'Primary Schooling in a Tribal District of Maharashtra: Some Policy Relevance'. *Journal of Education Administration and Policy Studies* 1 (5): 70–78.

Census of India. 2011. *PCA Maharashtra 2011*. Available at: http://pibmumbai.gov.in/English/PDF/E2013_PR798.PDF

Duary, N. 2010. *Education in Tribal India: A Study of West Bengal*. Delhi: Mittal Publications.

Government of India. 1956. *Report of Backward Classes Commission*. 1953–56. New Delhi: Government of India.

Goyal, P. 2014. 'Standing Committee on Social Justice and Empowerment of 15th Loksabha'. *Tehelka Magazine* 11 (48).

Jojo, B. 2011. 'Government Ashram Schools for Tribals, An Outcome Budget'. *The Indian Journal of Social Work* 72 (4): 605–616.

————. 2013. 'Decline of Ashram Schools in Central and Eastern India: Impact on Education of ST Children'. *Social Change* 43 (3): 377–395.

Joshi, S. D. 1980. 'Educational Problems of SCs and Scheduled Tribes of Baroda District'. In *Third Survey of Research in Education*, edited by M. B. Buch. New Delhi: NCERT.

Kamble, P. R. 1992. 'A Critical Study of the Effect of the Facilities Given by the Government to the Backward Class Pupils in Primary Schools in Devgad Taluka, Maharashtra'. MPhil dissertation. Pune: University of Pune.

MHRD. 2011. 'Statistics of Higher & Technical Education 2009–10'. New Delhi: Government of India, Bureau of Planning, Monitoring & Statistics.

————. 2012. 'Statistics of School Education 2010–2011'. New Delhi: Government of India, Bureau of Planning, Monitoring & Statistics.

Mehta, P. C., ed. 2006. *Development of Indian Tribes*. Delhi: Discovery Publishing House.

Mishra, B. C., and Dhir, A. 2005. *Ashram school in India: Problems and Prospects*. New Delhi: Discovery Publishing House.

Mutatkar, R. K. 2004. *Action Strategies for Health and Education in Tribal Nandurbar: Maharashtra Human Development Action Research Study*. Mumbai: The Indira Gandhi Institute of Development Research.

————. 2007. 'Social Group Disparities, Ethnicity and Poverty in India'. Unpublished PhD dissertation. Mumbai: The Indira Gandhi Institute of Development Research.

Patel, T. 1984. *Development of Education Among Tribal Women*. New Delhi: Mittal Publications.

TISS. 2015. *Educational Status of Scheduled Tribes in Maharashtra: Attainment and Challenges*. Unpublished report. A study sponsored by ICSSR, New Delhi. Mumbai: TISS.

————. 2015. *A Report on Status of Government and Aided Ashram Schools in Maharashtra*. Unpublished report. Mumbai: TISS.

Von Fürer-Haimendorf, C. 1982. *Tribes of India: The Struggle for Survival*. Berkeley, CA: University of California Press.

Chapter 4

Language as Instrument of Exclusion and Inclusion in Tribal Educational Development

Saumya Deol and R. R. Patil

Language can be formally defined as a pairing of a lexicon and a set of syntactic rules, being systematically governed at the level of sounds, words and sentences. A full appreciation of the role of language in education goes much beyond this definition. Language allows its users to decipher and unfold the world around them. When examined from a multidimensional holistic perspective of its structural, literary, sociological, cultural and psychological aspects, language becomes a potent tool of inclusion and exclusion in the society, especially in relation to the educational development of various population groups. A language education policy thus needs to fully envelope all the different elements of language—functional, aesthetic, fictional, narrative, metaphysical, rhetorical and so on.

From the point of view of validity of language, there is no difference between various languages, standard or pure languages, or different dialects. Where written knowledge is consciously monitored and frozen in time, spoken language is far more transient in nature. Still, there is no intrinsic sacrosanct relationship between language and script. Indeed, all the languages of the world, with minor modifications can be written in one script, just as any single language that can be written in all the scripts of the world. In spite of the fact that all languages as abstract systems are equal, the complex ways in which history, sociology, economics and politics interact confer some languages with a more prestigious status. Such languages become associated with socio-political power and become the standard language. It occupies dominant space in all the grammar, dictionaries and various reference materials. This not just makes the standard language national, official, and associate official languages to be used in education, administration, judiciary, mass media and so on, but it also enables those who wield power to create and perpetuate negative stereotypes about the languages of the underprivileged. In the process of enumeration of language in the Census, many mother tongues get subsumed under a dominant language because of power dynamics.

Article 343–351 of Part XVII and the 8th Schedule of the Constitution of India deal with the languages of the country. According to Article 343(1), 'The official language of the Union shall be Hindi in Devanagari Script'. Measures for the promotion of spread of Hindi have been mentioned in Article 351. English was given the status of an associate language in 1965. The Constitution also provides that English will be the language of the High Courts, Supreme Court, Acts of Parliament and so on. Article 350(A) (7th Amendment Act, 1956) also provides for adequate facilities for instruction in the mother tongue at the primary stage of education to children belonging to linguistic minorities. Children of linguistic minorities have a Constitutional Right to obtain education in their mother tongue(s) if they so desire and if the minimum number of such children is '10 in a class of 40 in a school' (Kothari Commission).

A three-language formula was thus evolved in 1961 at a meeting of the chief ministers of different states. The three-language formula was modified by the Kothari Commission (1964–1966). It was suggested in the National policy of Education 1968 that the medium of instruction at the primary stage should be the mother tongue and that the state governments should adopt, and vigorously implement the three-language formula which includes the study of modern Indian language, preferably one of the southern languages, apart from Hindi and English in the Hindi-speaking states and of Hindi in the non-Hindi-speaking states.

When education is imparted in the dominant language of the main linguistic groups, it can have serious implications for the marginalized ethnic groups. The three-language formula bears special significance for the tribal students, for whom all the three languages of Hindi, English and the state language might be alien all together. It is based on the assumption that children who speak a minority language at home must be accultured into the school language and thus it acts as a tool of assimilation into the dominant culture. The decisions about which languages will serve as the medium of instruction and the treatment of indigenous minority languages in the education system exemplify the exercise of power and the process of creation of marginalization.

While one of the main objectives of language is to equip learners with the ability to become literate, and read and write with understanding, language also remains the main source of cultural transmission. The linguistic and cultural patterns of social behaviour are largely subconsciously acquired and they gradually become constitutive of our identities. The question of identity becomes particularly relevant in the case of tribal population.

When the medium of instruction in the educational system for all the children including tribal children is dominated by the dominant language, one of the foremost dangers before anything else is the gradual disappearance of the mother tongue of the tribal. As tribal children get accultured into communicating in the dominant language, they become more alienated from their mother tongue, first by force, and then due to their socialization process that is actually socializing them in dominant values. As the level of alienation increases, it is not uncommon to find tribal children attaching very low prestige to their own language. Every time we lose a language, a whole literary and cultural tradition is likely to be erased.

When a tribal child enters the educational system with a language that he or she does not understand and with whom he or she has no contact outside of the classroom as the medium of instruction, the greater the degree of the difference of the language from the linguistic variety that the learner's community actually uses, the greater will be the problems that the learner would likely face.

Moreover, it is not just the learner who has to grapple with the language at school, as many teachers are equally unfamiliar with the language spoken by the learner at home. Sometimes, such teachers are unable to develop a positive appreciation for both the child's language and culture, which severely restricts their ability to create a conducive atmosphere in the classroom. Students are warned not to use their home language in school.

When it is not considered important that the teachers know the language of the students, or that the special measures be evolved to bridge the gap between the languages of home, neighbourhood and school. More often than not, classroom transaction is a one-way communication from the teacher to the student, with no guarantee of comprehension on part of the learners as the educational basics—textbooks, learning materials, and the teacher's language of instruction—are available primarily or entirely only in non-mother tongue languages.

When instruction, curriculum and materials are not in the mother tongue and do not take into account the child's known world, these result in widespread low-attendance, low levels of learning and achievement, and high levels of dropout and repetition. It is a wastage of child's potential as literacy is not simply being able to decode what is on a page, it is rather the intellectual process of gaining meaning from the text. When pre-existing pockets of marginalization intersect with schooling in an unknown language, children find little meaning in the classroom to keep them there. The failure to provide teaching in a language understood by the tribal child underscores and perpetuates the pre-existing inequalities. The language that children are taught often reflects broader societal inequalities and asymmetries in power.

While many factors influence learning outcomes at school, early literacy experiences are particularly important in later school achievement. Learning to read is a complex process and it is essential that it happens early. The situation turns dismal when children are expected to understand content that is incomprehensible, cognitively difficult and has little relevance to their lives.

Lack of confidence in development and usage of the dominant language in school can impair the communication skills of the tribal children. It creates a passive atmosphere in the classroom with minimal engagement, activity and enthusiasm as students tend to listen silently. The lack of enthusiasm can be attributed to not just the alien language, but sometimes the alien content has little relation with their actual lives as the textbooks are both contextualized in the dominant culture and imparted through a dominant language.

Learning through a tribal language and developing literacy skills in it does not limit a child's capacity to develop skills in a second or major language. States such as Odisha and Maharashtra have developed primers in the tribal languages to promote learning through a dual medium of instruction, where the dominant language can be introduced in the higher classes. However, it is worth nothing that changing to an unknown language too early or too abruptly in a child's schooling can also be damaging as the children might not be able to be successful in learning through either their mother tongue or in the dominant language. The primary task of a school should be to relate the home language to the school language. Thereafter, one or more languages can be integrated so that one can move into other languages without losing the first one. This would ensure a smooth transition from home language to school language in terms of discourse as the child moves from the known to the unknown and result in the maintenance of all the languages, each complementing the other.

It is recognized that a variety of advance level of linguistic skills are easily transferred from one language to another by the learner. The wide range of linguistic repertoire acquired through two languages also enables students to negotiate different social situations more effectively. Children's understanding of what is being taught and discussed in class significantly improves and they can focus on learning core skills, rather than struggling to learn in a language they do not understand. A curriculum is rooted in the child's known language, culture and environment with appropriate and locally developed reading materials, on the other hand, it stimulates interest and ensures greater participation and engagement. It encourages fluency and confidence in both the languages.

There is a convincing evidence that a second language is learned best when a first language is learned well as the child can utilize the same structures of organizing and comprehending the content. Learning to read requires a range of complex skills includes recognizing sounds, connecting sounds to symbols, developing vocabulary, understanding the content and developing fluency. Such children have a number of independent cognitive strategies at their disposal and exhibit greater flexibility in the use of these strategies to solve problems. Learning the dominant language later may ultimately be the more effective route.

The availability of good learning materials, written in a language and with a context relevant to the child is vitally important. This emphasises that the procurement of relevant reading and learning material is not just an act of translation from dominant languages, but that the content should also be culturally appropriate and relevant to the child, which he or she can relate to the outside world. Besides being important in children's learning, it can play an integral role in indigenous language revitalization, development and regeneration, and preservation of tribal culture and identity.

Mother tongue based instruction also has a positive impact on the child's self-esteem. It promotes a warm and secure learning environment where the child takes pride in his or her cultural and linguistic identity. When there is a linguistic and cultural discontinuity between home and school, minority language children may perceive that their language and culture are not valued—a perception that lowers their self-confidence and self-esteem and interferes with their learning. A smooth transition from home to school on the other hand fosters an emotional stability that translates to cognitive stability.

The potential cost of implementing mother-tongue learning is often cited as a reason for not introducing it: policymakers claim that it is financially impractical in resource-constrained countries. Certainly, in countries such as India, where there are many language groups, introducing early mother-tongue learning across the board may look economically challenging.

While exact costs depend on context and approaches, investment in mother tongue education is more than offset by improved educational performance. In the few cases where the benefits have been calculated, the savings from reduced school repetition and dropouts have considerably outweighed the incremental costs of establishing and maintaining schooling in local languages (production of learning materials, teacher training, etc.). Large amounts of teaching time, materials and infrastructure are wasted when children dropout, repeat grades, or fail to achieve learning outcomes. In Guatemala, for example, a study found that mother-tongue-based bilingual schooling created savings of US$5.6 million a year through reducing dropout and repetition, despite higher initial costs for introducing new materials and teacher training.

CASE STUDY

In the states of Andhra Pradesh and Odisha, with the support of Government, indigenous learning materials in minority languages had been developed for primary schools. The material included alphabet charts, primers, and big and small books for group and individual reading, majority of which were locally authored. Such materials were available in 10 minority languages in Odisha and in 8 minority languages in Andhra Pradesh. Materials for activities that aid in the reading process, such as picture/word cards and games, were also produced. The material developed for later primary years included mother tongue and bilingual textbooks and second language learning curriculum. The materials developed were based on community culture and knowledge and thus locally relevant and were developed with the support of local teachers and community. These measures brought a positive effect on the enrolment, attendance and achievement levels across the curriculum.

Additionally, in the programme, some schools were selected for specific research purpose under which additional materials was developed, focusing on fostering reading habit at both home and school, and increasing engagement of the community. It included the 'Read Together' programme, which sought to link oral traditions with written material.

Oral narratives on local history, ecology, and songs and stories were provided by the community and were incorporated in the content.

In the villages, community reading and learning resource centres were established and managed by the communities themselves. Such measures facilitated in developing the interest and engagement of the community in education of the children. Great improvements were observed in children's reading and learning attainment consequently.

Furthermore, in Odisha, the Government initiated a programme called Srujan which was aimed at increasing access to information, knowledge and materials for the multilingual education programme. It was a community-based approach to link indigenous community knowledge and practices with the curricular and extracurricular activities of the school, which included traditional games, art and craft, storytelling, nature walks, dance and music.

As a result of the programme, within 6 months, children studying in Class 1 showed ability to identify words and letters from a sentence, read a sentence with meaning and demonstrate creative thinking capacity. The children were able to relate what is taught in the classrooms with their own experiences and were thus better able to understand the content of the curriculum.

CHALLENGES

- Many indigenous languages do not have a written script due to either absence or loss of written version which poses a major hurdle in efforts at adaptation into a book as the pre-requisite to it is the development of a script of the indigenous language.
- It has been observed that in many communities, there are only a few proficient speakers of the indigenous language, if any at all, which is a major constraint in practicing the language in normative communicative contexts, in finding skilled teachers, and in developing complete range of adequate learning resources.
- Children being taught in more than one language are likely to promote the development of mixed languages, or localized versions of mainstream languages.
- The dominant language may be considered important by the parents, teachers and students for its role in professional success and upward social mobility. This might lead to students and parents

themselves resisting from what is being taught in the indigenous language and preferring the dominant-language medium.

- Since there are multiple indigenous languages, it makes provision of education in mother tongue a difficult task for the all children.
- There may be a lack of availability of teachers who are proficient in the academic instruction in the indigenous language and also appropriately trained.
- There may be a lack of availability of appropriate educational resources in the indigenous language.

DISCUSSION

A paradox is recently being observed in the educational scenario for tribal education in the debate on mainstream and vernacular/tribal language as the medium of instruction in schools. Many studies have reinforced the idea that concept formulation for children takes place in mother tongue; hence, there is a need to adopt home-language in the teaching pedagogy at least in the initial primary classes at school, which would improve the learning outcome of the tribal children. However, it is also observed that more parents of tribal children are increasingly aspiring to send their children to 'English-medium' schools that would equip their children with the language that is currently dominating the job market. Hence, a paradox arises as the importance of imparting education and concepts in mother tongue is juxtaposed against the rising demand of the parents to admit their children in English medium schools.

The medium of instruction in ashram schools is a very pertinent issue. Tribal languages ought to be viewed from a rights perspective. Language is an important component of one's identity and culture. Preservation of tribal languages thus should be encouraged. Education that gradually diminishes the number of speakers of a language can erase not just a language but an entire culture. Additionally, it has been empathized that the learning process that is based on a known home language is beneficial for children. In the absence of a known language, students must first put in efforts to understand the language in which the concept is being explained, and then try to understand the concept itself on the basis of their understanding, ranging from poor to excellent, of the language used as the medium of instruction. Such a home-language framework does not necessarily need to be exclusionary of other mainstream languages; rather, it can be complementary and assist in comfortable transition from home to school language at later stages of education.

On the other hand, tribal education must also be able to address the demands of parents of tribal children to obtain contemporary English medium education. While this definitely requires that the institutions of education for tribal be strengthened and upgraded with the contemporary times, however, it also indicates the need for an analysis of the dominant knowledge system. Market has been allowed to become the judge as education today is losing its true value and acquiring a mere 'Signalling Value'. This means that attaining a certain level of education is a 'signal' in the job market for possessing a certain skill set and this is the only purpose education has been reduced to. This 'signalling value' and dominant knowledge paradigm need to be questioned. Education must not be allowed to be judged by the market; rather, education should be allowed to evaluate the market. The knowledge system of the tribal must be respected and encouraged to be used as a vehicle for building their life skills, instead of just market-oriented skills. If one wants to empower the tribal, one must respect and include their pedagogy and their knowledge system.

RECOMMENDATIONS
Teachers

- Teachers should show an appreciation for the diversity in the classroom in terms of different backgrounds and varying cultures of the students, be positively inclined towards all the students and possess motivation to be positively involved in the teaching learning process.
- The feedback of teachers for designing textbooks and curriculum is very valuable as they represent the voices of the children and their parents. Teachers need to be trained to be sensitive observers in this context.
- When early literacy skills are imparted, their success depends on not only the availability of suitable materials, but also on how these

skills are introduced and taught. It is important that the teachers adopt instructional strategies which are engaging for children where they can be active participants in the learning process.

- Teachers' training also requires adequate attention and focus. Teachers need to be trained to be proficient in the language of instruction, and also possess teaching skills in the first and second languages. Teachers should also be trained the teaching methods that are learner-centred and interactive, and also designing and delivering curriculum that supports the acquisition of the skills in reading and writing.

Material

- Textbooks should be relevant and also interesting and challenging that encourage peer learning. The content of the textbooks should sensitize learners to socially relevant issues such as gender, AIDS, drugs, violence, politics and so on. The material should make a gradual shift from local culture to neighbouring cultures and then to the world culture.
- The material for textbooks is best developed by those who are aware of the aspirations and needs of the learners. Collaboration is required among teachers, innovative Non-Governmental Organisations and linguists to produce relevant study material.
- There exist quite some tribal languages which do not possess a script and thus such languages only have an oral tradition. The establishment of grammar and orthographies of such languages requires collaboration between educators, linguists and community members, which would also raise the status of the language itself as documentation of history, stories and local knowledge leads to the development of the language.
- The production of relevant and good quality material in tribal language must enlist community participation which would ensure inclusion of local and indigenous knowledge. Development of indigenous literature can be promoted through writing workshops, festivals, contests and so on. (e.g., Srujan in Odisha). Local artists can also be encouraged to produce illustrations that are relevant to the text and local context.

Pedagogy

- Children develop their language skills when they get a non-threatening and warm environment to practice their skills and listen to and use the language. Hence, the curriculum and pedagogy should enhance the listening and speaking skills of the students.
- Development of both home and mainstream language can be promoted through storytelling and singing rhymes in these languages.
- The charts in the classrooms can be labelled in both tribal and mainstream languages. This would build conceptual clarity and foster a learning environment.

Policy

- Bilingualism in schools should be promoted to promote conceptual clarity, ensure better cognitive growth, and foster healthier interpersonal communication skills.
- Multilingual classrooms can foster awareness and respect for linguistic and cultural diversity, and hence should be constructively utilized as a resource rather than being viewed as an obstacle.
- The survival of many tribal languages is being threatened by rapid social change and globalization and efforts are required to be made to ensure their preservation, sustenance and development.
- Reading habit must be encouraged in children through ensuring provision of relevant reading material in both tribal and dominant languages in all schools.
- Learning aids such as charts, cards, 'read aloud' books, can be developed in both tribal and mainstream languages which would facilitate learning. Interesting online and e-content can also be developed in indigenous languages as learning aids. The development of low-cost indigenous language learning material should be supported such as through making available printing paper to publishers at subsidized rates.

CONCLUSION

The functions of language go beyond literacy and communication. Language in itself is also a transmission of culture. While languages possess equal scientific validity, the complex socio-political forces make some languages more prestigious than others, used by the elite to wield power. Language can become an instrument of potential inclusion as well as exclusion. While languages such as English are becoming increasingly prestigious for professional and social mobility in the context of globalization, the language can also become a tool for exclusion when important educational concepts are imparted in a language that is incomprehensible to minority groups. In the backdrop of three-language formula, the medium of instruction in tribal schools holds significance as concerns of professional assimilation and social mobility need to be balanced with securing sense of identity and preservation of culture. The most crucial aspect here is making knowledge accessible in a medium comprehensible to the students so that no child is a mere spectator in the grand mission that is education.

Chapter 5

Living Conditions, Learning Status and Educational Performance of Tribal Students

Dhaneswar Bhoi

INTRODUCTION

Even after different specific policies, programme and schemes, the educational status of Scheduled Tribes (STs) is still low at different levels of education. Starting from their learning aids need to the residential school facilities, several policies, programmes and schemes are trying to bring the STs at par with the other categories at different levels of education. Despite these efforts, the STs still have very low access to enrolment, retention and evaluation (pass out/successful completion) at national as well as state and union territory levels. Jha (1985) argued about the schemes meant for tribals and that there are a number of problems in the ashram schools like the number of students admitted to the hostels had been much higher than the expected number of students. Moreover, the superintendents of these hostels were neither trained nor qualified for managing the hostel and teaching at ashram schools. The hostel rooms were also overcrowded and did not have basic facilities for a decent living. Raising the issue of gender, he argued that the scholarship given to girls were sometimes misappropriated and misused by their parents because of which the girl students were unable to utilize the money for the intended purpose. Apart from that, the money received by the ST students especially by the girls is not sufficient to fulfil their educational need. Thus, the prescriptions of the policies for the tribals have been unable to mitigate the needs of the tribal children. A number of incidents of death, poor health and unhygienic living condition are being reported in the media regularly. Therefore, a public interest litigation (PIL) has been filed in the Honourable Bombay High Court by the petitioners Mr Ravindra Umakant Talpe and others, alleging that proper arrangements have not been made in respect to basic public utilities which are provided in the *ashramshalas* all over Maharashtra. The Honourable Bombay High Court has directed the state government to make an assessment of the facilities available in the *ashramshalas* for the students by taking the assistance of non-governmental organizations (NGOs) in the field such as Tata Institute of Social Sciences (TISS) and other similar organizations. The State of Maharashtra was to make four zones and prepare teams either from Social Justice Department or Child Welfare Department along with members of the NGOs which are doing work in these areas (refer CRPIL 69 of 2013 heard on 18 June 2014).

As a result, a government resolution was issued by the Government of Maharashtra in July 2014 to carry out a survey with the technical assistance of Tata Institute of Social Sciences. The survey tool was designed by the Tribal Development Department (TDD) along with Tata Institute of Social Sciences. The state government formed a team of officials headed by the Child Development Project Officer of Integrated Child Development Services (ICDS), Women and Child Welfare Department in each district. The Deputy CEO (Women and Child Welfare) was designated as the nodal officer in each district. The team consisted of the following members:

TISS representative as an additional member as per the availability.

1. Child Development Project Officer, ICDS — Samiti Head
2. Extension Officer (Education), Panchayat Samiti — Member
3. Head Sevika, Child Development Project — Member
4. Social Welfare Supervisor Special Social Welfare Officer's Office (As per availability) — Member
5. Local SHG Representative of Maharashtra Financial Development Federation/MAVIM — Member

METHODOLOGY

The designated teams in each district of Maharashtra filled up the survey forms, visiting 1,076 *ashramshalas* in the months of August and September 2014. All the filled-in forms were collected at the Commissioner's Office, TDD, Nashik and were sent to TISS to tabulate, process and prepare the report. It was time consuming to do the data entry and processing the data as the survey gathered huge data. The data was entered online into a database, compiled and processed with the help of SPSS. The data has been analysed into the following areas: (a) Distribution of the *ashramshalas* covered under the study across the ATCs; (b) Profile of the *ashramshalas* and (c) Facilities in *ashramshalas*.

ASHRAMSHALAS COVERED UNDER THE STUDY

As the TDD has divided the state into four administrative zones under the Additional Tribal Commissioners (ATCs), the schools which are surveyed have been distributed across the four ATCs) in Table 5.1.

In Maharashtra, there are 1,108 ashram schools sanctioned out of which 552 are run by the TDD, Government of Maharashtra and 556 are aided or run by the NGOs. The study has covered 1,076 (523 government-run and 553 NGO-run) schools. Table 5.1 shows the distribution of the schools in different ATCs according to the different management. Out of the total schools studied, 51.4 per cent (553)

Table 5.1 *Distribution of Type of* Ashramshala *in ATCs*

Type of Ashramshala	ATCs				
	Nashik	Thane	Amravati	Nagpur	Total
Aided	209	71	128	145	553
	48.6%	35.7%	60.1%	62.0%	51.4%
Government	221	128	85	89	523
	51.4%	64.3%	39.9%	38.0%	48.6%
Total	430	199	213	234	1,076
	40.0%	18.5%	19.8%	21.7%	100.0%

schools are aided and 48.6 per cent (523) schools are government-run. The distribution across the ATCs shows that 40 per cent schools (430) are from Nashik, 18.5 per cent (199) are from Thane, 19.8 per cent (213) are from Amaravati and 21.7 per cent (234) are from Nagpur. In Nashik and Thane ATCs, the government-run schools are more than the aided schools whereas in Amravati and Nagpur there are more aided schools than the government-run ashram schools.

THE RESULT OF THE STUDENTS IN ANNUAL EXAMINATIONS

The data shows that the passing rate of boys was a little higher than the girls at the higher secondary level of education. The passing rate of males was comparatively higher in both government and aided schools. Likewise, the passing rate in government schools was slightly higher than the aided schools of boys and it is less for aided schools of girls (see Table 5.2).

Out of total schools, only in 394 (36.6%) schools, the students' attendance is more than 90 per cent and in 75 (7%) schools there is very low (less than 60%) attendance. In another 91 schools, the attendance could still be a concern as the attendance is between 60 and 69 per cent. In 255 (46.1%) aided schools, there is more than 90 per cent attendance but 33 (6.0%) schools have less than 60 per cent attendance of a student. On the other hand, in government schools, only 139 (26.6%) schools have more than 90 per cent attendance and 42 (8%) school have less than 60 per cent attendance (see Table 5.3).

Out of the total schools, there are 1,022 (94.98%) schools that have a blackboard in their classroom. There are 526 (95.1%) aided and 496 (94.85%) government schools that have blackboard whereas 27 (4.9%) of aided and 27 (4.9%) of government schools do not have blackboard in the classroom. This can have implication in the teaching and learning processes in the schools (see Table 5.4).

The maps and charts create a learning environment in the classroom. There are 589 (54.7%) schools which have charts and maps in their classroom and remaining 487 (45.3%) schools do not have them. Among them, 331 (59.9%) aided and 258 (49.3%) government schools have maps and charts in each classroom. But in 222 (40.1%) aided and

Table 5.2 School-wise Results of Students by Type of Ashramshala

Schools		Type of Ashramshala					
		Aided		Government		Total	
		Appeared	Passed	Appeared	Passed	Appeared	Passed
Secondary	Boys	5,290 35.1%	4,964 34.9%	9,773 64.9%	9,279 65.1%	15,063 9.36%	14,243 9.0%
	Girls	3,792 30.4%	3,477 29.5%	8,693 69.6%	8,320 70.5%	12,485 10.0%	11,797 9.6%
Higher secondary	Boys	862 32.5%	829 32.9%	1,787 67.5%	1,693 67.1%	2,649 1.7%	2,522 1.6%
	Girls	502 32.0%	472 31.6%	1,069 68.0%	1,021 68.4%	1,571 1.3%	1,493 1.2%

Table 5.3 *Students Attendance by Type of Ashramshala*

Students Attendance	Type of Ashramshala		Total
	Aided	Government	
Less than 60%	33 6.0%	42 8.0%	75 7.0%
60% to 69%	34 6.1%	57 10.9%	91 8.5%
70% to 79%	55 9.9%	106 20.3%	161 15.0%
80% to 89%	176 31.8%	179 34.2%	355 33.0%
More than 90%	255 46.1%	139 26.6%	394 36.6%
Total	553 51.4%	523 48.6%	1,076 100.0%

Table 5.4 *Classroom with Blackboard*

Classroom with Blackboard	Type of *Ashramshala*		Total
	Aided	Government	
Yes	526 95.1%	496 94.8%	1,022 95.0%
No	27 4.9%	27 5.2%	54 5.0%
Total	553 51.4%	523 48.6%	1,076 100.0%

265 (50.7%) government schools, there are no maps and charts in each classroom (see Table 5.5).

There are only 614 (57.06%) schools having two tubes/bulbs and fans in their classrooms and 462 (42.94%) schools do not have the tube light and fan facility. The distribution across the types of schools shows that only in 324 (58.6%) aided and 290 (55.4%) government schools

Table 5.5 *Classroom with Maps and Charts*

Classroom with Maps and Charts	Type of *Ashramshala*		Total
	Aided	Government	
Yes	331	258	589
	59.9%	49.3%	54.7%
No	222	265	487
	40.1%	50.7%	45.3%
Total	553	523	1,076
	51.4%	48.6%	100.0%

Table 5.6 *Tubes/Bulbs and Fans in the Classroom*

Two Tubes/Bulbs and Fans in Each Classroom	Type of *Ashramshala*		Total
	Aided	Government	
Yes	324	290	614
	58.6%	55.3%	57.0%
No	229	234	463
	41.4%	44.7%	43.0%
Total	553	523	1,076
	51.4%	48.6%	100.0%

there are two tubes/bulbs and fan in each classroom. Whereas 229 (41.1%) aided and 233 (44.7%) government schools do not have the two tubes/bulbs and fans in each classroom. As some of the schools use the rooms as classrooms in the day time and dormitory at night, non-availability of the lights and fans would make the life of residents very miserable at night (see Table 5.6).

LIVING CONDITION IN ASHRAM SCHOOLS

Out of the total schools, there are 601 (55.9%) schools who have not provided separate bed or bedding for each student in the boys' hostel. A total of 385 (69.6%) of the aided and 216 (41.3%) of the government schools are without this provision. As a result, students have to sleep on the floor without mattresses as seen in the photographs. Out of the total schools, there are 593 (55.1%) schools where the girls' hostel has not provided separate bed or bedding for each student, of which, 376 (68.0%) are of aided and 217 (41.5%) are of government schools. If there is a comparison between the boys and the girl's hostels, there is hardly any difference in their bedding facilities. However, it is to be noted that there is a higher percentage (68%–70%) of the aided schools who do not provide bedding facilities to each of the students. This would mean that the students either share the beds or manage on their own without the provision by the schools/hostels (see Table 5.7).

Out of the total schools, there are 390 (36.2%) schools boys' hostel that do not have one fan and one tube light in each room of which 169 (30.6%) are of aided and 221 (42.3%) are of government schools. There are 352 (32.7%) schools girls' hostel who do not have one fan and one tube light in each room. This is constituted by 162 (29.3%) aided and 190 (36.3%) government schools (see Table 5.8).

All the schools should have toilets for the students and the staff. The Swachh Bharat Abhiyan is a campaign for building toilets across the country so that people do not have to go out for open defecation and feel ashamed, embraced, harassed and become a victim of many diseases. Table 5.9 shows that in 307 (28.5%) schools the girls have the provision of one toilet for 20 girls and in 593 (55.1%) schools there is one toilet for 50 girl students. This could be a concern as with such ratio it might not be able to cater to the needs of the students, especially during morning time. The highest percentage of schools fall in this category across the schools. In addition, there are 176 (16.4%) schools where there are no toilets or the toilets are not in use. It is a serious situation. The situation for boys is no different. A very high per cent (272, 25.3%) of schools do not have toilets for boys or are unusable. There are certain commonalities on the availability of toilets for girls and boys. A very high percentage of schools have 50 students per toilet, across the type of schools and gender. However, most of the aided schools are in this category, even though the majority of the government schools also have a similar situation. On the other hand, the government schools are the ones leading without toilets for girls and boys (see Table 5.9).

Most of the schools have a water tank (57.7%), followed by a tap water (34.8%) and a vessel (4.1%). There are some schools who have

Table 5.7 Provision for the Separate Bed/Bedding for Each Student

Separate Bed/Bedding for Each Student	Girls Hostel			Boys Hostel		
	Aided School	Government School	Total	Aided School	Government School	Total
Yes	177 32.0%	306 58.5%	483 44.9%	168 30.4%	307 58.7%	475 44.1%
No	376 68.0%	217 41.5%	593 55.1%	385 69.6%	216 41.3%	601 55.9%
Total	553 51.4%	523 48.6%	1,076 100.0%	553 51.4%	523 48.6%	1,076 100.0%

Table 5.8 *Provision of Fans and Lights*

Provision of Fans and Lights	Girls Hostel					Boys Hostel				
	Aided School	Government School	Total		Aided School	Government School	Total			
Yes	391	333	724		384	302	686			
	70.7%	63.7%	67.3%		69.4%	57.7%	63.8%			
No	162	190	352		169	221	390			
	29.3%	36.3%	32.7%		30.6%	42.3%	36.2%			
Total	553	523	1,076		553	523	1,076			
	51.4%	48.6%	100.0%		51.4%	48.6%	100.0%			

Table 5.9 *Toilets for the Students in the Hostel*

Toilets	Girls			Boys		
	Aided School	Government School	Total	Aided School	Government School	Total
20 Students per toilet	151 27.3%	156 29.8%	307 28.5%	115 20.8%	109 20.8%	224 20.8%
50 students per toilet	347 62.7%	246 47.0%	593 55.1%	354 64.0%	226 43.2%	580 53.9%
Not available/not in use	55 9.9%	121 23.1%	176 16.4%	84 15.2%	188 35.9%	272 25.3%
Total	553 51.4%	523 48.6%	1,076 100.0%	553 51.4%	523 48.6%	1,076 100.0%

Table 5.10 *Provision of Drinking Water*

Sources Water	Nos. Schools	Percent
Tap	374	34.8
Water tank	621	57.7
Vessel	44	4.1
Others	37	3.4
Total	1,076	100

Table 5.11 *First-aid Box Available in the* Ashramshalas

Availability of First-Aid Box	Type of *Ashramshala*		
	Aided	Government	Total
Yes	461	382	843
	83.4%	73.0%	78.3%
No	92	141	233
	16.6%	27.0%	21.7%
Total	553	523	1,076
	51.4%	48.6%	100.0%

tube wells or open wells as the sources of drinking water. In about 66 per cent of schools, the drinking water facilities are proportionate to the number of students living in the hostel which means there are inadequacies related to drinking water facilities (see Table 5.10).

More than 78 per cent of the *ashramshalas* have the first–aid box with necessary basic medicines and materials. While around 83 percent of the Aided *shalas* have first aid box, it is 73 per cent of government *shalas* that have a first–aid box (see Table 5.11).

CURRICULAR PARTICIPATION OF THE STUDENTS

The participation reflects the accessibility of education system for the students. Participation in the classroom leads to involvement in the system. It also reflects the attachment with the school and education system. The quality of involvement of the students in the class can be gauged through the quantity and quality of the questions and answers by the students. The effects of the opposition of the banking system can be found out through this method of participation. The percentage of questions being raised in the class by the students increases with the increase in the standard of education (Rupavath 2016).

TISS (2016) study shows that many ashram schools do not have blackboards in the classrooms, nor maps and charts or proper lights and fans in each classroom. This can have implications in the teaching and learning processes in the schools. It has been observed that about 58 per cent of the students, irrespective of social categories, find difficulties in understanding classroom teaching mostly in language subjects followed by maths. It shows that more ST students are facing problems to understand classroom teaching than other students. However, about 42 per cent of the students do not find it difficult in classroom teaching.

CONCLUSION

A large number of tribal students (5,61,644 students for the academic year 2014–2015) are registered in more than 1,000 ashram schools of Maharashtra. Therefore, it is important to examine the situation of the ashram schools against their objectives of social, economic and educational advancement of the inhabitants in scheduled and remote areas. The state invests huge resources for the infrastructural, staff and the expenses for the students in the ashram schools. Unless and until the infrastructure, living condition, food and medical facility are enhanced in the ashram schools, it is very much difficult to expect a good performance of the tribal students in the ashram schools.

REFERENCES

Jha, P. 1985. *An Evaluative Study of the Hostels and Ashrams for Tribal Girl Students.* San Francisco, CA: Jossey-Bass Publishers.

Rupavath, R. 2016. 'Access to Education: Education Status of Scheduled Tribes in Andhra Pradesh: Attainments and Challenges'. *Review of Public Administration and Management* 4 (1): 1–7.

TISS. 2016. *A Report on Status of Government and Aided Ashram Schools in Maharashtra.* Mumbai: Government of Maharashtra.

Chapter 6

Insights on High Dropout Rates among Katkari Tribal Children in Maharashtra

S. N. Tripathy

BACKDROP

Education holds the key to economic growth and social transformation. It is remarkable to note that the total Scheduled Tribes (ST) population in the country, according to the Census 2011, was 8.6 per cent of the total population of the country. The states of Madhya Pradesh, Chhattisgarh, Maharashtra, Odisha, Jharkhand and Gujarat have more than half of the total tribal population of our country. In Maharashtra, the Katkari tribes are vulnerable primitive tribal group, regarded as the lowest in the social hierarchy by other STs in the region.

According to Census 2011, the tribal population constitutes 9.35 per cent of total population of Maharashtra and 10.08 per cent of total ST population of India. In the state of Maharashtra, out of 45 STs only three tribal communities such as Katkari, Kolam and Madia Gond have been listed as particularly vulnerable tribal groups (PVTGs). Katkari, also referred to as Kathodi, is the largest PVTG of the state which constitutes 3 per cent of total ST population of Maharashtra and 44 per cent of total PVTGs population. The Katkaris are among the most marginalized diminishing tribes of Maharashtra; their culture being in a transitional melting pot, grappling with alcoholism, cultural alienation and abject poverty.

BRIDGING SOCIAL CATEGORY GAPS IN ELEMENTARY EDUCATION

There has been a substantial increase in enrolment in elementary education of children from disadvantaged population groups such as Scheduled Castes (SC) and STs, children belonging to minority communities and children with special needs. Between 2000–2001 and 2013–2014, the gross enrolment ratio (GER) in primary education for SC children has increased from 96.8 per cent to 113 per cent, while the GER in upper primary education increased from 65.3 per cent to 98.3 per cent. The GER for ST children in primary education has increased by 12.1 percentage points, while the GER in upper primary education has increased by 31.1 percentage points during the period 2000–2001 to 2013–2014 (National University of Educational Planning and Administration 2014).

Review of Literature

Literature and studies on education of tribes give an insight into the extent of research conducted and identify the gap existing for further investigation. In this context, there have been several studies; a few of them have been outlined further.

Shyamlal (1987) and Sujatha K. (1996) both in their research opined that initiatives have been taken by the government in bringing low-cost primary schooling in the form of single- or two-teachers school in sparely populated tribal habitation. But this experiment does not bring desired results. When one or two teachers are expected to teach five classes, the quality of education becomes extremely poor. Hence, little or no learning takes place. In the classroom, teachers spend most of their time mainly in controlling diverse groups of children rather than communicating lessons effectively to them. Irregular attendance of teachers and frequent closure of schools are the most important causes for dropout of tribal children.

Sardamoni (1995) has highlighted that the children of migrant labourers, who often are a part of the labour process, and are on the move with their parents, have little opportunity to go to school. Migrant girls and women are also exposed to the risk of sexual harassment and exploitation. Women and children, who accompany these migrant workers, are even worse off. The overlapping of the migration cycle with the school calendar makes study impossible for these children.

Vinoba Gautam (2003) in his study examined education of tribal children in India and the issue of medium of instruction through a joint programme 'Janshala' for the universalization of primary education among educationally underserved communities. The programme was being implemented in nine Indian states. Records collected in schools in the Janshala programme areas indicated continuing high 'dropout' rates among tribal children. A crucial factor pointed out by him was the issue of language as the medium of instruction was regional language. Most tribal children do not understand the textbooks, which were generally in the regional language. The appointment of non-tribal teachers in tribal children's schools was another concern, as the teachers could not know the language the children spoke and children could not understand the teacher's language.

Tripathy and Pradhan (2003) have remarked that poverty and economic compulsions are the factors responsible for high dropout rates of tribal girls, as poverty-stricken parents do not possess adequate income to support their daughters to continue their education. The girls engaged in attending to younger siblings, which enabled their mothers to go out for wage earning and employment in the informal sector. Thus, the literacy level among tribes in general and tribal girls in particular were abysmally low.

Smita (2007) in her study reflected that for the children who migrate out with their parents—as there is only a small percentage of children who stay back in the village—their education is disrupted year after year, leading to dropping out of school entirely. Most of the children who do accompany their parents and families work in the sugar cane fields. The migrations force adults to take their children along, making them drop out of school and terminating the only opportunity available to them for an alternate future. Evidence indicates that such migrations are widespread and mounting, and the number of children below 14 years involved may be close to 9 million.

Tripathy (2012) in his study expressed that the migrant folk mostly consist of poor, illiterate and landless agricultural labourers, who do not have adequate income to meet the basic minimum requirements. The seasonality of the agricultural activities makes their life more miserable and they migrate to better-off places. The tribes constitute a major chunk of these migrants in all the states.

Haseena (2014) has studied on problems of tribal education and causes for dropouts. Tribal literacy is lagging behind because of their economic backwardness, social customs, lack of awareness about education, cultural ethos and distance between home and schools, etc. Thus, the policy framers have to focus on long-term strategies which should enhance the educational status of tribal children.

It is apparent from the foregoing analysis that there has been a plethora of studies on tribal education, but a study pertaining to tribal migrant children and specifically on Katkari children of Raigad district has not been conducted in the recent years. Hence, there is justification for the present chapter.

Objectives of the Study

The specific objectives of the present chapter are as follows:

1. To portray the background of the Katkari tribe of Raigad district of Maharashtra.
2. To examine the problems of educational attainment among the Katkari tribal children and the impediments encountered, resulting in high dropouts among them.
3. Finally, to suggest policy implication for betterment in the education through revamping the functioning of ashram schools/residential schools for Katkari tribal children.

Methodology

Methods adopted for collection of data in this study were both secondary and primary. Observation, direct small interview with the head of the households who had returned from the destination and participatory rural appraisal were resorted to collect the primary data. While secondary sources of data were collected from various published sources, primary data were collected with the help of interview schedule from 80 sample households of two sample villages. These two villages were Chandewadi and Sonarwadi under Konkan region, selected purposively due to the heavy concentration of Katkari households. While Chandewadi village is in Mangaon taluka, Sonarwadi village is in Mahad taluka located at a distance of 74 km and 117 km, respectively, from the district headquarters Alibag. There were 110 Katkari households in Chandewadi village, whereas there were 80 Katkari households in Sonarwadi village. Fifty households from Chandewadi village which comes to 45.4 per cent of the total Katkari households and 30 households from Sonarwadi village which comes to 37.5 per cent of the total Katkari households were identified for the study. The households having at least one school going children were selected for the purpose of data collection. Thus, out of 190 Katkari households only 80 households constituting 42.1 per cent were interviewed during February–March in 2016 at their place of origin (Table 6.1). There were 84 Katkari children in the age group of 5+ to 14 years supposed to be enrolled in the *ashramshalas*. Because of the grassroots relationship and bonds of rapport stimulated during the field visits, two focus group discussions (FGDs) with the key leaders of the villages, consisting of both men and women, one in each village were resorted to. The rapid appraisals have helped in studying the extent of educational deprivations and dropout among the children of Katkari tribe.

DISTRESS MIGRATION AS A COPING MECHANISM FOR THEIR LIVELIHOOD

The concept of migration is an old social phenomenon with human civilization. Migration is one of the dynamic constituents of population change and a vital component of development (Tripathy 2005: 24). It may consist of the crossing of village or town boundary as a minimum condition for qualifying the movement as integral migration (Tripathy 2005: 1). An important group of circular migrants consist of 'seasonal migrants' who combine activities in several places according to seasonal labour requirements and availability of seasonal work opportunities

(Tripathy 2006: 2). Such seasonal migration is an outcome of environmental degradation, acute poverty, indebtedness to the moneylenders or brick kiln owners (Gadgil and Guha 1995).

In the context of Katkaris of Raigad district, rural to urban migration of the poor Katkari tribe along with their family has been manifested as a significant aspect of survival strategy. This coping mechanism has been resorted to compensate for the insecurity of livelihood. The Katkaris are engaged in multiple occupations ranging from charcoal making to brick kiln labourers or daily wage labourers. Labour contractors, engaged every year to find workers, use cash advances to allure for brick production work and to keep them tied down to it.

The brick kiln owner appoints the *mukadams* (supervisors) to monitor the labourers. The *mukadams* take attendance, delegate work among the labourers, supervise the work done, maintain the record and ensure that labourers do not leave or run away from the kiln. The supervisors are paid according to the number of labourers they have to supervise and are responsible for controlling and keeping them under surveillance. Conditions of unemployment, landlessness and poverty constrained the Katkari tribes to work under the contractors and brick kiln owners under subhuman living conditions.

ENABLING EDUCATION FOR THE TRIBAL CHILDREN

Article 46 of the Directive Principles of State Policy manifests that the state shall promote with special care the education and economic interests of the STs and protect them from social injustice and exploitation.

After four decades of planning, it was felt imperative to initiate educational promotion drive so as to promote literacy among tribal students by providing hostel accommodation to such students who were not in a position to continue their education either because of the remote location of their villages or because of their poor economic condition. While the construction of tribal girls' hostels was started during the Third Plan period, a separate scheme for the construction of hostels for tribal boys was launched in 1989–1990 to provide an environment conducive to learning to the students belonging to the STs and to arrest the dropout rates in primary, middle and secondary stages (Jha et al. 2015).

Thus, ashram schools/residential schools for tribal children were established in tribal sub-plan areas from 1990–1991 onwards.

In order to provide quality education to the tribal students, a part of funds under Article 275 (1) of the Constitution of India was utilized for setting up of 100 Eklavya Model Residential Schools in 20 states from Class 6 to Class 12 in different states. This initiative was embarked upon during 1997–1998 with the objective of enabling tribal students for availing the facility of reservation in higher and professional education courses as well as in higher level jobs in the government and different public sector undertakings. The government interventions in education-related plans and programmes were to support the tribal community in building their confidence and making them at par with other community in terms of socio-economic development considerations.

In the aforementioned backdrop, before penetrating the problems of tribal education, we can shed light on the constraints and problems of education in the context of non-tribal children. According to the 2011 Census, more than 65 million children in the 6–17 age group are out of school. Out of every 100 children who enrol in Class 1, about 20 per cent dropped out before reaching Class 5 and around 47 per cent before reaching Class 10. The dropout rate is much higher among ST children (31% in primary education and 62% before reaching Class 10; MHRD 2014). While persistence of the quality gap in physical infrastructure of government schools has been a crucial reason for the high dropout rate (Ministry of Statistics and Programme Implementation (MoSPI) 2015), the existence of 7.5 per cent single-teacher schools, 4.2 per cent single-classroom schools (Mehta 2016), more than 0.5 million vacant teacher posts and 20 per cent of teachers untrained at the elementary level (MHRD 2016), only 57.3 per cent elementary schools that had an electricity connection and only 26 per cent of the schools that had a computer (Mehta 2016), etc., are the supply constraints and roadblocks in the path to success of Sarva Shiksha Abhiyan, one of the flagship programmes of the government after its inception in 2000–2001.

Kasturba Gandhi Balika Vidyalaya (KGBV) is the public sector educational development scheme aimed at reaching the 'most marginalized', largely to dropout girls. The number of such schools/

facilities and the enrolment of girls there is higher than that in Jawahar Navodaya Vidyalayas and lower than that of ashram schools. Thus, ashram schools/residential schooling has emerged as a major system of providing school education to tribal children spread over all parts of the country and these access their funding from union and state governments.

In the perspective of Katkari tribes of Maharashtra, as per 2011 Census, total literacy percentage of the Katkari is 41.7 per cent with its male literacy 49.4 per cent and female literacy 34 per cent. Katkari literacy rate is lower than the state's tribal literacy, that is, 65.7 per cent. Even male and female literacy percentage of Katkari group is lower than the state's tribal literacy rate.

RESIDENTIAL ASHRAM SCHOOLS IN MAHARASHTRA

The Tribal Development Department (TDD) is running the functioning of residential ashram schools in hilly and remote tribal concentrated regions of Maharashtra for social, cultural and educational development of tribal children. In Maharashtra, the TDD is operating 1,078 ashram schools to cater to the educational, health, nutritional and sociocultural needs of 0.425 million tribal children. There are 556 aided ashram schools administered by non-governmental organizations (NGOs), catering educational services to 225,576 tribal students, that is, 135,628 boys and 89,948 girls (Waghmore 2014).[1]

The concept of ashram school has originated from the traditional Indian *gurukuls* in which the teacher and the students live together having close interface with the sublime intention of serving the teacher in the development of complete personality and in sharpening their abilities. The foremost objectives of ashram school as envisaged by the numerous committees and commissions are as follows: to impart general formal

---

[1] This work explores the persistent exclusion and deprivation of Katkaris in the districts of Raigad and Thane region, following mixed methods and a review of secondary literature. It details the extreme vulnerabilities faced by Katkaris in the present time. The report also suggests culturally and economically sensitive government measures for inclusion and development of the Katkaris.

education, to encourage tribal traditions such as folk songs and dances so that the schools are not only learning places but also centres of cultural activities, to decrease the dropout rate and to increase the retention capacity of the school. Accordingly, ashram schools are anticipated to reduce the incidence of absenteeism, wastage and stagnation, and expand the standard of education at primary level (Waghmore 2014).

IMPEDIMENTS IN ACCESSING EDUCATION TO KATKARI CHILDREN

It is lamentable to note that the Katkaris out of schoolchildren were deprived of education and on the contrary were helping their families to make their living at the destination in the brick kiln.

Migration adversely affects the educational access of children considerably and, as a result, the Katkari children are deprived of their childhood too early due to economic compulsions. This is mirrored in the educational levels among the Katkaris. The *ashramshalas* could be a great source of relief for the Katkaris if they are provided culturally and socially sensitive environment along with quality education and living. *Ashramshalas* have, however, failed to do so. Thus, there has been an overwhelming absence of the Katkaris in *ashramshalas*. Further, lack of incentives, schemes, jobs and secured future for educated Katkaris has only discouraged the Katkaris from taking on the challenge of higher education.

Table 6.1 *Sample Villages in Raigad District and Selection of Households*

Hamlet/ Villages in Raigad District	Distance of the Villages from Alibag (in km)	Number of Katkari Households	Households Interviewed	Percentage
Chandewadi	74	110	50	45.4
Sonarwadi	117	80	30	37.5
Total	191	190	80	42.1

Source: Field study.

Table 6.2 *Educational Profile of the Sample Migrant Katkari Households (N = 80)*

Socio-economic Profile	No. of Members	Percentage
Age group		
Below 5 years	66	17.74
5–14 years	84	22.58
15–45 years	92	24.73
46 years and above	130	34.95
Total	372	100.00
Level of literacy		
Illiteracy	192	62.75
Knowing only signature	44	14.37
Read and write	70	22.88
Total	306	100.00

Source: Field study.

Table 6.2 demonstrates the socio-economic profile of the Katkari sample households. It is revealed that there is an aggregate of 372 members from 80 sample households.

There were 66 members (17.74%) in the age group of below 5 years. In the school going age of 5–14 years, there were 84 members constituting 22.58 per cent of the total members from among the sample households. A maximum of 92 members (24.73%) are in the productive age group of 15–45 years who are physically sound to perform the strenuous work, whereas in the age group of 46 years and above there were only 130 members which includes aged parents, widows, etc. (34.95%).

In the present chapter, excluding the members belonging to the child category below 5 years, there were 306 members. Illiteracy was rampant among the Katkari members as 192 members (62.75%) were illiterate. Out of the illiterate members, the number of children not enrolled in school has been significant. While 44 members (14.37%) were only able to put their signature by practice, there were 70 members, constituting a meagre percentage of 22.88 per cent who could read and write.

SOCIO-ECONOMIC AND OTHER INDICATORS CAUSING DROPOUTS

Over dependence on subsistence and uncertain agriculture, absence of rural non-farm employment, increasing deforestation and recurring droughts have resulted in abject poverty in the tribal dominated districts of Raigad. It has been observed that the development of economic infrastructure such as irrigation, electrification, banking, communication, which could have generated direct economic benefits to the people for sustainable form of livelihood in the district has not been followed up in the right perspective.

The backwardness of tribal regions, widespread poverty of the tribes and problems of integrating them with the mainstream of civilization, etc., are the stumbling blocks in the path of educational development of Tribes (Tripathy 1989). In the tribal regions, a high frequency of dropouts because of lack of awareness about the significance of formal education is conspicuous.

Thus, it was further ascertained that poverty of the migrant households constitute the crucial factor for dropout of the children and non-enrolment of their children in *ashramshala* and, as such, they are deprived of their right to education.

It is depicted in Table 6.3 that the dominant reasons for non-enrolment of tribal children in the *ashramshalas* are to earn money to support the family income (26.19%), followed by failure in the class (21.43%) and lack of awareness and dislike of parents for study (14.29%).

Though primary education through *ashramshala* is within easy reach in many areas, secondary schools are not that widespread to be within easy reach of most of the villages. A communication gap exists between the teachers and the students on the one hand and the textbooks and the students' mental preparation to receive anything from them on the other, especially at the primary education stage.

The magnitude of educational development of tribes largely depends on a wide range of factors; mainly on the nature of tribal life (settled,

Table 6.3 *Reasons for Non-enrolment of Tribal Children in the Ashramshalas (N = 84)*

Sl. No.	Reasons for Non-enrolment	Response/ Percentage
1	Distance from home	10 (11.90)
2	To earn money to support the family income	22 (26.19)
3	Sibling care	06 (07.14)
4	Failure in class	18 (21.43)
5	Lack of awareness and dislike of parents for study	12 (14.29)
6	Gender discrimination	06 (07.14)
7	School is not attractive	10 (11.90)
7	Total	84 (100)

Source: Field study.

semi–settled, practising shifting cultivation, migratory), the *ashramshala* administration and environment, cultural barriers (assimilated tribes, tribes in transitions and primitive tribes), domestic and household economic use of the children, staff pattern, difficult communication, etc. The reasons which have contributed for high dropouts of tribal children in the study district have been portrayed in Table 6.3.

REASONS FOR GAP IN LITERACY AMONG TRIBAL GIRLS AND THEIR DROPOUTS

It was revealed from the FGD that the crucial reasons for the non-enrolment and dropping out from schools among the tribal children as a whole and tribal girls in particular were social, economic and cultural. The array of reasons found was:

1. Boys are given preference over girls in education due to gender discrimination. This disparity is particularly marked in rural areas and in urban when opportunity costs are high.
2. Girls are made to help in domestic activities earlier than boys. They are expected to look after the younger siblings, collect firewood or

fuel and fodder, fetch water, etc., in order to free the mother for productive activities. They are also needed to shoulder domestic responsibilities.

3. When girls attain puberty, fear for their safety rises and conservative cultural norms make parents withdraw them from school.
4. Early marriage ends schooling.
5. Parents are unwilling to send their daughters to co-educational schools and schools where there are no female teachers.
6. If schools are far away from home, parents are worried about the girl's safety. Sending an escort with her is not always practical.
7. The goal of a girl's life is marriage wherein she will be required to take care of the family. Thus, the parents feel that education does not have any value and is not relevant to the life of girls. Moreover, the school curriculum is also not relevant to the needs of the girl.

FINDINGS FROM THE FGDs

There were revelations from the FGDs pertaining to numerous stumbling blocks which obstruct the socio-economic development of tribes which in turn impact their educational attainments. These impediments were inter alia (a) lack of organization at the village or community level among the Katkaris, and exploitation by outsiders, (b) prevailing situation of landlessness, indebtedness, bonded labour, (c) illiteracy among the Katkari households, (d) lack of basic amenities in Katkari hamlets, deplorable housing conditions, food and nutritional insecurity, (e) inaccessibility to proper healthcare facilities, (f) inaccessibility to legal documents such as caste certificates, ration card and BPL certificate.

1. It is revealed from the FGDs that land alienation, failure of crops, ineffective implementation of government plans and programmes such as land reform measures and Forest Rights Act are contributing factors for large-scale landlessness and poverty of the Katkari households.
2. Explanations for influencing the educational achievement of tribal children were lack of ownership rights (private as well as community) over land, water bodies and forests, loss of access and control over natural resources traditionally harnessed coupled with a lack of alternate options (assured wage labour and employment), threat

of evictions and displacement, lack of information and awareness, inadequate education, and social and psychological insecurity.

3. The study revealed that impoverished living conditions, uncertain livelihood, lack of provision for basic education in destination point of work site due to seasonal migration of parents in search of work are crucial features for low literacy of tribal children.

4. It is further inferred from the FGDs that when the basic needs of the Katkaris are denied, the government is supposed to intervene with remedial measures, mostly in the mode of welfare schemes. But there are ways which mislead eligible beneficiaries out of the purview of their rights to food, such as (a) lack of awareness about the schemes themselves, (b) an eligibility criteria with selection in the hands of local elites, (c) tardy programme implementation and (d) corruption and pilferage of development funds. Invariably manifested in all tribal regions of our country with variation in degree, all these factors deprive the needy and poor marginalized Katkari tribes the benefits of food security. The reason for negligible literacy among the Katkari children is due to their migration and non-availability of schools in the migrant areas. The Katkaris believe that children are added assets to the families. They believe that employment to their children even at an age of 11–15 years could bring the families food baskets.

5. Educational achievement among Katkari children is abysmally low compared to other neighbouring tribal community of the state. Katkari children are forced to undergo series of vulnerabilities and social atrocities within the school circles.

CONCLUDING OBSERVATIONS

The Katkaris of today are fragmented and very scattered community, highly dependent on others for their livelihoods and for a place to live. Most Katkari are landless workers with only periodic and tenuous connections to their original nomadic, forest-based livelihoods. Many have become bonded labourers working on the brick kilns and charcoal units serving the urban and industrial interests of Greater Mumbai.

Residential schools as an access strategy for girls from marginalized communities have been part of programmes under the Department of Education. Besides, residential schools are also included in policies under the (a) Department of Social Welfare, (b) Department of Tribal Affairs and (c) Department of Women and Child Development. Kasturba Gandhi Balika Vidyalayas (KGBVs) and *ashramshalas* are the two most important residential school programmes for girls. KGBV in particular is important for its focus on empowerment.

The validation came not only from the need for covering the living costs and making it potential to have access to physical, residential space and food in order to be able access the schooling facilities but also from the need for providing a conducive environment for education where these children are not expected to participate in work and other chores. Although there is no definite policy on residential schooling in general or for girls in particular, several residential schooling strategies exist for girls in the public school system in India. There also exist certain small-scale residential schooling strategies outside the state sector, funded either through public funds or other avenues. While a few of these have some interlinkages, many have evolved independently of each other drawing their rationales from a variety of experiences within and outside the country. The information on the performance of these schemes/programmes/initiatives remains uneven, isolated and sporadic.

The benefits of this paradigm of development have been disproportionately cornered by the dominant sections at the expense of the poor, who have borne most of the costs. Development which is insensitive to the needs of these communities has invariably caused displacement and reduced them to a subhuman existence. In the case of tribes, in particular, it has ended up in destroying their social organization, cultural identity and resource base and generated multiple conflicts, undermining their communal solidarity, which cumulatively makes them increasingly vulnerable to exploitation.

Displacement deprives the vital sustenance of the tribal people who are dependent on the land, forests and common property resources for their livelihood and finally their long-term sustainability is also endangered.

The key factors explaining the highest incidence of poverty in tribal regions are: (a) tribes' low bargaining capacity; (b) their low degree of political representation and poor quality of local governance and (c) constrained access to forest, land and water. The issue of control, power and access to natural resources is contentious both at economic and political level for tribal groups, apart from deep-rooted corruption and massive pilferage of development funds by the government officials (Tripathy 2014).

From the earlier discussion, it also transpires that despite development efforts, the benefits of development have not percolated to the Katkari tribe, rather it has adversely affected their lifestyle, leading to the violation of human rights, miserable living standard of the tribes, restricted the community's rights over natural resources and their own forest resources and, finally, culminated in identity crisis of the tribes. The reckless and indiscriminate exploitation of natural resources by the non-tribes who dominate the government machinery in the tribal areas results in not only a threat to tribal survival but also leads to depletion of resources in the tribal regions.

SUGGESTIONS

Relevant suggestions with implications for policies that focus on the solution to socio-economic and education problems of the Katkaris are:

1. Improving the infrastructural facilities of tribal ashram school, as well as improving the quality of education and adequate provision for classroom, bathroom and drinking water should be made.
2. Adequate number of teachers should be recruited. Especially, it is better to recruit from the local area itself so that they can teach in the local dialect. Vocational training courses should be introduced to attract more tribal students.
3. There is a need to have a partnership between government, NGOs and private sector in education as government also is not capable of providing all services. Partnership, however, does not mean subcontracting but working as equal partners. Hence, it is suggested that the teachers should have sincerity of purpose and dedicated attitude to serve the tribal students.
4. The income of Katkari (PVTG) farmers needs to be enhanced through the development of agriculture, horticulture and cultivation of vegetables in collaboration with the dedicated NGOs in Raigad district. Cashew plantations in the hill slopes, grafted mango

tree plantation, pineapples, banana, lemon and papaya, etc., are essential for horticulture development to generate additional sources of income of the Katkari tribes.

5. The Katkari tribal youths need to be imparted training for upgradation of technical competence for their development. Improving the quality of human resources is essential for effective administration to ensure freedom from exploitation and finally to enrich the quality of life. The training component should include leadership management, natural environmental protection, maintenance of health and hygiene, household management, chidcare, etc., for bettering their way of life. Tribes evolved local specific livelihood strategies based on their indigenous knowledge. There is a need to change the school curriculum with reference to the richness of tribal culture to arrest the dropout rate of PVTG children.

6. Efforts are being made to generate a community demand for tribal girls' education and enabling conditions for people's and women's participation to create the push factors necessary to guarantee girls education. Motivation and mobilization of parents and the community at large, enhancing the role of women and mothers in school-related activities and participation in school committees and strengthening the linkages between the school, teachers and communities are some of the ways in which the enabling conditions are being created.

REFERENCES

Gadgil, Madhav, and Ramachandra Guha. 1995. *Ecology and Equity: The Use and Abuse of Nature in Contemporary India*. New Delhi: Routledge.

Gautam, Vinoba. 2003. *Education of Tribal children in India and the Issue of Medium of Instruction: A Janshala Experience Coordinator*. New Delhi: UN/Government Janshala Programme.

Haseena, V. A. 2014. 'Scope of Education and Dropout among Tribal Students in Kerala—A Study of Scheduled Tribes in Attappady'. *International Journal of Scientific and Research Publications* 4 (1): 1–23.

Jha, Jyotsna, Geeta Menon, Puja Minni, and Shanmuga Priya. 2015. *Residential Impact on Girls' Education and Empowerment*. Bangalore: Centre for Budget and Policy Studies (CBPS); IPE-Global.

Mehta, Arun C. 2016. *Elementary Education in India: Where Do We Stand?* Analytical Report and Analytical Tables, District Report, State Report Cards. New Delhi: National University of Educational Planning and Administration.

MHRD. 2014. *Educational Statistics at a Glance*. New Delhi: Planning & Monitoring Bureau, Ministry of Human Resource Development, Government of India.

MoSPI. 2015. *Status of Education and Vocational Training in India*. NSS Report No. 566 (68/10/6). New Delhi: National Sample Survey Office, Ministry of Statistics and Programme Implementation.

National University of Educational Planning and Administration. 2014. *Education for All: Towards Quality with Equity*. New Delhi: Ministry of Human Resources Development.

Sardamoni, K. 1995. 'Crisis in the Fishing Industry and Woman's Migration: The Case of Kerala'. In *Women and Seasonal Labour Migration, Indo-Dutch Series on Development Alternatives*, edited by Schenk–Sandbergen, 79–154. New Delhi: SAGE Publications.

Shyamlal. 1987. *Education among Tribal: Tribal education in Rajasthan*. Jaipur Print Well Publishers.

Smita. 2007. *Locked Homes, Empty Schools*. New Delhi: Zubaan.

Sujatha, K. 1996. *Single Teachers Schools in Tribal Areas*. New Delhi: Vikas Publishers.

Tripathy, S. N. 1989. *Bonded Labour in India*. New Delhi: Discovery Publishing House.

———. 2005. *Tribal Migration*. New Delhi: Sonali Publication.

———. 2006. *Dynamics of Tribal Migration*. New Delhi: Sonali Publication.

———. 2012. 'Socio–Legal Aspects of Migrant Labourers: A Study in Maharashtra'. In *Changing Dimensions of Social Justice in New Global Era*, edited by Kamlesh Gupta, Trivikram Tiwari and Nandini Basistha. New Delhi: Pentagon Press.

———. 2014. 'Naxalism and the Development of Tribal Youths'. *Tribal Studies: A Journal of* COATS 2 (2): 27–36.

Tripathy, S. N., and P. Pradhan. 2003. *Girl Child in India*. New Delhi: Discovery Publishing House.

Waghmore, Suryakant. 2014. *Socio-Economic Issues Facing Katkaris: A report prepared for Rest of Maharashtra Development Board*. doi:10.13140/RG.2.1.3629.6722. Available at https://www.researchgate.net/publication/290438347 (accessed on 3 April 2020).

Chapter 7

Education of Scheduled Tribes in Residential Schools in Manipur

Chipemmi Awung Shang and R. R. Patil

INTRODUCTION

Educating the tribal population is of great importance. Every Census report shows that the literacy rate of Scheduled Tribes (STs) is always lower as compared to other categories. The Constitution of India has made special provisions for promoting education among the Scheduled Castes (SCs) and STs. Article 15 (4) empowers the state to make any special provision for the advancement of any socially or economically backward class of citizens or for the SCs and STs. Article 46 contains a directive to the state governments to promote with special care the educational and economic interest of the weaker section of the public and, in particular, of the SCs and STs, and protect them from social injustice and all forms of exploitation.

The Government of India had initiated many policies, programmes and schemes to bring the tribals into the mainstream. Ministry of Tribal Affairs and Ministry of Human Resource Development had introduced special educational schemes and residential facilities such as ashram schools, Eklavya Model Residential Schools, Kasturba Gandhi

Balika Vidyalaya, Jawahar Navodaya Vidyalayas and various vocational training centres were opened in remote tribal areas. Apart from the government-run residential schools, many non-governmental organizations (NGOs), missionary organization and private agencies also run the residential schools for the overall development of ST children.

In order to enhance education among tribal children, residential schools/ashram schools facilities were introduced by the central government in tribal areas. The idea of tribal residential schools/ashram schools goes back to the education system in ancient India termed as ashram also known as guru (teacher) where students were living in teacher's household. Residential schools/ashram schools were in one sense a continuation of the home where the teacher offered personal affection conductive for the natural growth of tender life (Singh 1991). During the freedom movement, Mahatma Gandhi realized the suffering of the SCs and STs; he brought forth other social measures for their upliftment and favoured their educational advancement. Mahatma Gandhi exhorted social reformers like Thakkar Bapa to play a crusading role in the field of tribal education. In 1922, he started ashram schools to educate the tribals in Gujarat. From the very beginning, free boarding and lodging were given to the tribal students (Singh 1991).

The establishment of residential schools/ashram schools was envisaged as a direct intervention to tackle the socio-economic and geographic inequality of the tribal population by providing educational opportunities. The concept of ashram schools stemmed from the objective of providing an atmosphere in which the inmates are offered full opportunities to develop their personality towards their own community. In addition to formal schooling, these institutions aim at communication of new ideas and fostering leadership and decision-making ability among the inmates. The concept of ashram school combines both functional and literary aspect-based education, relieving the tribal parents off the burden of feeding, clothing school going children besides providing a congenial school environment. Further, it is expected to inculcate in the pupils a sense of service to society and link school learning with household and community activities (Mishra and Dhir 2005).

REVIEW OF LITERATURE

There had been many studies conducted on tribal education with special reference to residential schools/ashram schools in India. Sujatha (1990) conducted a study on tribal education with special reference to tribal residential schools/ashram schools in the state of Andhra Pradesh. The findings of the study reveal that most of the primary stages at ashram school are run in a rented house. Moreover, there was no adequate teaching aid material such as blackboard, maps, charts, globe, audiovisual aids and games materials. It also found out that the dropout rate in ashram school was alarming in spite of providing free boarding and lodging facilities. Sahoo (1992) in a study of tribal residential schools/ashram schools in Odisha found that most of the ashram schools faced the shortage of financial allotment, poor educational condition and lagged far behind the set norms. The study also reveals the shortage of teachers and teaching aid material; however, it stated that the academic achievement level of students is quite satisfactory and academic achievement levels of boarders are higher than that of day scholars. Ananda (1994) in a study of tribal education in Chenchus tribe of Nallamala Hills in Andhra Pradesh reveals that tribal residential schools/ashram schools in Nallamala Hills did not have proper facilities and equipment, buildings and accommodation, teaching aid, games and sports equipment and playgrounds. Lack of trained teachers and teaching aid contributes to absenteeism, stagnation and dropout among the Chenchus tribes. In addition, due to poor economic condition, parents could not send children to school but rather engaged them for earning a livelihood.

Lakshmaiah et al. (1995) in a comparative study of educational facilities provided by the government and non-governmental schools in the tribal area of Ranchi found that the residential schools/ashram schools located in Tamar block of Ranchi could not function properly due to lack of financial support from the government. Some residential schools/ashram schools had been closed down due to lack of fund, and this sudden closure of schools had a direct impact on the education of tribal children which led to the incidence of high dropout among the inmates. Panda (1998) and Yadappanavar (2003) carried out a study on education of the tribals in Odisha and

Andhra Pradesh, respectively. The findings of the study revealed that the number of educational institutions in the tribal villages is not adequate considering the total area and population. There was a problem of transportation and communication in most of the tribal areas and many of the interior forest tribal villages have limited schools, which makes them greatly handicapped with little scope of education. Children have to walk a long distance to attend school in other villages. Most of the tribal parents are not aware of residential schools provided by the government and though some are aware, they faced trouble in admitting children at residential schools due to seat limitation. The facilities provided in the residential schools are not at all sufficient; rooms are overcrowded, with inadequate beds and utensils, low quality of tables and chairs, and even the food provided is below standard and with poor medical facilities for tribal children. Shah (2005) in a study of tribal education too shows that there is an unequal distribution of educational institutions and facilities among the tribals in the same state in different regions, in the same region in different tribes and in the same tribe in different social strata. Even in the tribal community, those belonging to upper strata always take more advantage than the lower ones.

Pathak (2000), Nagi B. S. (2000), Narayan (2005) in a study of tribal education and residential schools/ashram schools found that many schools had no proper school buildings, boundary wall and some of the schools did not have sufficient classrooms, no separate toilet and teaching materials such as charts, maps and playing materials are inadequate. Ambashat (2001) in a study of 'Tribal Education: Problems and Issues' has pointed out the problems of instruction and curriculum followed in tribal school. Tribal children failed to understand the teaching process because the medium of instruction used is mostly other than their mother tongue. In the same way, the curriculum followed in tribal areas has not reflected tribal life. Moreover, the economic burden is another factor that hinders tribal education; many tribal families hardly get two meals a day and thus cannot imagine sending their children for education. Likewise, a study on the 'Role of Ashram School in Tribal Education' by Indira and Barak (2012) also shows that poverty is a major contributing factor for educational backwardness among the tribal community. It has been observed that parents of more than

60 per cent children of the ashram schools are labourers, 20 per cent are farmers and only 10 per cent are employees in the coal mines or government servant.

Jojo (2013) in a study 'Decline of Ashram Schools in Central and Eastern India: Impact on Education of ST Children' shows that many tribal ashram school buildings are in a bad condition without proper maintenance. Hostel rooms are congested and 2–3 students share the same bed. Food provided in the school is poor in quality and many schools do not follow the prescribed menu chart. Teaching–learning material such as map, chart, blackboard, tables and chairs are either inadequate or in poor condition. Most of the schools have electricity facilities; however, there is no regular power supply and inverters are used as an alternative. Toilet facilities in most of the schools are old and not in use due to unavailability of water, which makes students and teachers resort to open defecation. It is also observed that students are suffering from unhealthy and unhygienic environment in the hostel. Most of the school do not have provision for regular health check-ups and there are no special classes for health education and hygiene. Haseena and Mohammed (2014) in a study of education among tribal students in Attappady, Palakkad district of Kerala reveal that the existing educational system in tribal area does not match the learning styles, because, in most of the tribal culture, learning is an active enjoyable event mostly carried out among peers by giving more importance to music, dance and other types of entertainment prevalent in the community. The linguistic problem was another factor contributing to dropout because tribal children hardly know additional languages other than their mother tongue. Most of the tribal parents are illiterate and have low socio-economic status with little awareness on the importance of education; instead, they are more interested in giving household responsibilities to their children at a young age. The attitude of teachers towards the tribal student was another reason for dropout. It was observed that most of the students did not want to go to school due to the punishments they received in the classroom.

From the aforementioned literature review, it is known that several studies had been conducted on tribal education particularly on residential schools/ashram schools. Moreover, various studies have stated the numerous issues and problems of tribal education and tribal residential schools/ashram schools that are concentrated mostly in the tribal populated Indian states such as Andhra Pradesh, Odisha, Kerala, Jharkhand, Uttar Pradesh and Karnataka. Very few studies had been conducted on tribal residential/boarding schools in the north-east region, especially in the state of Manipur. Therefore, it is very significant to conduct a study on tribal residential/boarding schools from the north-eastern region perspective.

RATIONALE OF THE STUDY

As mentioned earlier, there have been many studies conducted on tribal education and particularly on tribal residential schools/ashram schools in different parts of India. However, very few studies on residential schools/ashram schools in the north-east region have been conducted and it is significant to have the viewpoint of the north-eastern part of the country, which has geographical isolation and cultural differences. This study examines the existing conditions of infrastructural facilities, staff management, teaching and learning pattern, curriculum and extra-curricular activities and dropout cases. It studied the best practices and contribution of these residential/boarding schools in the educational development of tribal children in the north-east region. The study also pointed out the issues and challenges of residential schools/ashram schools in the selected region/locality. Thus, this study will contribute with some kind of insights and knowledge of the tribal residential schools located in the north-east region and thus add to the ideas for the effective implementation of tribal residential schools/ashram schools schemes and policy in future.

Objectives of the Study

1. To study the existing condition of residential/boarding schools such as infrastructural facilities, administration and staff management.
2. To examine the teaching and learning pattern, curriculum and extracurricular activities, tribal sub-group representation including age, gender enrolment and dropout rate.

3. To examine the best practices of residential schools and also to find out various issues and challenges of residential schools.

Research Methods

This is a comparative study of residential schools run by government, NGO and Christian missionary organization/private in selected tribal areas of Manipur. The study used a descriptive design to describe the present status of residential schools as accurately as possible. Simple random sampling was used to select the types of residential schools, run and managed by different agencies in the tribal areas of Manipur.

Table 7.1 presents the sample size, which consists of 14 residential schools selected from two tribal inhabited districts of Manipur; four government-run residential schools, four Christian missionaries-run residential schools, four private-run and two NGO-run residential schools were selected for the study. Interview schedule was administered to all the selected residential school's principals and observation checklist was used for confirmation.

Table 7.1 *Residential Schools in Ukhrul and Churachandpur Districts of Manipur*

	Type of Residential Schools	No. of Schools Selected for Study
Ukhrul District	Government run	2
	NGOs run	1
	Missionary run	2
	Private run	2
Churachandpur District	Government run	2
	NGOs run	1
	Missionary run	2
	Private run	2
	Total	**14**

Source: Field-based data from selected districts of Manipur.

Data Analysis and Interpretation

1. *Infrastructural facilities:* Table 7.2 shows the infrastructural facilities of residential schools located in Ukhrul district of Manipur. In Ukhrul district, the government-run and Christian missionaries-run residential schools have pukka (concrete) buildings, while the private-run residential boarding schools are constructed in wooden building. It also shows that the residential schools in Ukhrul district have adequate rooms with separate study room, kitchen, dining hall and toilet facilities.

   It was observed that residential schools have electricity connection; however, generator and solar light is also installed to use whenever it is required. The main source of water supply in residential schools is a pipeline and wells; still, many residential schools face the problem of proper water supply from the pipeline. Government-run and Christian missionaries-run residential schools have wall/fencing and a security guard in the school compound, while NGOs and private-run residential schools do not have proper wall/fencing and a security guard in the school campus. Regarding medical facilities, first aid is available in all residential schools for immediate assistance, and district hospital is used for further medical treatment.

   Table 7.3 represents the infrastructural facilities of residential schools located in Churachandpur district of Manipur. In Churachandpur district, all the residential schools have pukka (concrete) buildings and have adequate rooms with separate study room, kitchen and dining hall and toilet facilities. All residential schools have electricity connection; moreover, generator and solar light are installed to use whenever it is required. Water pipeline and wells are the main sources of water supply in residential schools. All the residential schools have proper wall/fencing in the school compound. A security guard is available in the government-run residential schools, while other residential schools have no security guard in the school campus. First aid is available in all residential schools for immediate assistance and district hospital is used for advanced medical treatment.

2. *Administration and staff management:* Government-run residential schools in both the district are managed by state and central

Table 7.2 *Profile of Residential School in Ukhrul District, Manipur*

Infrastructural Facilities	Government	NGOs	Missionary	Private
Type of building	Pukka	Semi-pukka	Pukka	Semi-pukka
Sufficiency of rooms	Yes	Yes	Yes	Yes
Electric connection	Yes	Yes	Yes	Yes
Separate study room	Yes	Yes	Yes	Yes
Separate kitchen	Yes	Yes	Yes	Yes
Toilet facilities	Yes	Yes	Yes	Yes
Wall/Fencing in school compound	Yes	No	Yes	No
Security guard in school compound	Yes	No	Yes	No
Playground facilities	Yes	No	Yes	No
Source of drinking water	Pipe/Well	Pipe/Well	Pipe/Well	Pipe/Well

Source: Field-based data from Selected districts of Manipur.

Table 7.3 Profile of Residential School in Churachandpur District, Manipur

Infrastructural Facilities	Government	NGOs	Missionary	Private
Type of building	Pukka	Pukka	Pukka	Pukka
Sufficiency of rooms	Yes	Yes	Yes	Yes
Electric connection	Yes	Yes	Yes	Yes
Separate study room	Yes	Yes	Yes	Yes
Separate kitchen	Yes	Yes	Yes	Yes
Toilet facilities	Yes	Yes	Yes	Yes
Wall/Fencing in school compound	Yes	Yes	Yes	Yes
Security guard in school compound	Yes	No	No	No
Playground facilities	Yes	No	Yes	No
Source of drinking water	Pipe/Well	Pipe/Well	Pipe/Well	Pipe/Well

Source: Field-based data from Selected districts of Manipur.

government with school's principal as the head of institute. Christian missionaries organizations run and manage their own residential schools for tribal children. NGO and civil society organization working on tribal education also run residential schools in tribal areas, and they are managed by committee and schools' principals oversee the functioning of the schools. Some individuals who are interested in education also run and manage their own private residential/boarding school for tribal children. The study observed that all the residential schools have adequate staff in the school and there are no issues with regard to the sufficiency of teachers in the residential schools.

3. *Teaching–Learning pattern:* Classroom teaching is the common way of teaching and learning process. In all the schools, English is used as a medium of instruction; however, in exceptional cases, local dialect is used to make students understand the topic. Homework is assigned on a regular basis, but project works are rarely assigned. Evaluation of students is conducted on a regular basis; additionally, there are two major examinations, half-yearly and final examination. Half-yearly examination is mostly conducted in the month of June and the final examination is conducted in the month of November every year.

4. *Curriculum and extracurricular activities:* In Manipur, most of the residential schools follow the curriculum directed by the State Education Department that comes under the Board of Secondary Education Manipur. However, some residential schools like Jawahar Navodaya Vidyalayas and schools affiliated to centre follow the Central Board of Secondary Education pattern. With regard to syllabus content, many principals and teachers stated that there are some subjects that talk about tribal culture, tradition and way of life. However, they too felt the need for including more topics related to tribal life and culture. Tribal children love extracurricular activities and every residential school used to organize extracurricular activities such as singing, dancing, games and sports.

5. *Student enrolment and tribal sub-group representation*
Table 7.4 shows that the government residential schools have a higher rate of student enrolment as compared to Christian missionaries-run and NGO/private-run residential/boarding schools.

Table 7.4 *Type of School and Student Enrolment*

Type of Residential School	Student Enrolment Rate					
	Less than 25	26–50	51–100	101–200	300 and Above	Total
Government	–	–	1	–	3	4
NGOs	1	1	–	–	–	2
Missionary	2	–	1	1	–	4
Private	1	2	1	–	–	4
Total	4	3	3	1	3	14

Source: Field-based data from selected districts of Manipur.

All the government residential schools have more than 300 student enrolments, while Christian missionary and NGOs/private schools have less than 100 students. The reason is that government schools have less educational cost as compared to that of private and missionary schools. With regards to tribal sub-group representation, in Ukhrul district, Tangkhul community has the highest tribal sub-group representation and enrolment in residential schools, while in Churachandpur district, Kuki community has a higher rate of enrolment in residential schools as compared to other sub-tribes.

6. *Gender enrolment rate and age:* The study observed that in the majority of the residential/boarding schools, boys have a higher rate of enrolment as compared to girls. Most of the residential/boarding schools provide seats starting from Class 6 to Class 12. Minimum age of admitting in residential/boarding schools is at the age of 9–10 years and students studying in Class 6 can get admission in most of the residential schools.

7. *Dropout case and reason for dropout:* The data reveal that in the majority of the residential/boarding schools, boys have a higher rate of schools dropout as compared to girls (Table 7.5).

Some of the common factors that contribute to dropping out of tribal children include poverty and financial difficulties, poor scholastic performance, peer group influences, seasonal agriculture work, lack of family motivation and encouragement, and inability to adjust with the rules and regulations of the school.

Table 7.5 Dropout Case and Reason for Dropout Cross-tabulation

Sl. No.	Dropout Case	Poverty/ Financial Issues	Poor Scholastic Performance	Peer Group Influence	Lack of Motivation	Adjustment Problem with School System	Total
				Reason for Dropout			
1	Boys	2	2	1	1	4	10
2	Girls	0	3	0	1	0	4
	Total	**2**	**5**	**1**	**2**	**4**	**14**

Source: Field-based data from selected districts of Manipur.

8. *Best practice of residential/boarding schools:* Residential/boarding schools provide good educational opportunities and facilities for tribal children in Manipur. Government-run and missionary-run residential schools had been operating for a decade in tribal areas, while many new private residential/boarding schools have established in recent years. It is found that residential/boarding schools have provided better educational facilities to tribal children and have produced many good students.

   Government- and some missionary- and NGOs-run residential/ boarding schools have been providing free education facilities to talented and economically backward tribal children. Table 7.6 shows that Christian Missionary-run residential schools have better teachers' attendance, students' scholastic performance percentage and overall school achievement rate, which was followed by private-run, government- and NGOs-run residential schools. It also found that besides providing educational facilities, all the residential/ boarding schools have been contributing in overall personality development of the tribal students by providing skills development training, training disciplines, teaching basic hygiene and cleanliness, and making children learn a new language (besides mother tongue) to enhance socialization with others.

9. *Issues and problems faced in residential schools:* The data stated that most of the residential schools run by the government and socio-religious organizations have better infrastructure as compared to that of the residential/boarding schools run by private agencies. Lack of proper infrastructure and inadequate building are the main problems faced by the private-run residential/boarding schools. Most of the private-run residential/boarding schools are constructed in wooden building, while the government-run and socio-religious organizations-run residential schools are constructed in concrete building. Some of the residential schools run by the government and socio-religious organizations face the issue of overcrowding of students during the admission and enrolment process. While some of the residential schools run by private agencies faced the problem of parent's inability to pay the boarding fees, other common issues and problems of residential/boarding schools include irregularity of electricity, lack of safe drinking water from pipeline and sometimes also faced problem with ration supplies due to frequent bandh, strike and road blockage in the tribal areas.

10. *Challenges in running residential schools in the tribal area of Manipur:* Based on the information acquired from the present chapter, it is revealed

Table 7.6 *Best Practice of Residential Schools*

Infrastructural Facilities	Government	NGOs	Missionary	Private
Type of building	Pukka	Semi-pukka	Pukka	Semi-pukka
Adequate teacher	Yes	Yes	Yes	Yes
Teacher's attendance	Regular	Regular	Very regular	Regular
Teacher's training	Occasionally	Rarely	Regularly	Occasionally
Student's personality development	Yes	Yes	Yes	Yes
Student's skills development	Yes	Yes	Yes	Yes
Students scholastic performance (%)	85	85	95	90
Overall school achievement rate	Good	Good	Very good	Good

that there are many challenges in running a residential/boarding school in the tribal areas in Manipur. Some of the major challenges include lack of sponsors from government agencies as well as from the NGO, lack of awareness among the tribal parents on the importance of residential/boarding schools and also lack of finance among the private agencies in managing the residential/boarding schools. Last but not the least, shortage of affordable residential facilities for many economically weaker tribal children is a challenge.

FINDINGS/RESULTS OF THE STUDY

Some of the significant findings of the study are as follows:

1. The study found that there are less government residential schools in both the districts, considering the population of tribal children.
2. Many poor and talented tribal children are unable to access the government residential facilities due to shortage of schools and limited seat allotments. This shortage of government residential schools give way to many private agencies to establish residential/boarding schools with high educational cost.
3. It is observed that the overall infrastructural facilities of residential/boarding schools in Churachandpur district are better as compared to that of residential/boarding school in Ukhrul district.
4. Lack of proper residential building is the major problem of NGOs and private-run residential schools in Ukhrul district.
5. In both the districts, Christian missionary-run residential schools have better teachers' attendance, better percentage of students' scholastic performance and overall school achievement rate, as compared to private-run, government and NGOs-run residential schools.
6. In both the districts, government residential schools have higher student enrolment rate as compared to other residential schools due to less educational cost.
7. In most of the residential schools, boys have a higher number of students' enrolment; however, boys' dropout rate is also higher as compared to girls. A major reason for dropout among boys is found to be poor scholastic performance and inability to adjust with the residential schools' rules and regulations.
8. Parents are ignorant of the availability of residential facilities for tribal students.

SUGGESTIONS AND RECOMMENDATION FOR POLICY INTERVENTION

Residential/boarding schools have become a major system of providing education among tribal children in India. In Manipur, government-run residential schools had been running for a decade in tribal areas while unaided private residential/boarding schools have been booming in recent years. These residential schools access their funds from different sources, including union and state government, private agencies and NGO. Residential and boarding schools have contributed much in the overall development of the tribal students in Manipur. On the other hand, the study found that many young intelligent tribals are unable to get access in government and NGOs residential schools due to a shortage of residential schools and limited seat allotment, while unaided private residential schools are charging high fees. Based on the findings of the study, the following suggestions and recommendations are made that can enhance the education of tribal children in the north-east region in general and Manipur in particular.

1. The study suggests to the state and central government for urgent policy intervention to address the problem of shortage of residential schools/ashram schools in tribal areas of Manipur.
2. It recommends to the state and central government to establish more residential schools/ashram schools with games and sports facilities, so that along with education, many young talented tribal children can build their future career in sports activities too.
3. It suggests to the concerned government for strengthening missionary- and private-run residential schools through financial assistance and material aid, as they are highly contributing towards the overall development of tribal children.
4. It recommends to the NGO and civil society organizations working on education to take more interest, particularly in tribal educa- tion, by sponsoring additional residential schools facilities for tribal children.
5. It suggests to the concerned education board to include more topics on relevant tribal life and culture in the upcoming curriculum.
6. It suggests to local-based student organization to generate extra awareness programme on availability and opportunity of tribal residential facilities to parents and students.

CONCLUSION

This chapter concludes that in spite of some issues and challenges, the residential and boarding schools have contributed much in the overall development of tribal students in the north-east region, particularly in Manipur.

REFERENCES

Ambashat, N. K. 2001. *Tribal Education: Problems and Issues*. New Delhi: Venkatesh Prakashan.

Ananda, G. 1994. *Ashram Schools in Andhra Pradesh: A Case Study of Chenchus of Nallamalai Hills*. New Delhi: Commonwealth Publishers.

———. 2000. 'Educating Tribals: An Ashram School Approach'. New Delhi: Commonwealth Publishers.

Haseena, V. A., and A. P. Mohammed. 2014. 'Scope of Education and Dropout Among Tribal Student in Kerala—A Study of Scheduled Tribes in Attappady'. *International Journal of Scientific and Research Publications* 4 (1): 1–23.

Indira, Garnaik, and Niranjan Barak. 2012. 'Role of Ashram School in Tribal Education: A Study of Block in Jharsuguda District'. *Odisha Review*. 85–89.

Jojo, Bipin. 2013. 'Decline of Ashram Schools in Central and Eastern India: Impact on Education of ST Children'. *Social Change* 43 (3): 377–395.

Lakshmaiah, T., Bhupinder, S., & Neeti, M. 1995. '*Tribal Education in India*'. New Delhi: Inter-India Publication.

Mishra, B.C., & Dhir, A. 2005.'*Ashram Schools in India. Problems and Prospects*'. New Delhi: Discovery Publishing House.

Narayan, S. 2005. *Sustainable Development*. New Delhi: Commonwealth Publishers.

Nagi, B.S. 2000. '*Educating Tribals in India: A Study of Ashram Schools*'. New Delhi: Kanishka Publishers and Distributors.

Panda, S. C. 1998. *An Empirical Study of Education of Tribal*. New Delhi: Radha Publications.

Pathak, Nilpa. K. 2000. *A Study of Organisation of Ashram school in Baroda District*. New Delhi: NUEPA.

Sahoo, R. 1992. *A Critical Study of Ashram Schools of Orissa*. Pune: Centre for Educational Studies Indian Institute of Education.

Shah, B.V., and Chacko, Pariyaran. M. 2005. *Tribal communities and social changes*. New Delhi: Sage Publication.

Singh, S.N. 1991. *Tribal Education in India*. New Delhi: Uppal Publishing House

Sujatha, K. 1990. 'Education in Ashram Schools: A Case of Andhra Pradesh'. NIEPA Occasional Paper No. 18. New Delhi: National Institute of Educational Planning and Administration.

Yadappanavar, A.V 2003. *Tribal Education in India*. New Delhi: Discovery Publishing House.

Chapter 8

Status and Functioning of Tribal Ashram Schools

Prakash Chandra Jena

INTRODUCTION

For the development of a society, there is the need of inclusive progress of all the sections of the society, and from this perspective, education has been regarded both as an end in itself and a means of realizing other desirable ends. It develops the personality and rationality of individuals and qualifies them to fulfil certain economic, political and cultural functions, thereby improving their socio-economic status. It has been recognized as a major instrument which societies can use to direct the process of change and development towards desired goals. It provides vertical mobility and can thus help to equalize status between individuals coming from different social strata. Education imparts knowledge of self-identity and human environment that infuse a sense of confidence, courage and ability among the weaker sections of the society to know and overcome their problems associated with exploitation and deprivation and avail socio-economic and political opportunities extended to them (Pradhan 2011). Under Article 46 of the Indian Constitution, the government is committed to promoting, with special care, the educational as well as the economic interest of the weaker sections of the society, in general, and of the Scheduled Tribes (STs) and Scheduled Castes (SCs), in particular (Pattajoshi 2010). The Indian Constitution assigns special status to STs. Traditionally referred to as Adivasis, Vanvasis, tribes or tribal, STs constitute about 10.4 per cent of the Indian population. There are 573 STs living in different parts of the country, having their own languages, different from the one most spoken in the state where they live. There are more than 270 such languages in India (Dyson, 2002).

Recognizing the importance of education for STs, the Government of India has been initiating efforts to achieve education for all, particularly for the groups which have lagged on the economic scale. A major step was taken in 2002 when by virtue of the 86th Amendment to the Constitution, Article 21(A) was inserted making free and compulsory education for the children of 6–14 years age group a fundamental right. In pursuance thereof, Sarva Shiksha Abhiyan (SSA), a flagship programme, was launched for the achievement of universal elementary education (UEE) in a time-bound manner. It had a special focus on the education of tribal children. Recently, the Right to Education (MHRD 2009) of children to free and compulsory education was enacted which describes the modalities of the importance of free and compulsory education for children between 6 and 14 years. STs are one of the principal categories of backward classes or historically disadvantaged bottom groups of society. Despite the government's initiatives and efforts to promote education among STs, the literacy rate among STs, as compared to national average, has remained low and the female literacy rate has been even lower compared to national female literacy rate.

As given in Table 8.1 literacy rate for the total population in India has increased from 28.30 per cent to 72.99 per cent during the period 1961–2011, whereas the literacy rate among STs has increased from 8.53 per cent to 58.96 per cent. Among STs, male literacy rate increased from 13.83 per cent to 68.53 per cent and female literacy increased from 3.16 per cent to 49.35 per cent during the same period. It is seen that the percentage gap in literacy rate, which was 19.77 per cent in 1961, increased to 27.22 per cent in 1981, though there has been a reduction in the gap to 14.03 per cent in 2011.

Table 8.1 *Literacy among STs and All Social Groups as per Census 2011*

Year	STs %			All Social Groups			Gap %
	Male	Female	Total	Male	Female	Total	
1961	13.83	3.16	8.53	40.40	15.35	28.30	19.77
1971	17.63	4.85	11.30	45.96	21.97	34.45	23.15
1981	24.52	8.04	16.35	56.38	29.76	43.57	27.22
1991	40.65	18.19	29.60	64.13	39.29	52.21	22.61
2001	59.17	34.76	47.10	75.26	53.67	64.84	17.74
2011	68.53	49.35	58.96	80.89	64.64	72.99	14.03

Source: Census of India, 2011.

Scrutiny of data of literacy rates among STs in various states reveals that in most of the north-eastern states, namely Meghalaya, Mizoram and Nagaland, STs are at par with the general population, while in some of the other states, namely Madhya Pradesh, Maharashtra, Odisha, Tamil Nadu and West Bengal, which have sizeable ST population in remote areas, the literacy gap is still as high as 18–26 per cent shown in Table 8.2.

The Ministry of Human Resource Development is mandated to promote education in the country and take initiatives to improve opportunities for education of disadvantaged groups. The Ministry of Human Resource Development has addressed the issue of educational deprivation of ST children through creating better provisions, relaxing norms for opening primary schools in tribal hamlets, establishing residential facilities, opening Kasturba Gandhi Balika Vidyalaya in tribal areas, etc. Besides, the Ministry of Tribal Affairs makes all efforts to supplement the efforts of the Ministry of Human Resource Development, which is the line ministry, and the state governments/union territory (UT) administrations by administering various schemes with the objective of enhancing access to education through provision of infrastructure by way of construction of hostels for ST students, establishment of ashram schools, Eklavya Model Residential Schools, vocational training centre as well as to maximize retention of ST students within the various stages of school education and promoting higher learning

Table 8.2 Literacy Rate for General Population and STs as per Census 2011

India/State/UT	Literacy Rate (%) 2011 (General Population)			Literacy Rate (%) 2011 (STs)		
	Person	Male	Female	Person	Male	Female
1. Andhra Pradesh	67.02	74.88	59.15	49.21	58.35	40.09
2. Arunachal Pradesh	65.38	72.55	57.7	64.58	71.48	57.96
3. Assam	72.19	77.85	66.27	72.06	78.96	65.10
4. Bihar	61.8	71.2	51.5	51.08	61.31	40.38
5. Chhattisgarh	70.28	80.27	60.24	59.09	69.67	48.76
6. Goa	88.7	92.65	84.66	79.14	87.16	71.53
7. Gujarat	78.03	85.75	69.68	62.48	71.68	53.16
8. Haryana	75.55	84.06	65.94	–	–	–
9. Himachal Pradesh	82.8	89.53	75.93	73.64	83.17	64.20
10. Jammu and Kashmir	67.16	76.75	56.43	50.56	60.58	39.73
11. Jharkhand	66.41	76.84	55.42	57.13	68.17	46.20
12. Karnataka	75.36	82.47	68.08	62.08	70.14	52.98
13. Kerala	94	96.11	92.07	75.81	80.76	71.08
14. Madhya Pradesh	69.32	78.73	59.24	50.55	59.55	41.47
15. Maharashtra	82.34	88.38	75.87	65.73	74.27	57.02
16. Manipur	79.21	86.06	72.37	77.36	82.08	72.71
17. Meghalaya	74.43	75.95	72.89	74.53	75.54	73.55
18. Mizoram	91.33	93.35	89.27	91.51	93.59	89.47

19.	Nagaland	79.55	82.75	76.11	80.04	83.11	76.91
20.	Odisha	72.87	81.59	64.01	52.24	63.70	41.20
21.	Punjab	75.84	80.44	70.73	–	–	–
22.	Rajasthan	66.11	79.19	52.12	52.80	67.62	37.27
23.	Sikkim	81.42	86.55	75.61	79.74	85.01	74.27
24.	Tamil Nadu	80.09	86.77	73.44	54.34	61.8111	46.80
25.	Tripura	87.22	91.53	82.73	79.05	86.43	71.59
26.	Uttar Pradesh	67.68	77.28	57.18	55.68	67.08	43.72
27.	Uttarakhand	78.82	87.4	70.01	73.88	83.56	63.89
28.	West Bengal	76.26	81.69	70.54	57.93	68.17	47.71
	Union Territories						
29.	Andaman and Nicobar Islands	86.63	90.27	82.43	75.58	80.87	69.92
30.	Chandigarh	86.05	89.99	81.19	–	–	–
31.	Dadra and Nagar Haveli	76.24	85.17	64.32	61.85	73.62	50.27
32.	Daman & Diu	87.1	91.54	79.55	78.79	86.23	71.23
33.	NCR of Delhi	86.21	90.94	80.76	–	–	–
34.	Lakshadweep	91.85	95.56	87.95	91.70	95.69	87.76
35.	Puducherry	85.85	91.26	80.67	–	–	–
	India	**72.99**	**80.89**	**64.64**	**58.96**	**68.53**	**49.35**

Source: Census of India, 2011.

by providing monetary incentives in the form of scholarships such as pre-matric scholarship, post-matric scholarship, scholarship for top class education, Rajiv Gandhi National Fellowship and National Overseas Scholarship for ST students.

HISTORICAL BACKGROUND OF ESTABLISHING ASHRAM SCHOOLS

Ashram schools are residential schools for tribal children from a cluster of habitations. Based on the Gandhian philosophy of self-reliance, it was first experimented by Thakkar Bapa, a Gandhian in Panchamahal district of Gujarat in the pre-Independence days (Ananda 1994). Ashram schools were found effective as (a) it was not feasible to open full-fledged schools in very small and scattered habitations, (b) it created congenial atmosphere for teaching and learning as it is assumed that the tribal households do not have such an environment and (c) it helped to develop the total personality of the child and impart vocational skills to improve employment opportunities. Ashram schools generally provide admission to children from habitations at least 6–8 km away from the school. If children from nearby villages are admitted, they are not provided with boarding. The curriculum of Ashram schools includes agriculture and other life skills in addition to general subjects. Ashram Schools are imparting primary, middle and secondary education to ST boys and girls. The ashram Schools which are run by state governments have been an important tool to give formal education to ST children at the elementary level. The National Policy on Education, 1986, and the Programme of Action, 1992, accorded priority for the establishment of ashram schools on a large scale. Many parents in Jharkhand, Odisha and Gujarat preferred ashram schools as they provided free food, clothing and boarding. Some parents said that the education of their wards in ashram schools was not obstructed when parents migrated for work (Jha and Jhingran 2002).

CENTRAL SCHEME OF ESTABLISHMENT OF ASHRAM SCHOOLS IN TRIBAL SUB-PLAN AREAS

To supplement the efforts of state governments, the Ministry of Tribal Affairs has implemented a scheme, 'Establishment of Ashram Schools in Tribal Sub-Plan Areas', under which grant-in-aid is given to states for construction of school buildings. The scheme is in operation since 1990–1991 and has been revised with effect from the financial year 2008–2009.

Salient Features

- The scheme is operational in the TSP states/UT administrations. Twenty-two states, that is, Andhra Pradesh, Assam, Bihar, Chhattisgarh, Goa, Gujarat, Himachal Pradesh, Jammu and Kashmir, Jharkhand, Karnataka, Kerala, Odisha, Madhya Pradesh, Maharashtra, Manipur, Rajasthan, Sikkim, Tamil Nadu, Tripura, Uttar Pradesh, Uttarakhand and West Bengal and two UTs, that is, Andaman and Nicobar Islands and Daman and Diu are identified as TSP areas for implementing the scheme. Table 8.3 provides further details related to the status of ashram schools in India.

Table 8.3 *Status of Ashram Schools in India*

Name of the State Government	No. of Ashram Schools Sanctioned	No. of Ashram Schools Completed	No. of Ashram Schools Incomplete
Andhra Pradesh	78	41	37
Chhattisgarh	134	73	61
Gujarat	164	154	10
Goa	1	0	1
Jharkhand	2	0	2
Karnataka	19	17	2
Kerala	11	7	4
Madhya Pradesh	242	172	70
Maharashtra	87	87	0
Odisha	82	52	30
Rajasthan	9	0	9
Tripura	19	3	16
Uttarakhand	12	10	2
Uttar Pradesh	2	0	2
Total	862	616	246

Source: Statistical Survey Report, Ministry of Tribal Affairs, 2016.

- The scheme allows for construction of ashram schools for the primary, middle, secondary and senior secondary stages of education as well as upgradation of existing ashram schools for ST boys and girls including Primitive Tribal Groups (PTGs).
- 100 per cent funding for the establishment of ashram schools, that is, school buildings, hostels, kitchen and staff quarters for girls in TSP areas. In addition, 100 per cent funding for the establishment of ashram schools for boys in only the TSP areas, (if any), of the Naxal-affected districts identified by Ministry of Home Affairs from time to time. All other ashram schools for boys in the TSP states continue to be funded on 50:50 basis. 100 per cent of the funding is provided to UTs.

Financial assistance on 50:50 basis given for other non-recurring items of expenditure, that is, purchase of equipment and furnishings, purchase of a few sets of books for a small library for use of inmates of the hostels, etc. The scheme is need based and demand driven and funds are released on receipt of proposals indicating the mandatory details from states governments/UTs, and subject to availability of funds under the scheme. Therefore, there is no sate-wise allocation under the scheme. Table 8.4 provides details related to the Budget for the Establishment of Ashram Schools from 2008 to 2014.

Table 8.4 *Budget for the Establishment of Ashram Schools (₹ in Crore)*

Year	Budget Estimate (RE)	Revised Estimate (RE)	Expenditure
2008–2009	30.00	30.00	30.00
2009–2010	41.00	41.00	41.00
2010–2011	75.00	65.00	65.00
2011–2012	75.00	75.00	75.00
2012–2013	75.00	61.00	61.00
2013–2014	75.00	–	–

Source: Statistical Survey Report, Ministry of Tribal Affairs, 2016.

While the Ministry of Tribal Affairs administers the scheme and releases grant-in-aid for construction of buildings and procuring equipment, furniture, books, etc., the maintenance and running of ashram schools is the responsibility of the concerned state government/UT administration.

- The ashram schools are required to be completed within a period of two years from the date of release of the central assistance. However, for the extension of existing ashram schools, the period of construction is 12 months.

Mode of Operation

- Plan of the ashram school along with the location must be duly approved by the competent authority in the state government/UT administration. The plan must indicate a layout of the compound, including the kitchen, vegetable garden and plantation (fruits and nutritional trees such as Moringa and citrus) areas. States are encouraged to use fuel saving or renewable energy technologies in the school by availing schemes of the Ministry of New and Renewal Energy. A certificate to the effect that matching provision exists in the state budget for the scheme, wherever necessary.
- Unencumbered land is made available free of cost by the concerned state government for construction of an ashram school.
- State governments bear the required matching share of the cost of the building based on the current schedule of rates of either State Public Works Department or Central Public Works Department.
- The location of new ashram schools and the admission policy should be so decided as to give priority to ST girls, children of PTGs and migrant STs.
- Utilization certificate and physical progress report in respect of grants released during previous years.
- A few rooms/blocks of the hostels should be constructed barrier free and facilities like ramps should be included in the design of the construction for the convenience of the ST students with disabilities.
- In case any state government is unable to provide the required matching share from its budget, any Member of Parliament/Member of

Legislative Assembly can provide the state's share from his/her Members of Parliament Local Area Development Scheme/Member of Legislative Assembly Local Area Development Scheme fund.

- Preference will be given to State Governments who commit annual maintenance expenditure, as per reasonable norms.

Funding Pattern

Under the scheme of Establishment of Ashram Schools in TSP Areas, state governments are eligible for 100 per cent central share for construction of all girls' ashram schools and also for construction of boys' ashram schools in Naxal-affected areas. The funding pattern for the other boys' ashram schools is on 50:50 basis, while cent per cent assistance is given to UTs for construction of both girls' and boys' ashram schools.

Facilities in Ashram Schools

The ashram schools of the state governments/UT administrations are mandated to provide all necessary facilities such as drinking water, bedding and mattress, good quality food, toilets, security arrangements, laboratory, library, computer room, watchman, sweeper and health check-up of ST students.

Security of Students in Ashram Schools

On the issue of the security arrangement for students studying in ashram schools, especially in the Naxal-affected areas, the central government provides financial assistance for the construction cost of ashram schools. The running and maintenance including security arrangement for students studying in ashram schools, especially in the Naxal-affected areas, are the responsibility of the state governments.

Selection of Teachers

Selection and posting of the right kind of teachers are crucial when the education of disadvantaged children is considered. Issuing guidelines for selection and posting of teachers in ashram schools is the responsibility of the concerned state governments/UT administrations. Such responsibility on the part of the concerned state governments/UT administrations encompasses the areas of teachers' recruitment, students' enrolment, syllabus, affiliation to the education board, management of dropout rates and general functioning of the schools.

As per the information from the Ministry of Human Resource Development, following are practices under SSA for STs:

- Development of educational material in local languages using resources available within the community.
- Textbooks in mother tongue for children at the beginning of primary education where they do not understand the medium of instruction.
- Incorporation of local knowledge in the curriculum and textbooks.
- Teaching in the local language by recruiting native speakers as teachers.
- Training of teachers in multilingual education. Special training for non-tribal teachers to work in tribal areas, including knowledge of tribal dialect.
- Sensitization of teachers to tribal cultures and practices.
- Establishing resource centres in tribal-dominated states for providing training, academics and other technical support for the development of pedagogic tools and educational materials catering to multilingual situations.
- Creating spaces for cultural mingling within schools so as to recognize tribal cultures and practices and obliterate feelings of inferiority and alienation among tribal children.
- Involvement of community members in school activities to reduce social distance between the school and the community.
- Anganwadis and balwadis in each school in tribal areas so that the girls are not required for sibling care.
- Special plan for nomadic and migrant workers.

STRATEGIES AND APPROACHES IN SSA

The national programme of SSA, which aims to achieve UEE, has a special focus on education of the tribal children. Tribal children are an important constituent of the special focus group under SSA; other focus groups include girls, SCs, working children, urban deprived children, children with special needs, children below the poverty line and migrating children. These groups are not mutually exclusive and they overlap.

The broad strategies under SSA reiterate that there will be a focus on the participation of children from SCs/STs and minorities, urban deprived children, children with special needs, working children and children in the hardest to reach groups. SSA recognizes the varied issues and challenges in tribal education in view of the heterogeneous structure of the tribal population in the country. The issues and challenges in tribal education can be categorized as external, internal, socio-economic and psychological. The external constraints are related to issues at levels of policy, planning and implementation, while internal constraints are with respect to the school system, content, curriculum, pedagogy and the medium of instruction. The third set of problems relate to the social, economic and cultural background and psychological aspects of tribal first-generation learners. STs are at different levels of socio-economic and educational development. The planning teams at the state and district levels under SSA have been sensitized about the approach adopted and provisions made in the SSA framework for the education of ST children. The assessment of the problems, issues and challenges relating to tribal education is made through the household surveys and micro-planning exercise. The *Manual of Appraisal of Plans* has been brought out by the Ministry of Human Resource Development and monitoring tools have also been developed to ensure that programmes for education of tribal children are implemented as planned. A checklist to address the equity issues, especially focusing on the education of ST children, has also been developed.

Some of the interventions being promoted in states under SSA include the following:

- Setting up schools, education guarantee centres and alternative schools in tribal habitations for non-enrolled and dropout children.
- Textbooks in mother tongue for children at the beginning of the primary education cycle, where they do not understand the regional language. Suitably adapt the curriculum and make available locally relevant teaching–learning materials for tribal students.

- Special training for non-tribal teachers to work in tribal areas, including knowledge of tribal dialect.
- Special support to teachers as per need.
- Deploying community teachers.
- Bridge Language Inventory for use of teachers.
- The school calendar in tribal areas may be prepared as per local requirements and festivals.
- Anganwadis and Balwadis or creches in each school in tribal areas so that the girls are relieved from sibling care responsibilities.
- Special plan for nomadic and migrant workers.
- Engagement of community organizers from ST communities with a focus on schooling needs of children from specific households.
- Ensuring a sense of ownership of school communities by ST communities by increasing representatives of STs in Village Education Committee/Parent Teacher Association, etc. Involving community leaders in school management.
- Monitoring attendance and retention of children.

Provisions under SSA

SSA provides for ₹1.5 million per district per year for specific interventions for the education of SC/ST children. It also provides free textbooks up to ₹150 for girls and SC/ST children (SSA Framework for Implementation 2002). The other components under the broad framework of SSA which have an impact on the education of tribal education are: (a) school/EGS (Education Guarantee Scheme) like alternative facility to be set up within one kilometre of all habitations; (b) upgradation of EGS to regular schools after two years; (c) mainstreaming camps, bridge courses/residential camps for out of school girls, SC/ST children under the alternative and innovative education component; (d) provision of process-based community participation with a focus on the participation of women and SC/ST; (e) free midday-meal to all children at primary stage and (f) interventions for early childhood care and education.

COMMUNITY MOBILIZATION/INVOLVEMENT

As for all other population groups and areas, community mobilization and awareness generation on issues of enrolment, education of girl children, retention of children in schools and school involvement are carried out in tribal areas. The specific features of such mobilization in tribal areas are as follows:

- Use of tribal/folk art forms (Kerala, Assam, Bihar, Odisha)
- Meetings of mothers and family meetings and involvement of tribal youth volunteers (Assam, Kerala, Odisha)
- Leaflets, posters, *kalajathas* or folk theatre and videocassettes in tribal languages (Kerala, Assam, Orissa, Gujarat, Andhra Pradesh, Karnataka, etc.).
- Organization of meetings in tribal haats/bazaars and use of tribal fairs and festive occasions to discuss primary education issues (Assam, Gujarat)
- Involvement of traditional tribal organizations in the mobilization effort (Assam, Odisha)
- Involvement of the community including VECs members in the documentation of local folklore, history, traditional medicine and agricultural practices (Assam)

EVALUATION BY INDIAN INSTITUTE OF PUBLIC ADMINISTRATION

An evaluative study of 'ashram schools' in Odisha, Madhya Pradesh, Chhattisgarh and Jharkhand was conducted by the Indian Institute of Public Administration during the year 2006–2007. It was recommended that the number of ashram schools need to be increased based on demand, focusing on areas where children continue to be unenrolled, and quality of ashram school ensured with required infrastructure. Other suggestions include ensuring access to institutions of higher learning proper sanitation facilities and provision of requisite support staff in the form of teacher/warden staying in the school campus.

EVALUATION BY NATIONAL INSTITUTE OF RURAL DEVELOPMENT

The Ministry of Tribal Affairs conducted a study on education and its related schemes run by them, including the scheme of 'Establishment of Ashram Schools in TSP Areas'. It has been entrusted to National Institute of Rural Development, Hyderabad, for their continuation in the Twelfth Five-Year Plan. Central government should bear the recurring and non-recurring costs of the ashram schools established in TSP areas for better quality of education.

- Admissions to ashram schools should be in the ratio of 80:20 between tribal and non-tribal students for proper mix and integration.
- 10 per cent of ashram school seats should be earmarked for the local students as day scholars with day boarding and other facilities to have local community support.
- All ashram schools should have provision of early childhood education facility for mainstreaming the tribal children.
- Ashram schools should be provided with annual building maintenance grant for school and hostel buildings.
- Career guidance and counselling facility to be provided.

CONCLUSION

Realizing the educational needs of STs, which are one of the most deprived and marginalized groups, a host of programmes and measures have been initiated by the central as well as state governments ever since India's independence. A number of schemes and programmes have been implemented for the promotion of education among STs. Governments have also emphasized and taken steps for the opening of more and more tribal ashram schools and upgrading some ashram schools to high schools and high schools to higher secondary schools. In order to bring quality in ashram schools, it is suggested that like other schools such as model schools, Eklavya schools, Kasturba Gandhi Balika Vidyalayas, Navodaya Vidyalayas, provisions and facilities should be provided and maintained in all tribal ashram schools. Above all, firm determination with the dedication of the teachers, government and community can make the Ashram school a role model like 'Shantiniketan' which can give sight to the tribal children and empower the tribals to look at their problem in civil societies. As the name 'ashram' suggests a powerful symbol throughout the Hindu society where the Hindu kings entered in 'gurukul' to learn the art of warfare with education, the modern ashram school should be maintained in this way in a natural surrounding by giving value-based education to create brave, faithful *jawan* (hero) for future whose potentialities can be best utilized for the nation. They will be the valuable human resources of our country.

REFERENCES

Ananda, G. 1994. *Ashram Schools in Andhra Pradesh: A Case Study of Chenchus of Nallamalai Hills.* New Delhi: Commonwealth Publishers.

Dyson, K.K.(2002) India Education Report, Oxford University Press, New Delhi.

Jha. J., and D. Jhingan. 2002. *Elementary Education for the Poorest and Other Deprived Groups: The Real Challenge of Universalization.* New Delhi: Centre for Policy Research.

MHRD. 2009. *The Right of Children to Free and Compulsory Education Act (RTE).* 2009. New Delhi: Government of India.

Ministry of Tribal Affairs. 2016. *Statistical Survey Report.* New Delhi: Ministry of Tribal Affairs, Government of India.

Ministry of Human Resource Development. 2011. '*Sarva Shiksha Abhiyan: Framework for Implementation Based on the Right of Children to Free and Compulsory Education Act*' (2009). Ministry of Human Resource and Development, Government of India.

Pattajoshi, A. 2010. 'Globalization of Education as an Empowering Tool for Tribal Women'. *Orissa Review.* http://magazines.odisha.gov.in/Orissareview/2010/September/engpdf/53-56.pdf (accessed 2 April 2020).

Pradhan, S. K. 2011. 'Problems of Tribal Education in India'. *Kurukshetra* 59 (7): 26–31.

Chapter 9

Educating Tribal Children
Issues

R. Vasundhara Mohan

In the context of educating children of Scheduled Tribes (STs), ashram schools constitute an important component. Ashram Schools are residential schools which impart education up to the secondary level to children belonging to STs.

The concept of Ashram Schools for tribal children has been derived from the traditional Indian *gurukuls* and the Gandhian philosophy of basic education, in which the teacher and the taught live together and have close interaction. This type of closeness helps the students not only in sharpening the capacities but also in full personality development (Sujatha, 1990).

As early as in the 1920s, Amrutlal V. Thakkar, popularly known as Thakkar Bapa, a close associate of Mahatma Gandhi and member of Gokhale's Servants of India Society, worked among the Adivasis and the downtrodden sections of the society. Exhorted by Mahatma Gandhi to play a vital role in the field of tribal education, Thakkar Bapa, who condemned untouchability, set up schools for the children of labourers in Ahmedabad and tribals in Gujarat. Tribal children were provided free boarding and lodging. These schools were opened in natural surroundings in *kuccha* houses to present a picture of traditional ashram. The school and hostel were run in the same campus.

EDUCATIONAL BACKWARDNESS OF TRIBAL CHILDREN

The problem in educating tribal children lies in the fact that the Indian tribals depend on agriculture or traditional economic activities for their livelihood. The income that they derive from such activity is not enough to send their children to good schools located at far-off places, as the tribal population lives in isolated hilly and forest areas where educational facilities are not available. Even if the parents are willing, the children have to travel long distances on foot. As the distance deters the children from joining the schools, it leads to absenteeism and dropouts. They would, instead, prefer to stay with and help their parents in agricultural activities. Being illiterate and ignorant, tribals do not know the value of education. Their main concern is the survival of the family. They think that their children also should earn for the betterment of the family.

Thus, poverty is the major factor contributing not only to the educational backwardness of the tribals but also to their inability to bear the cost of educating their children; for, apart from boarding and lodging expenses, the parents have to meet additional costs towards the purchase of notebooks and stationery, dress, shoes and the cost of travel from home to school and back, if there is a public transport. Such expenditure puts economic pressure on the poor tribals forcing them to rather make their children work in the fields and forests. This is where the ashram schools, which provide free boarding and lodging facilities, come to the aid of the tribal. The ashram schools are expected to provide an environment conducive to the education of tribal children.

CONSTITUTIONAL BACKING

Realizing that the needs and problems of the STs are different from those of the Scheduled Castes, the framers of the Constitution felt that a special approach is required to bring about all-round development of the STs. Consequently, the Constitution has special provisions for STs in Articles 244 (Fifth and Sixth Schedules) and 275(1) (Grants from the Union to certain States). Article 339 provides for the appointment of a commission by the president to report on the administration of Scheduled Areas and the welfare of STs in the states, at the end of 10 years of the commencement of the Constitution.

During the First Five-Year Plan (1951–1956), there was an attempt by the Government of India to open such schools. However, the momentum in opening ashram schools started increasing only from the Third Five-Year Plan onwards.

The first commission mandated under the Constitution was set up in 1960 under the chairmanship of U. N. Dhebar. In its 1961 report, the commission reviewed the functioning of ashram schools in Maharashtra and Gujarat and found that they were successful and suitable for educating tribal children. The commission recommended the establishment/expansion of ashram schools in more interior, inaccessible and sparsely populated areas. It was also emphasized that these schools should act as centres for crafts/vocational education and cultural activities, apart from general education. The report also envisaged that ashram schools should serve the most disadvantaged among the tribal groups. Later the Education Commission (1964–1966) also recommended the opening of ashram schools.

THE SCHEME OF ASHRAM SCHOOLS

Based on the above recommendations, a centrally sponsored scheme of ashram schools was initiated in different states and later it was transferred to the respective state governments.

The state governments are responsible to assess the requirement of ashram schools and seek central assistance. The state governments are eligible for 100 per cent assistance for the establishment of ashram schools for girls (including school buildings, hostels, kitchen and staff quarters) and 50 per cent for ashram schools for boys in non-Naxal tribal areas. In addition, 100 per cent central funding is available for the establishment of ashram schools for boys in only the tribal sub-plan (TSP) areas, if any, of the Naxal-affected districts identified by the Ministry of Home Affairs from time to time. All other ashram schools for boys in the TSP states continue to be funded on 50:50 basis. Union territories (UTs) are provided with 100 per cent funding.

The main objectives of establishing ashram schools are as follows:

- To admit ST students who are unable to continue their education without the assistance of the government and impart formal education.

- To wean the children away from an atmosphere which is generally not conducive for the development of their personality and outlook and standard of life.
- To improve and develop their talent, make them aware of their inner strength, capacity and build self-confidence among them.
- To impart socially useful vocations/crafts in addition to general education.
- To protect and encourage tribal traditions such as folk songs and dances.
- To provide close interaction between the teachers and the children through increased individual attention.
- To reduce the dropout rates and improve the retention capacity of the school.

Apart from the above objectives, there are some other secondary objectives which are as follows:

- To ensure that the ashram school children do not develop snobbery as this may separate them from the other village boys. If they develop snobbery, the ashram school boys would prefer going away from their homes, villages and also look down upon their parents and elders. This trend is witnessed among the Oraons of Sundargarh district of Odisha.
- The ashram schools are also expected to fulfil the fundamental needs like building up a team of tribal who, with a broad and liberal outlook, will be able to administer their own areas and fill the posts which are occupied by non-tribals.
- Produce well-trained tribal officers to develop their own areas.
- See that the tribals do not feel disappointed and frustrated after education.
- To emphasize the strong community feeling that generally binds the villagers in tribal areas.

Ashram schools offer the best opportunities to translate the above aims and objectives into action among the tribals.

The scheme, in operation since 1990–1991, is managed by the Ministry of Tribal Affairs, Government of India, with a special accent on areas that have been identified as having a high concentration of tribal population.

It will be seen that besides providing formal education, the ashram schools are also expected to provide craft-based or vocational education in the fields of agriculture, horticulture, spinning and weaving and other trades. The ashram schools are also expected to train them for self-employment. But craft-based vocational education requires craft equipment, employment of special teachers and above all, large investment. Unfortunately, due to alleged economic constraints, vocational education in ashram schools has remained wishful thinking.

NUMBER OF ASHRAM SCHOOLS IN INDIA

There are two types of ashram schools, namely (a) those maintained and financed by the government (b) those maintained by the voluntary social organizations and assisted by the state government. According to information furnished to the Lok Sabha on 18 December 2017 by the Minister of State for Tribal Affairs, Government of India, there were 1,205 ashram schools supported by the Ministry of Tribal Affairs, Government of India, and 3,272 schools supported by the state governments and UTs (Table 9.1).

STATUS OF ASHRAM SCHOOLS

While the aims and objectives of the scheme for setting up ashram schools are laudable and have a solid constitutional backing, there are a number of aspects that are affecting the achievement of the objectives. These include both paucity of funds and apathy and negligence of personnel responsible for the implementation of the scheme. Such negligence starts with the construction of ashram schools itself. For instance, according to reports, by the beginning of 2014, the Maharashtra government had constructed only 66 of the 382 residential schools sanctioned for tribals (Biswas, 2014).

An Audit report has noted that in the absence of proper buildings, the students had to face much hardship. Reports also show that a visit to two government-owned (Devargaon taluka and Trimbakeshwar, Nashik)

Table 9.1 *Number of Ashram Schools in India*

| S. No. | State/UT | Number of Ashram Schools Supported by | | |
		Ministry of Tribal Affairs, Government of India	State Government/ UT	Total
1.	Andhra Pradesh	180	136	316
2.	Assam	3	–	3
3.	Chhattisgarh	157	1,058	1,215
4.	Gujarat	164	–	164
5.	Jharkhand	11	83	94
6.	Karnataka	28	5	33
7.	Madhya Pradesh	405	784	1,189
8.	Maharashtra	95	463	558
9.	Odisha	97	684	781
10.	Rajasthan	9	10	19
11.	Sikkim	1	–	1
12.	Tripura	24	29	53
13.	Uttar Pradesh	7	5	12
14.	Uttarakhand	12	10	22
	Total	1,205	3,272	4,477

Source: Annual Report, 2017, Ministry of Tribal Affairs, Government of India.

and one aided ashram school (Waghera) had revealed that a large number of students were living in a single room, and in the absence of separate hostel facility, they lived in classrooms after the lectures were finished for the day (Ibid). The delay is attributed to lack of supervision and coordination between the tribal department and the Public Works Department (PWD), which is entrusted with the construction work. According to tribal rights advocates, the delay was one of the many ills plaguing the department. According to Lok Sangharsh Morcha, corrupt practices were preventing the funds meant for tribals from reaching them (Parth, 2017).

A 2015 report by Tata Institute of Social Sciences, Mumbai, which studied the functioning of 1,076 ashram schools in Maharashtra, revealed:

'Merely 6 percent aided and 3.6 percent of the government tribal schools served breakfast according to the Government approved menu. Further, while 33 percent of the schools had their gas facility and utensils in good condition, the kitchens themselves were unhygienic' (Ibid).

While PWD is just a building contractor, the Tribal Welfare Department which is directly responsible for implementing the scheme obviously did not seem to bother whether the schools are constructed or not and whether the children are facing problems. More than the two government departments which are faceless, the teachers employed in the ashram schools are directly responsible for the welfare and education of the tribal children. But activists point out that besides being beaten up and ill-treated, sexual exploitation of the tribal children was also rampant in the ashram schools (Ibid).

QUALITY OF FOOD

The apathy and negligence towards educating tribal children are also reflected in the quality of food served to the children. In fact, a public interest litigation (PIL) was filed in the Bombay High Court on this aspect and the absence of safety conditions. According to PIL, 793 children from ashram schools had died in the last decade due to snake and scorpion bites, fever and other illnesses. A division bench comprising Justice Sawant and Sadhana Jadhav commented:

This is really a pathetic state of affairs. All the money and funds (meant to provide facilities) are with bureaucrats. We cannot have such a situation where children are dying due to such reasons like taking bath in cold water, eating food poisoned because of rodents, snake bites and so on (Sequeira, 2017).

TEACHERS

Irrespective of the apathy and negligence of the government departments towards ashram schools and tribal education, it is the commitment of the teachers that is essential if the objectives of establishing ashram schools are to be achieved. There are problems relating to the teachers employed in ashram schools. First, the absence of suitable accommodation in tribal locations compels the teachers to come from far-off places, resulting in absenteeism among the teachers and defeats the aim that teachers and students stay together in ashram school campuses.

Further, the teachers complain that they are a neglected lot. Their commitment and capacity to teach the tribal children in the ashram schools being a separate issue, the neglect shown in appointing competent teachers in time and paying their salaries regularly is another aspect that is affecting the system. For instance, according to a report in the newspaper *Indian Express* dated 23 June 2018, as many as 1,936 contract teachers working in ashram schools of Andhra Pradesh were at the risk of losing their jobs. Most of the teachers, who have been working in the schools for the last 15 years, have been left in the lurch with the government not renewing their services. M. Shobhan Naik, state president of Girijan Sangham said that since their appointment in 2003, the teachers had been neglected by the government and paid low wages despite the heavy workload. The committee recommended that: (a) ST youth be encouraged to take up teaching in ashram schools and (b) special training be provided to non-tribal teachers.

TRIBAL LANGUAGE

Statistics show that a large number of ST children were dropping out of schools. On average, the dropout rate is about 55 per cent at the elementary level and 71 per cent at the secondary level. This is 22 per cent higher than the national average. Assuming that the children were dropping out because they do not understand the language in which they were being taught, the Dhebar Commission had recommended developing local language textbooks and teaching children in their local language with a gradual shift to Hindi or English to address the problem of dropouts.

In fact, Article 350A of the Constitution directs the state to take steps to provide adequate facilities for instruction in the mother tongue at the primary-level, particularly to the children belonging to the linguistic minorities, with a view to preserving their language and facilitate better understanding. A tribal child is relatively less exposed to other languages at the age of its entry to the school. A tribal child entering the school for the first time sees a completely different environment. The building pattern with closed walls and sitting arrangement are alien to him. The teacher, his apparel and language, unseen and incomprehensive, create a sense of suspicion and fear in the child initially. Moreover, the teachers' (mostly non-tribal) treatment makes it impossible for the child to continue in the school' (Johari, 2016).

The problem is that the tribal languages have no script. With the exclusion of the constitutionally recognized languages, the rest of the Indian languages can be considered as minor languages and most of the minor languages are spoken by the tribals. The attitude of the dominant ethnic groups towards tribal languages is its outright rejection in a bilingual context and ridiculing the tribals for using their mother tongue in public places. The attitude of tribals towards the majority languages is total recognition and learning it for intergroup communication and acceptance as a language of social mobility, economic emancipation and status.

However, an attempt is being made in Odisha (by Pratham Books) in collaboration with tribal writers. Such books are being published in the tribal languages in a bilingual format using Odia script and additionally in Hindi and English. The latest to join the list is Maharashtra, which has published a series of 12 educational books for primary school children in 10 Adivasi languages. According to officials at the Maharashtra State Council of Education Research and Training in Pune, the books were being distributed in 15 districts for Adivasi children speaking Gondi, Warli, Bhili, Pavri, Korku, Nihali, Bhiroli, Mawachi, Kolami and Katkari (Ibid).

A study of the ashram schools in Andhra Pradesh has revealed that 50 percent of the students from Class 4 to 5 are drop out. The highest number of dropout rate was recorded in the case of Medak district, where the dropout rate of students was around 70 percent. On the other hand, the Vizianagaram district accounted for the lowest percentage of dropout of tribal boys and girls. Data also shows that Mahboobnagar district stands first with the highest dropout rate of 87 percent. Here again, the dropouts include more than 90 percent of girls and 83 percent boys. The high dropout rate clearly mirrors the lack of awareness about the fruits of education among the ST boys and girls. A study revealed that 'owing to lack of awareness on the part of the parents, children do not maintain regular school-going habits. (Midatala, 2000).

PRIVATE ASHRAM SCHOOLS

Since the mid-1990s, many corporations have started establishing and running residential tribal schools as a part of their corporate social responsibility policies, with a strategic interest in the tribal lands. Most private-run residential schools receive large funds from companies which wrest control over tribal lands. In fact, residential schools have become a new-age displacement mechanism, under the pretext of an assimilationist education system. Even the state governments are involved in grabbing tribal lands and displacing the tribals on the pretext of development. Among the 60 million people displaced due to development projects in the past decades, 40 per cent are tribal population.

EDUCATING TRIBAL CHILDREN IN THE DEVELOPED WORLD

Before we conclude, we may look at the status of educating tribal children in the developed world; for, apart from India, high-income countries such as the USA, Canada, and Australia have sizeable tribal populations, who differ from the mainstream population in terms of language, culture and traditions. Does the non-indigenous population of these countries treat the indigenous population on an equal footing? How different is the system of educating tribal children in the USA?

Observers of the tribal education system in the USA agree that the basic principles behind establishing schools for the Native American children are laudable. The schools are child-centric and provide culturally appropriate education through bilingual textbooks to speed up an understanding of modern life. The schools devote half a day to academics and half a day to the vocational curriculum. To prevent high dropout rates of the native children, separate community colleges were set up in 1978. There are 35 tribal colleges in 13 states of the USA.

But it appears that all is not well with the tribal education system in the developed world, including the USA. We may recall UNESCO's Global Education Monitoring Report, which states that 'Education systems should not encourage *unsustainable lifestyles* and can learn much from indigenous communities: they should respect local cultures and plural knowledge systems, and provide instruction in local languages'(UNESCO, 2016). However, there was a time when the American-Indian children were forced into boarding schools which imposed manual labour and aimed at eradicating students' Indianness by teaching that their cultures and languages were inferior. While the American-Indian community desires that their children need to have an inclusive culture in the classroom, that is, an infusion of their ways of knowing and their culture within the curriculum and lesson plans, it is alleged that 'for most Americans the educational and social issues that challenge Native students in rural villages, homelands, and reservations are invisible'(Castagna, 2014). (11) The teaching methods, therefore, are not always appreciated by the non-indigenous society. This threatens community-based education, as students are encouraged to embrace more mainstream methods.

Reports show that the performance of the US Bureau of Indian Education (BIE), responsible for overseeing nearly 200 schools serving approximately 50,000 Native American children in 23 states of the USA, is not up to the mark. Writing in in the *Washington Post*, Emma Brown called the BIE 'a long dysfunctional corner of the federal bureaucracy'(Brown, 2015). (12) This is evident from the statement made by Rep. John Kline (Republican, Minnesota) before the committee on the management of government Native American schools. He said, 'You have got collapsing roofs, leaking roofs, buckling floors, exposed wires, popping circuit breakers, gas leaks. That is totally unacceptable'. The very fact that BIE was headed by 33 different people in 36 years shows the disinterestedness of bureaucracy to handle the subject. BIE is reported to be plagued by limited staff capacity, poor communication and inconsistent accountability.

Not only the US Federal Government has acknowledged its failure to provide adequate education to the Native American children, but it was also dragged to the court by nine Native American children complaining:

- The elementary schools did not teach any subject other than English and Maths.
- There were not enough books in the library.
- There were no sports activities.
- There were frequent teacher vacancies resulting in the children being taught by non-certified staff, including the janitor.

It was also complained that the tribal community members were excluded while taking decisions concerning tribal children. Among other things, it was alleged that the 'boarding schools have become notorious for their efforts to assimilate Native American students into white culture, punishing them for speaking native languages and practicing native traditions' (Brown, 2017).

One of the main barriers for tribal children, both in schooling and beyond, is overwhelming racism and bias. Katie Dupere writes: 'Indigenous children around the world have long been denied the right to celebrate their roots while getting a comprehensive education. They are up against major inequalities, from structural racism embedded in school systems to inaccurate retellings of history' (Dupere, 2016).

One of the most important aspects of educating tribal children is their language; their mother tongue. Indigenous communities speak an overwhelming majority of the world's 7,000 languages, a clear indicator of rich culture and deep history that can aid any learning environment. Yet these languages are threatened when teachers discourage young children from speaking in their own language in the classrooms. Non-indigenous modes of education—both public and private—often ignore or discourage the culture, languages and practices of native students, which are vital to success (Ibid). Such discouragement of native languages is found even in India. For instance, a recent study of the Oraon tribal community in Odisha by Fr. Nirmal Dhanasamy has shown that the Oraon students are so badly ridiculed when they talk in their own language (Kurukh) that they have stopped using their own mother tongue even when they speak among themselves.

It is not only the language but also the customs and traditions of the tribal that the non-tribal population ridicule. Discussing the state of affairs of the indigenous population in Canada, Rajaraman Sundaresan writes: (Sundaresan, 2018)

> The European settlers in Canada believed that they were a superior civilization as compared to the indigenous people. They felt that the indigenous people were savages and lacked what the Europeans possessed – civilization. This deeper sense of cultural racism was one of the primary reasons for the European settlers to think of a solution to the Indian problem, which was the forceful exchange of their lands for civilization. This became one of the primary reasons for establishing residential schools in the 1850s and after. In many ways, the residential schools became one of the greatest sites of acculturation in order to grab hold of the land of the indigenous people. It was a conscious effort to efface the histories, identities, lifestyles, livelihoods and the knowledge that the indigenous communities of Canada held.

We agree with Rajaraman Sundaresan's teacher, who said that: (Ibid)

> We see the world through the lens of the West. We were trapped in a history that moved in concentric circles, and right at the epicenter, was the West, with its own projection of itself, and how it sees the others, the non-West.

CONCLUSION

While the literacy gap at the national level between STs and other groups in India has decreased to 14 per cent, there is a significant inter-state variation with the literacy gap at 28 per cent in some states. Over a period of time, the literacy rates of both STs and all social categories are increasing. In the year 1961, the literacy rate of STs was 8.53 per cent and in 1991 it increased to 29.6 per cent. In 2011, ST literacy rate increased to 58.96 per cent.

The idea of educating tribal children may be noble, but it is not easy to gather enough tribal children to run a school, as the tribals live in remote hilly areas and in the thick of forests. One of the striking features of the tribal areas is the sparseness of the population or small size of habitation in widely scattered hamlets. The tribals are economically backward and their children work in the farms along with their parents to supplement the family income. The distinct culture and traditions, their abject poverty and their disconnect with the outside world does not encourage them to get their children educated. They are far removed from modern civilization and think that their children have nothing to gain from formal education.

In the above context, the idea of establishing ashram schools for educating tribal children is laudable. However, the scheme can only function well if the parents and children are motivated properly. Tribal parents have to be made to understand the value of education. Keeping in view the poor economic status of the tribals, scholarships should be granted to enable the students to purchase study materials, dress, shoes, etc. It is necessary to establish hostels with necessary amenities for boys and girls so that they need not commute over long distances from their homes to attend the schools. Similarly, it is necessary to provide teachers with suitable accommodation close to the ashram schools so that they are always available to the students and can devote more attention to their work.

Poor economic status is not the only reason for the high dropout rate among tribal children. Reports indicate that the high dropout rate in most states is the result of the medium of instruction in the ashram schools, which is usually the regional language. As most tribal children do not understand the textbooks, they feel out of place and stop attending the schools. Similarly, either the non-appointment of teachers in time or the appointment of non-tribal teachers in tribal schools is another problem; the teachers do not know the language the children speak and children do not understand the teacher's language.

Thus, language is a major problem in the context of tribal education. While it is argued that a uniform policy with respect to regional language use in schools can alone ensure the integration of tribal children in the mainstream, others perceive it as a constraint in the process of schooling. As the tribal children get marginalized by the formal education system, serious thought needs to be given to this aspect.

An important development in the policy towards the education of tribals is the National Policy on Education, 1986, which specified, among other things, the following:

- Priority should be accorded to opening primary schools in tribal areas.
- There is a need to develop curricula and devise instructional material in tribal languages at the initial stages with arrangements for a switchover to regional languages.
- Tribal youth should be encouraged to take up teaching in tribal areas.
- Incentive schemes should be formulated for the STs, keeping in view their special needs and lifestyles.

Reverting to Indian ashram schools, the state of tribal children in these residential schools is a source of serious concern. Students in these schools are being stripped off their identities and even after several exposés on deaths and sexual abuse cases in government-run residential tribal schools in Maharashtra, Chhattisgarh, Odisha and Assam, no concrete measures are taken to prevent such cases. Instead, the government plans to set up more residential schools by 2022 under the garb of tribal education and development.

There is a need to look at the painful experiences that the tribal communities have gone through since independence and construct a different future. But education is being used as a tool to further the developmental agenda and for mainstreaming tribal children. There is a dire need for a dialogue to construct epistemically sensitive curriculums. This is possible only when the tribal population is involved in the constitutive rules of pedagogies. The schools must become inclusive and open in order to interact with other knowledge cultures without categorizing them as non-scientific and primitive. It is in this context that the South African scholar and UNESCO educator Catherine Odora Hoppers has said, 'developing a knowledge paradigm of the future has to begin with reaching out to those excluded. It is a compassionate but strategic evolution through contemplation during which the outer voice of possibility meets the inner voice of disenfranchisement'.

In India, the question of tribal education is not debated or discussed much in mainstream forums, except when it comes to reservation policies.

This sad silence stems primarily from the belief that Adivasi societies are lagging behind when compared to mainstream society, which is advancing at a rapid pace. Education is only seen as a rite of passage to becoming a part of society, and not as a means for achieving social justice. Catherine A. Odora Hoppers said, (Hoppers, 2008) 'Attempts at introducing the idea of education for sustainable development have so far ended up focusing on environmental degradation and climate change with little reference to diverse traditions that are ecologically coded and are paradigmatically more congruent with the reality of sustainable living'.

Apart from the above reasons, what is primarily required is a commitment on the part of the state governments, Tribal Welfare Department's officials and teachers. In the absence of such commitment, any number of committees and commissions cannot help the situation.

UN Declaration on the Rights of Indigenous people (there are about 370 million indigenous people around the world living across 90 countries) protects the right to education to the indigenous people. But while it is written in print, advocates say that education equality in practice is still a fallacy. It is alleged that the bias against the indigenous people often leads to non-indigenous people ensuring that the indigenous students are unable to succeed academically. Educating tribal children is a means of civilizing them. But civilizing does not mean ignoring the language and culture of the tribal.

REFERENCES

Biswas, P. 2014, May 21. 'Of 382 ashram schools okayed for tribal, only 66 come up in 10 years'. *Indian Express,* Pune.

Brown, E. 2015, May 19. 'Washington is taking notice of Crumbling Native American Schools'. *Washington Post,* Washington.

Brown, E. 2017, January 12. 'US Government has dismally failed to educate Naïve American children, lawsuit alleges'. *Washington Post,* Washington.

Castagna, A. 2014.'TeachforAmerica'. Available on: https://www.teachforamerica.org/stories/why-are-native-students-being-left-behind

Dupere, K. 2016. '5 issues that Indigenous students face globally—and how you can help'. Available on: https://mashable.com/2016/08/08/indigenous-education-inequality/

Hoppers, C. A. O, 2015, 'The future of development education – perspectives from the South', International Journal of Development Education and Global Learning 7 (2), Research Chair in Development Education at the University of South Africa. Available on: https://files.eric.ed.gov/fulltext/EJ1167844.pdf

Johari, A. 2016. 'By introducing bilingual education, Maharashtra hopes to keep Adivasi children in school', in Scroll.in, October 28. Available on: https://www.scroll.in/article/819962/by-introducing-bilingual-education-maharashtra-hopes-to-keep-adivasi-children-in-school

Midatala, R. 2000. 'Tribal Languages and Tribal Education', Social Action, 50 (4): 414–419. Available on: http://el.doccentre.info/eldoc/n00_/01oct00SOA7.pdf

Parth, M.N. 2017. 'Tribal schools of Maharashtra: Students live and study in abysmal conditions', in First Post, January 22. Available on: https://www.firstpost.com/india/tribal-schools-of-maharashtra-students-live-and-study-in-abysmal-conditions-3213706.html

Parth, M.N. 2017. 'The Headmaster of Aswali village of Palghar district came to the class drunk and kicked the children', Tribal schools in Maharashtra, Part:3, December 31. Available on: www.firstpost.com/

Sequeira, R. 2017, January 13. 'Maharashtra government says no funds to compensate for Ashram school deaths, draws HC Ire', Times of India, Mumbai.

Sujatha, K. 1990. 'Education in Ashram Schools: A Case of Andhra Pradesh', NIEPA Occasional Paper 18, National Institute of Educational Planning and Administration, New Delhi.

Sundaresan, R. 2018. 'Can India Learn From Canada's Dark History of Residential Schools for Indigenous Children'? in the Wire, October, 27. Available on: https://thewire.in/education/can-india-learn-from-canadas-dark-history-of-residential-schools-for-indigenous-children.

UNESCO, 2016. 'Global education monitoring report, 2016:Place: inclusive and sustainable cities'. Available on: https://unesdoc.unesco.org/ark:/48223/pf0000246230

PART II

Innovation and Best Practices in Tribal Education

Chapter 10

Balancing Indigenous Culture and Formal Education
Ashram Schools in Kerala

Noorjahan Kannanjeri and Alkha Dileep

INTRODUCTION

This study is an attempt to explore the current status and the educational system of two ashram schools run by the Government of Kerala in Wayanad. Ashram schools aim at empowering tribal students in education by preserving their culture. The Government of Kerala is running 20 model residential schools (MRSs) including 5 ashram schools in the State of Kerala. Among these few ashram schools, two ashram schools are situated at Noolpuzha and Thirunelli in Wayanad district. Wayanad district of Kerala has the highest number of tribes (45.41%, 136,062), and is thus known as the homeland of various tribal communities in Kerala. There are a total of 2,167 tribal settlements spread over all the four Block Panchayats of Wayanad district. Paniya, Adiyan, Kurichian, Kuruman, Mallukuruma, Uraly, Vettakuruman, Kattunayika and Kadar are the significant tribal groups located in the Wayanad district.

The concept of ashram schools for tribal children has been derived from the traditional Indian *gurukulam* and the Gandhian philosophy of basic education, in which the teacher and the student live together and have close interaction. The two ashram schools in Wayanad district are for particular tribal communities. Rajeev Gandhi Memorial Model Residential School at Noolpuzha particularly aims at the education of Kattunayakan tribe, whereas Government Ashram School Thirunelli especially aims at the education of Paniya and Adiya communities.

A vast majority of tribes in Kerala belong to the Paniya tribal sector. Paniya (Paniyar) is the largest of the 35 major tribes. The Paniyas were once sold along with plantations by the landlords as bonded laborers. They were also employed as professional coffee thieves by higher castes. The name 'Paniyaan' means 'worker' as they were supposed to have been the workers of non-tribes. The Adiyas were known as 'Ravulayar' traditionally. The Adiya, like the Paniya, is one of the slave sects in Kerala. The literacy rate and educational attainment among Paniyas indicate their educational deprivation. Paniya has an overall literacy rate of 48.47 per cent which is far below the state-level Scheduled Tribes (STs) literacy rate of 64.4 per cent (Census of India 2001). Although males have high literacy rate compared to females, it is also far below than the state average. The female literacy is even far below the national literacy rate of STs.

Kattunayakan, a significant tribe in the district classified as 'Primitive Tribal Group' by the government, depends mostly on the forest for their livelihood. It constitutes nearly 9 per cent of the total Adivasi population of Wayanad. The population of Kattunayakan is 14,715 and 81 per cent of it is concentrated in Wayanad district (Census of India 2001). They are found in the deep forests of Kidangad, Purakadi, Pulpalli, Noolpuzha, Maruthonkara, Tharuvana, Nallanad and Kattikkulam areas of Wayanad district. The Kattunayakan were also called Jenn Kuruman, then Kurumban and Sholanayakan. As their name denotes, the Kattunayakan were the kings of the jungle regions engaged in the collection and gathering of forest produces. They are known as Jenn Kurumar since they collect honey from the forest. They have all the physical features of a hill tribe. They use Kattunayakan dialect which is close to Dravidian language Kannada for conversing within the community, but the younger generation can converse in Malayalam (Government of Kerala 2016). The literacy rate of Kattunayakan stands far below the state as well as national literacy average of STs. Out of the total population aged 7 and above, only 40.18 per cent of them are literate (Census of India 2011). The female literacy rate also shows the pathetic condition of education among them, as it is only 35.72 per cent.

REVIEW OF LITERATURE

Education of the tribes has been discussed since the pre-independence period. The low literacy rate of the tribes, compared to the general population of India, which has the single largest tribal population of the world, has been studied a lot with various approaches. While 83rd Amendment of the Constitution made free elementary education a fundamental right of all citizens of India, official statistics indicate that compared to the literacy rate of 29.34 per cent of the general population, only 6 per cent of the tribes are literate. That means a vast majority of the tribes are denied the important fundamental right. The situation of Kerala which is the most literate state of India is also not so hopeful. According to the 2011 Census, while the state occupies around four lakh tribes in the land, the literacy rate is comparatively low (Census of India 2011).

Education problems and backwardness of the tribes have been studied using various approaches. Geographical isolation, cultural differences and exploitative practices are major factors behind low human development and educational backwardness of ST population in India (PRS Legislative Research n.d.; Sujatha 2002). The measures adopted for educational development of tribal communities fail to adequately address the specific disadvantage characterizing the tribal population. Sujatha criticizes the dual system of administration in which Tribal Welfare Department deals with tribal life and culture and administrative development work at the local level including education, whereas the Education Department is in authority for the planning of education development. She also analyses and criticizes the uniform pedagogy and curriculum transaction of the tribal education system with the point that this has mostly put the tribal children at a disadvantage.

Kuldeep Singh Rajput (2017) contends that tribal students are the major victims of the socio-psychological and language barriers of communication. He argued that due to the language barrier, students are unable to participate in the learning process effectively and the language which is used as the medium of instruction should be flexible enough to meet their demand. He also found that tribal students face problems in communication with teachers who are mostly not tribal. Students are not comfortable to have a personal relationship with them.

Sahu (2013), in his study among the tribal areas of Sundargarh and Keonjhar, suggested the importance of the introduction of tribal teachers in the school and preparation of the syllabus texts in the tribal language, so that tribal children have easy access to the text, thus enhancing their learning capabilities. Besides all these observations, financial problem, parental negative attitude and illiteracy, environmental problems and language problems are the common factors which many of the researchers pointed out.

In order to minimize exclusion and marginalization of STs in education, in general, and their integration in mainstream formal education, in particular, various attempts have been made by the Government of India through various legislations, policies, schemes and programmes. More specifically, in order to provide better access to formal schooling system with residential/boarding facilities, the ashram schools/residential schools for ST students have been opened in remote and tribal areas under the central scheme of 'Establishment of Ashram Schools in Tribal Sub-Plan Areas' by Ministry of Tribal Affairs since 1990–1991. Similarly, the Ministry of Tribal Affairs also introduced a scheme of 'Eklavya Model Residential Schools' for ST students in 1998 to provide quality middle- and high-level education to ST students (Sujatha 1990).

The concept of ashram schools for tribal children has been derived from the traditional Indian *gurukulas* and the Gandhian philosophy of basic education, in which the teacher and the taught live together and have close interaction. It hypothesizes that this type of closeness helps the students not only in sharpening the capacities but also in their full personality development. These schools are residential in which free boarding and lodging along with other facilities and incentives are offered to the inmates. One of the major thrusts of ashram school is imparting skills in crafts and vocational training, apart from providing general education.

The objectives of an ashram school include the following:

- To wean the children away from an atmosphere which is generally not conducive for the development of their personality and outlook.
- To impart general formal education.
- To impart socially useful vocational crafts along with the general education.
- To encourage tribal traditions like folk songs and dances so that the schools are not only mere learning places but also centres of cultural activities.
- To provide close interaction between the teacher and taught through increased individual attention.
- To reduce the dropout rate and to improve the retention capacity of the school, (Government of India 1966).

There are 20 ashram schools/MRSs in Kerala; among these, two of the ashram schools are situated at Wayanad district, one at Thirunelli and the other at Noolpuzha (A Digital India Initiative 2016).

RESEARCH METHODOLOGY

A case study has been used as a research strategy in this study since the study is a deep investigation of two cases containing various elements. 'Case study is an empirical inquiry that investigates a contemporary phenomenon within its real-life context when the boundaries between phenomenon and context are not clearly evident, and in which multiple sources of evidence are used' (Yin 1984).

The study aims at close and deep analysis of the system of ashram school, teaching methods, curriculum, people's attitude including teachers and students in it.

The study investigated two ashram schools in the district of Wayanad in Kerala. They are Rajeev Gandhi Memorial Model Residential School at Noolppuzha, and Government Ashram School Thirunelli. The researchers used a qualitative approach to conduct the study.

Major data collection methods used to do the study are semi-structured in-depth interviews, semi-structured observation, focus group discussions

(FGDs) and documents. According to Yin (2003), there are six possible sources of evidence for case studies: documents, archived records, interviews, direct observations, participant observation and physical artifacts.

We interviewed the headmasters, principals, office staffs, counsellors, mentors and managers. We conducted one FGD among students of higher secondary level in each school. We observed the play behaviour and other activities of students out of classrooms. Field notes were prepared based on observation. We have also reviewed the documents related to tribal education and ashram schools.

DESCRIPTION OF THE CASES

Case Number 1: Rajeev Gandhi Memorial Model Residential School, Noolppuzha

Rajeev Gandhi Memorial Model Residential School was established in 1991 and it is the first ashram school of Wayanad. This is the only school which is exclusively for the primitive tribe, Kattunayakka in Kerala. The school aims at the holistic development of Kattunayakka students. Currently, 515 students are studying in the school. Both boys and girls are studying in the school. The school is from standard one to twelve. The school is situated in a village area of Noolppuzha Panchayat, near Muthanga Reserve Forest, Wayanad, Kerala.

The school has 389 students and 7 teachers in high school session. In higher secondary session, there are 10 teachers in which 6 of them are permanent staff including the Principal and four teachers are working on temporary basis. There are eight non-teaching staff members including one mentor, two counsellors and one manager. It is a residential school where only one student is a day scholar due to some disciplinary issues. Most of the students get admitted in lower primary classes. But students get admission in higher secondary school by a single window system of the higher secondary education department. There are students from various parts of Wayanadu, Nilambur and Malappuram districts (where Cholanaykkar and Kattunayakkar are living) studying in the school.

Higher secondary session of the school started in 2016. Commerce and Humanities are the two streams running in the school. There are six permanent teachers and one contract teacher in higher secondary session.

The school follows the state school syllabus and curriculum. Teachers follow the normal teaching methods which are adapted in general schools. Besides the academic activities, the National Service Scheme, National Cadet Corps, Red Cross and Scout are active in the school. Besides these, science club, Haritha club, IT club, natural club, Malayalam club exist in the school, though their activity level is a little bit doubtful.

The First Secondary School Leaving Certificate (SSLC) batch passed out from the school in 2000–2001 and the higher secondary batch of commerce was started in the academic year of 2008–2009 for the higher education of Kattunayakkar. Humanities batch started in 2015–2016. The school received an award for the best website in 2010 from the president of India.

Absenteeism is a major issue in the school. Among the enrolled 515 students, 16 students are yet to come to the school. Moreover, once they go home for the long and short term vacation, they are reluctant to comeback to school again. They get back to the school with the help of mentors and counsellors.

The school authority is trying to teach, train and mould the students. Special classes and tuitions are given in school and hostels with the help of residential teachers. Although the normal class time is 9:30–3:30, the class is extended to 4:30 for extra classes. Tuitions are given in the hostel under the supervision of the manager. Teachers have a special duty for that. Besides the academic training, students are engaged in various extracurricular activities too. Special coaching for spoken English and yoga is being given to the students. The students are encouraged to participate in various arts and sports competitions held at school, district and state levels. But no vocational training is being given to the students.

All teachers are qualified teachers according to the general criteria of the Public Service Commission. Only two of them are from Kattunayakka tribe. The remaining teachers are from the general category and so their eligibility, experience and attitude for teaching the 'tribal children' who have a distinct culture and language are a matter of question. Although teachers are supposed to stay with the students, but here, most of them do not stay with the students.

Generally, teachers use common teaching methods in classrooms. They use Malayalam for instruction with which the students are not so familiar. Except for teachers of Kattunayakka (only two teachers are there), no other teacher knows the language Kattunayakka. So the mentor acts as a translator in lower primary classes. Students pick up Malayalam in later years. The school authority says that this is how they overcome the language problem. The school uses blackboards, charts and oral teaching as teaching methods. Higher secondary classrooms are smart classrooms, and audio–visual aids are used in Higher Secondary Schools.

There is a mentor teacher who is an alumnus of the same school. He aids the backward students in studies and tries to get back the absentees to the schools. As he is from the same tribal group and knows the sociocultural aspects better than anyone, he is a really helpful resource in the school. But it is a very poor ratio as there is just one mentor for 515 students. There are two professional counsellors who are qualified masters of social work. They work for the social and psychological well-being of the students.

Case Number 2: Government Ashram School, Thirunelli

The Thirunelli MRS was established in 2000 to cater to the educational needs of 'Adiya' and 'Paniya', who are far behind among tribal communities. Thirunelli MRS consists of 351 students ranging from 1st to 10th standard including boys and girls. There are 4 permanent staff and 12 contractual staff in the teaching section. Also, there are contractual posts of junior public health nurse, counsellor and mentor teacher. There are also eight non-teaching staff in the institution. In the 2017 year, the SSLC batch achieved a pass percentage of 100. Students from this MRS frequently achieve state- and district-level medals in athletics. Also, 3 students from this school were among the 18 students selected all over from Kerala by the state government for 'Operation Olympia', aiming at medals in the upcoming Olympics.

The institution takes up activities for quality improvement in education and follows up on the students who pass out from there. In this regard, the institution conducts career counseling, motivation classes, appreciation events, uniform and dress distribution, book distribution, etc. There are ongoing infrastructural developments in the institution for better hostel and academic facilities. The administration of the institution is done by an executive committee under Scheduled Castes and Scheduled Tribes Residential Education Society.

MAJOR FINDINGS AND DISCUSSION

Isolating from the Natural Habitat: Does It Help the Tribal Students?

An important and accepted hypothesis about ashram schools is that the separation of the tribal students from the unhealthy atmosphere of their natural inhabiting is helping them to have more positive development with regards to their education, sociocultural and personality aspects (Government of India, 1966). This is somewhat proved as true while considering the increasing rate of their literacy. The free lodging education and other facilities are giving them a better opportunity to have primary education. But it is observed that a high majority of the students are not preferring ashram schools. They point out that it blocks their opportunity of co-living with their community as well as the general community and is thus adversely affecting their personality and socio-cultural development. Inhibition, fear of general community, inferiority complex, identity crisis and stigma are the main issues of the students which are clearly reflected in the verbatim of the students during FGDs.

'As we all are from the same tribe, it is decreasing our very chances of interacting with other tribal and general students. This is cutting our confidence down. Now we feel inhibited to interact at general occasions where there are lots of people', Mr. P said.

Most of the students agree to this point. Head teacher and counsellors also reported that the stigma of being a tribal and inferiority complex are affecting their confidence level largely and these are some of the reasons for their discontinuation of higher education.

Another important observation is that because of this residential school life away from the home, the tribal children are being denied of the opportunity of co-living with their community and thus are denied the opportunity to learn and acquire many skills and learning which are rooted in their culture and tradition. The mentor of the school, who is a tribal, agrees to this.

Are the Syllabus and Curriculum Culturally Friendly with the Tribe?

It is a true and well-known reality that the school is following the syllabus and curriculum of the general school system in order to main-stream the tribal students. Sujatha (2002) says it is not desirable to have a separate syllabus which is determined on wider consideration due to reasons such as certification, equivalency, mobility and credibility. But is this curriculum and syllabus inclusive of the unique tradition and sociocultural features of these tribal students? Unfortunately, we found no elements of inclusion of the beneficiary's culture and tradition including language, celebrations, festivals, food, dress and traditional skills and vocational training, except that some amount of effort is made for preserving their traditional songs and traditional dances in school youth hostels. As Balagopalan and Subrahmanian (2003) have pointed out, inclusion does not mean inclusion in enrolment. Understanding beyond it would require that we look at the ways in which children and parents are both able and not able to feel a degree of comfort in the school space. Developing a culturally responsive educational frame-work is the most challenging task here. Rathnaiah (1977) pointed out that poverty and geographic distribution are generally considered as constraining factors in the education of the tribal children, whereas it is also important to accept that the schools did not address tribal festivities and celebrations and this is a major contributing factor for the high level of absenteeism of students in certain seasons.

Do They Need a Specially Prepared Teaching Methodology?

The most distinctive feature of the tribe is that they live in the forest and nearby places in harmony with nature. Especially Kattunayakka tribes have a distinct way of life which is not at all limited to four walls. Their children used to live and learn in the forest which enriched their knowledge and experience related to their natural living place, community, animals, plants, foods and various unique skills. Now what the ashram schools are doing is replacing that living and learning system with a closed classroom system which is very strange and difficult for them. In her study, Sujatha (2002) argued that with respect to pedagogy, it has been found that the rigid systems of formal schooling, which emphasize discipline, routine norms, teacher-centred instruction, etc. have made the children wary of school. This goes against the culture of free interaction and the absence of force as embedded in tribal ethos and culture prevalent at home.

The situation is not so hopeful in these two ashram schools. No specialties were found in teaching methodology, teacher–student relationships and the effectiveness of teaching. Teachers and counsellors are reporting that most of the students are slow learners.

'No matter how hard we work to teach them, they won't reach to up to the mark.'

'They are basically slow learners while compared to the general children. I wonder that these students have generally low IQ.'

Irrespective of the hard work, facilities and serious efforts, if the students are still remaining backward in academic activities, then the methods and ways, including the attitude of both parties to each other and to the education should be rechecked and reanalyzed. Unless the methods of teaching and communication are drawn from the tribal life situation, the perception and performance level of tribal children will continue to be low. Designing a socioculturally appropriate teaching methodology can cause an effective development in their learning process.

Sujatha (1990) rightly pointed out that though separate syllabus is desirable and practical, teachers in ashram schools are free to change its curriculum and pedagogy. She argues that 'the organization of the teaching–learning process is completely in the hands of teachers and they can make changes by orienting it to their milieu, and life, combining craft with education'. The variety of life situations of the tribes can be woven into the curriculum which then becomes a suitable education to tribes. For instance, teachers are reporting that the Tribal students have a unique skill in memorizing the music, songs or other things. They can remember things which are told to them in comparison to remembering the material they read. They have difficulty in writing and reading materials in Malayalam and English. This special skill can be used as an effective teaching methodology. In Tribal culture, oral tradition is highly followed rather than written documents. Besides that, art and motifs in all their magnificent forms are used for transmitting information and knowledge from one generation to another. This tradition can be well converted to more interesting and effective teaching methods. Thus, the methodology will be more student friendly than system friendly. That is the core objective of the ashram school and basic essence of *gurukualm* which is totally absent here.

Why the Tribal Students Are Not Preferring Ashram Schools?

Most of the students reacted that they want to go back to their *oouru* (tribal settlement). We asked the focus group that if they were given an option of selecting their schools, which would they select. All the students of the group reacted that they would opt for a school near their *oouru* so that they can live in their community. This answer implies many things including forced education. It directly implies that the ashram school system is not attractive for them and the reason can be the absence of tribal-friendly attitude, curriculum, syllabus, teachers and even their different perceptions about education. In short, what they want is not being provided by the existing education system, while they are forced to receive what they are provided with.

Do the Tribal Students Need Specially Trained Teachers?

Teachers are considered as second parents and good teachers are the most essential element of the integral development of any student. Teachers can highly contribute to and influence the academic and non-academic development including the personality of the student. Do tribal students usually get these sort of teachers? Well, it is doubtful. The observations of this case study are in agreement with Sujatha (1990) who stated that the knowledge of social reality, particularly related to the social structure of tribes, is quite essential for the teacher to play his/her role effectively. Except for two, other teachers are non-tribal teachers who are experienced in teaching non-tribal students. Most of them are not friendly with the sociocultural unique features and abilities of tribal students. They are not getting any sort of special training to develop a more tribal children-friendly attitude and skills to deal with them. Moreover, they tend to compare tribal students with the general students which is a highly foolish and dangerous activity. A clear gap between teachers and students is evident. So these teachers with an alien language and culture often become the most serious impediment in the tribal children's learning process (1990).

In short, teachers should be specially trained in order to deal with tribal students more effectively. Tribal students need more positive regard and a positive attitude, not neglect, unhealthy comparison and labelling. Most alarmingly, against the very base of the ashram schools, the majority of the teachers are not ready to stay in the school. This tendency is breaking the chief objective of the ashram school (Government of India 1966), that is, to provide close interaction between the teacher and taught through increased individual attention. Then how can we distinguish ashram schools from other general schools?

SUGGESTIONS AND RECOMMENDATIONS

1. Ashram school should adopt a curriculum and teaching methodology which are inclusive of the unique sociocultural features of the particular tribe.
2. The school should adopt programmes to preserve the culture and tradition of a particular tribe, like adopting their skills as vocational skills. Efforts should be made to include their festivals, celebrations, foods, language, etc. in the school.
3. A number of teachers from the tribe should be trained and included in the teaching as well as the development of curriculum, methodology and training programmes. This may help to produce a healthy result in terms of the student's integral development.
4. The government should plan a proper system of follow up on the tribal students after their schooling. It is found that there is such a system that is exists and also heard an unofficial report that very few students continue their education after schooling.

5. Inclusion and preservation of their language in the education system are very important in terms of preserving their language and culture, as well as imparting the students more confidence in communication. Moreover, it is very important to preserve their traditional songs, art forms, craft works, food, dressing style, etc. as a part of preserving the rich culture. It is the major aim of ashram schools to impart general formal education while preserving their culture as well.

CONCLUSION

M. K. Gandhi (1937) said, 'By education, I mean an all-round drawing out of the best in child and man-body, mind, and spirit. Literacy is not the end of the education or even the beginning'. No other quote is suitable to end the discussion of this chapter. Although ashram schools could increase the literacy rate of the tribe considerably, it is unfortunate that the system could not impart the essence of education to them. Instead of educating them in their culture, the system is trying to fit them into a foreign education system, which is neither culturing them nor enabling them to make their life dignified.

REFERENCES

A Digital India Initiative. 2016. Retrieved from https://data.gov.in/resources/state-vise-list-tribal-asrham-residential-schools-april-2016-ministry-tribal-affairs

Balagopalan, S., and R. Subrahmanian. 2003. 'Dalit and Adivasi in Schools: Some Preliminary Research Themes and Findings'. *IDS Bulletin* 34 (1): 43–54.

Census of India. 2001. 'District Total Tribal Population'. https://mahades.maharashtra.gov.in/files/report/CensusReport.pdf (accessed on 2 April 2020).

———. 2011. 'PCA Maharashtra 2011'. http://pibmumbai.gov.in/English/PDF/E2013_PR798.PDF (accessed on 2 April 2020).

Government of India. 1966. *Report of the Education Commission 1964–66*. Education and National Development, Ministry of Education.

Government of Kerala. 2016. 'Tribes in Wayanad'. Available at https://www.wayanadu.com/pages/tribes-in-wayanadu (accessed on November 2018).

PRS legislative research. (n.d.). Available at https://www.prsindia.org/report-summaries/working-ashram-schools-tribal-areas

Rajput, K. S. 2017. 'Learning with Burden: Analysis of Language Problem Faced by Pawara Tribal Students'. *An International Peer reviewed and Referred Schoarly Research Journal for Interdisciplinary Studies* 4 (32): 490–496.

Rathnaiah, E. V. (1977). *Structural Constraints in Tribal Education*. New Delhi: Sterling Pubishers.

Sahu. (2103). 'Educational Advancement in Tribal Area through PPP. A Case study of Odisha'. *Odisha Review*, 73–80.

Sujatha, K. (1990). 'Education in Ashram Schools: A Case of Andhra Pradesh'. NIEPA Occasional Paper 18. National Institute of Educational Planning and Administration, New Delhi.

———. (2002). 'Education among Scheduled Tribes'. In *India Education Report Progress of Basic Education*, edited by R. Govinda and Mona Sedwal. New Delhi: Oxford Universty Press.

Yin, R. K. 1984. *Case Study Research: Design and Methods*. Beverly Hills, CA: SAGE Publications.

———. 2003. *Case Study Research, Design and Methods*. Vol. 5, 3rd ed. Thousand Oaks, CA: SAGE Publications.

Chapter 11

Ashram School Codebook
Framework for Qualitative Management

Rajashri Tikhe and Buveneswari Suriyan

INTRODUCTION

Ashram schools in India have a long history since the pre-independence period. They were initially started by Gandhian disciples like Thakkar Bapa with the objective of imparting formal education along with craft-oriented vocational education to help children lead self-reliant, self-sufficient lives in future. In the decade of 1953–1954, state governments provided support to 12 ashram schools started by private trusts. Forty government ashram schools were started in the year 1972–1973.

Initially, these schools were in the jurisdiction of the education department of the state government. In 1975–1976, they came under the administration of the social welfare department, followed by the Tribal Development Department (TDD) taking the charge, as it came into existence in 1984.

Initially, codes of secondary schools of education department were followed for administering the residential tribal ashram school. In 1995, considering the different nature of residential schools, especially started for children of Scheduled Tribes, the need for independent guidelines or codebook was identified by the TDD.

The committee for drafting guidelines was formed in 1995 which comprised of officers from TDD and representatives of private-aided ashram school. The draft submitted by this committee was issued on 14 September 2001 as *Codebook*. The need for revising this draft was again felt in 2003 because of the gaps observed in the draft as well as the changed policies of the government. The committee to revise the *Ashram School Codebook* was formed in 2003. The committee was chaired by the commissioner, TDD, and it mainly consisted of the authorities in education department, namely director (primary and secondary) education; director, MSCERT; director, (MPSP), along with the representatives of private-aided ashram school. Revised codebook came into action in 2006–2007. At present, the same version of the codebook (2005) is being used in tribal residential ashram school.

NEED FOR REVISION

TDD realized the need to revise the codebook again in 2014 mainly to align with the Right to Education (RTE) norms and to respond to other situational needs such as increasing demand for security measures in ashram school.

1. **To Align with RTE Norms**

   Right to Education Act (1 April 2010), which covers schools of all management and all medium, provides a clear mandate for admission in age-appropriate classes, and the appointment of appropriately trained teachers. It specifies the duties and responsibilities of appropriate Governments, local authority and parents in providing free and compulsory education. Similarly, it specifies norms for assessing children in a comprehensive and continuous manner, making the child free of fear, trauma, and anxiety through a child-friendly and child-centred system. The guidelines in *Ashram School Codebooks* needed to be revisited to align them with RTE.

2. **To Align with GRs Issued after 2005**

   TDD, while responding to the situational needs and changing context, has issued about 115 government resolutions (GRs) post the enactment of *Ashram School Codebook*. These GRs can be broadly classified into five subgroups, namely (a) approval and expansion of schools, (b) HR provisioning for ashram schools at various levels, (c) infrastructure development in the schools, (d) monitoring (quality of infrastructure and of education), (e) provisioning of amenities for students, (f) nutrition, (g) quality enhancement of education, (h) community participation in management and monitoring of ashram schools and (i) financial provisioning for administration and management.

The codebook needed to be revised either to align with changed rules or to accommodate newly added rules and regulations set by some of the newly issued GRs.

3. Inputs from Field Research

Tribal education and governance of ashram schools have been an important theme for renowned institutions and researchers across the country, and hence, there is a wide variety of study reports on both these aspects. These reports pertain to key aspects relating to tribal education, in general, and governance and quality of education in government schools, in particular. They provide useful insights. These reports also consist of practical suggestions for improving the governance of ASs and enhancing the quality of education imparted to the students. Reports (Government of Maharashtra, 2014; Government of Maharashtra 2016; UNICEF-CBPS 2017; TISS 2015; YASHADA 2006) focusing on Maharashtra (post-2005) assume special significance for the *Ashram School Codebook*.

In short, 1,048 (502, government; 546, private aided) ashram schools in Maharashtra serve to 4.43 lakh tribal children in the age group of 6–18 years. The objective of revising the Codebook was to have a strong, child-centric Codebook in order to ensure the effective functioning of these schools and provide quality education in a safe, secure and child-friendly environment.

THE REVISING PROCESS

As described in Figure 11.1 the process of revising *Ashram School Codebook* was a highly intensive process with a child-centric approach and inviting representation from different stakeholders including government and non-government institutions.

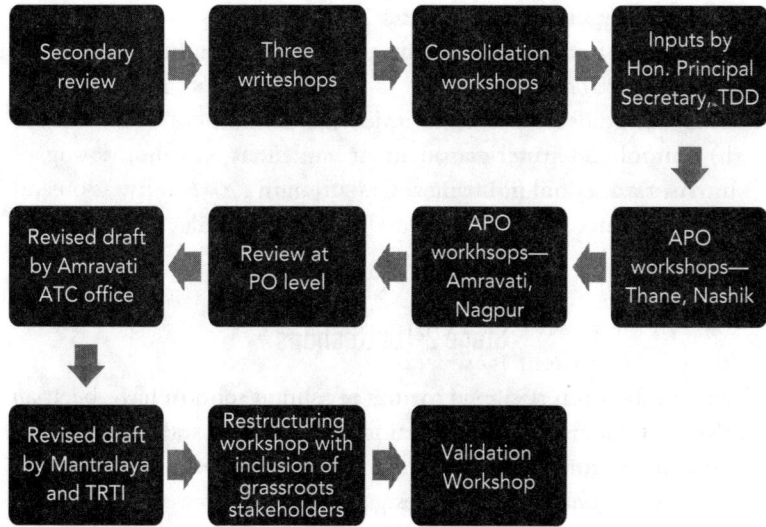

Figure 11.1 *The Revising Process*

Source: Ashram School Codebook, TDD, Government of Maharashtra, 2014.

Initially, it was led jointly by TDD, Maharashtra, and civil society led by UNICEF, Mumbai (Figure: 11.1).

Stage 1: Desk Review of Secondary Data

This was done at the UNICEF level. Desk review included the study of the following documents:

1. Right to Education Act, 2009
2. TDD GRs (2005–2017)—administration, infrastructure, nutrition, ashram school code, quality of education, protection
3. Research studies
   a. Functional review of Maharashtra state departments (YASHADA 2006)
   b. Report of the high-level committee on balanced regional development issues in Maharashtra (Government of Maharashtra 2013)
   c. Status of government and aided ashram schools in Maharashtra (TISS 2015)

    d. Government of Maharashtra 2016

    e. Status of education in tribal areas of Maharashtra (UNICEF–CPBS 2017)

4. Relevant guidelines of other residential schools

    a. School and hostel management guidelines, Odisha

    b. Ashram school guidelines, Chhattisgarh (2016)

    c. Guidelines for Kasturba Gandhi Balika Vidyalaya, Maharashtra (2012)

Stage 2: Writeshops

A broad outline was designed for the revised version of *Ashram School Codebook* on the basis of insights gained from the secondary review. As per suggestion from TDD, the next step planned was writeshops for drafting revised chapters as per designed outline.

Total three writeshops were conducted in which representatives from the following sectors participated and made valuable contributions in drafting the chapters:

1. Members from the non–government sector having experience in tribal issues, education, health, protection, child rights, etc.
2. Representatives of RTE forum
3. Officers of different cadres from TDD
4. Officers of the education department
5. UNICEF consultants

Representation from different government and non–government sectors made this process inclusive, transparent and grounded. Inputs collated in the consultation by RTE forum were also referred to in the writeshops and relevant inputs were incorporated in the drafts.

The primary drafts were discussed further for refinement and finalization, jointly by the team of UNICEF consultants and TDD consultants. The outline and chapterization were also revised at this level.

The revised structure and content of writeshops were presented to the secretary, TDD, and other officers on 5 August 2017. The draft was revised based on the suggestions by the secretary, TDD. UNICEF submitted final zero-level draft on 16 August 2017.

Stage 3: Presentation for Hon. Principal Secretary, TDD, Maharashtra

Draft of *Ashram School Codebook* was presented to Hon. Principal Secretary, TDD, Maharashtra. As per her guidance, the further process was planned which included feedback from administrative officers as well as end users, that is, ashram school staff.

Stage 4: APO Workshops

Workshops with Assistant Project Officer (APO), Education, were conducted to get the inputs from stakeholders by the department. Workshop at Nashik covered APOs, Education, from Thane and Nashik region, while workshop at Amaravati covered the APOs from Nagpur and Amaravati region. Apart from APOs, Education, Tribal Development Department (TDD) authorities such as Project Officers (POs), Additional Tribal Commissioner (ATCs), joint commissioner, commissioner and deputy secretary also participated in the workshops and provided important inputs.

These workshops helped to get field insights from the departmental angle and gave practical tone to the document.

The inputs gained through APO workshops were filtered and incorporated in a joint meeting of consultants of TDD and UNICEF.

Stage 4: Review at PO Level

Draft 1 of *Ashram School Codebook* was shared with PO offices. They were supposed to conduct feedback sessions with headmistress, teachers and superintendents from randomly selected government and private-aided Schools.

Stage 5: Redrafting by Amaravati ATC Office

The entire draft was reviewed by Amaravati ATC office to include grassroots suggestions, relook from administrative angles and ensure continuity. Draft 2 version was handed over to Mantralaya.

Stage 6: Redrafting by Mantralaya and Tribal Research and Training Institute

Draft 2 submitted by Amaravati ATC Office was reviewed by Mantralaya officers with a specific focus on administrative aspects for both government and private-aided schools as a milestone decision of unique codes for all schools had been implemented.

At the same time, it was reviewed by Tribal Research and Training Institute (TRTI) focusing on the content on quality of education, health and security of children. Internal as well as external domain experts were involved in this process.

Stage 7: Restructuring Workshop

Draft 3 version of the *Ashram School Codebook* jointly revised by Mantralaya, Mumbai, and TRTI, Pune, was restructured in a workshop with a specific focus on making it user-friendly. The attempt was not to interfere with the content but to refine the flow of the content and make the structure more logical from the administrative angle.

Stage 8: Validation Workshop

Very select members including deputy secretary, commissioner, TDD and TRTI, joint director, TRTI, along with consultants read every single line of the document to validate its legal standing. Extension officer from directorate primary education was also invited to validate codes related to school management.

Stage 9: Validation Workshop

The final draft of *Ashram School Codebook* was submitted to Mantralaya for ratification.

MAJOR FEATURES OF THE PROCESS OF REVISING

The main features of this process were as follows:

1. *Inclusive:* Wide variety of stakeholders were involved including TDD (right from teachers to deputy secretary, Mantralaya), representatives of education department, domain experts from the field of education,

health, child protection, representatives from non-government organizations and movements, RTE forum and UNICEF.

2. *Transparent:* Different perspectives were discussed and understood. Civil society representatives were involved until the stage of draft revision by TRTI.

3. *Grounded:* Feedback was taken on every draft version by the end user, that is, ashram school staff.

The policy is majorly criticized for its top-down approach. The major strength of the *Ashram School Codebook* is that it considered approaches of the majority of stakeholders, not just from within the system but also from outside the system, not just elites but also grassroots implementers.

STRUCTURE OF THE CODEBOOK
The Content of the Revised Ashram School Codebook

1. Introductory Chapters
Introductory chapters include:

- Background
- Vision and Objectives
- Jurisdiction
- Definitions

As described in Figure: 11.2 for the first time, the vision of the department towards ashram schools and education of Adivasi children

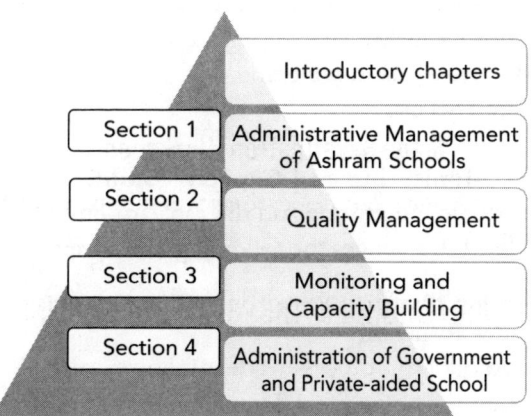

Figure 11.2 *Structure of the Codebook*

Source: Ashram School Codebook, TDD, Government of Maharashtra, 2014.

was clearly defined in the Codebook. The vision acknowledges the strengths of tribal communities in Maharashtra. It states the clear aim of tribal ashram schools, that is, to create multilingual, multicultural and student-centric education system by integrating the natural capacities of students in formal learning. The objectives of the Code are also revised to make them more elaborate and positive and sensitive towards the tribal community.

After the introductory chapters, the chapters in the Codebook are classified into four sections as follows:

2. Section 1: Administrative Management of Ashram Schools

The first section covers administrative management of ashram schools in the following five chapters:

a. Basic Infrastructure
b. Human Resource Management
c. Admission Process
d. School Administration
e. Hostel Administration

3. Section 2: Quality Management

Section 2 focuses on soft areas, namely quality of education, health and safety and security of children. It includes the following three chapters:

a. Educational Quality
b. Health, Hygiene and Nutrition
c. Safety and Security

4. Section 3: Monitoring and Capacity Building

Section 3 covers the monitoring and the capacity-building part at the management level. It includes the following four chapters:

a. Monitoring and Mentoring
b. Grievance Redressal
c. Social Audit
d. Continuous Professional Development of Ashram School Staff

5. **Section 4: Administration of Government and Private-aided School**

The last section is again for higher level management for administrative issues. It is divided into three parts:

a. Common Administrative Aspects
b. Administrative Aspects Specific to Government Ashram School
c. Administrative Aspects Specific to Private-aided Ashram School

MAJOR FEATURES OF THE CONTENT OF THE CODEBOOK

As described in figure 11.3, the major features of the content of the codebook are as follows:

1. *Common guidelines and codes to government and private-aided ashram schools except for administrative issues:* This is the major feature of the Codebook. There were different chapters for government ashram schools and private-aided ashram schools in the old Codebook. In the new Codebook, codes and guidelines related to administrative management, quality management, monitoring and capacity building are same for the schools of both the management. Different codes will apply only with regard to staff recruitment, service conditions, grants, etc. Thus, expectations regarding quality of infrastructure, basic amenities and facilities, education, health and safety/security of children will be equal for government and private-aided ashram schools.

2. *Academic approach:* The old Codebook missed the academic approach which resulted in a high level of ignorance even at the implementation level. The revised Codebook has gone beyond educational management and school administration, to include academic guidelines to improve academic quality in ASs. It has also acknowledged the presence of higher secondary schools and included codes and guidelines for this section separately.

3. *Holistic approach towards health:* In the old Codebook, guidelines related to health were scattered in different chapters. There was a lack of proper guidelines on the treatment of health problems. The revised copy includes an independent chapter on health which has elaborate guidelines regarding maintaining good health and prevention of health problems. However, it also has a separate section which provides guidelines and codes of action in case any health problem arises.

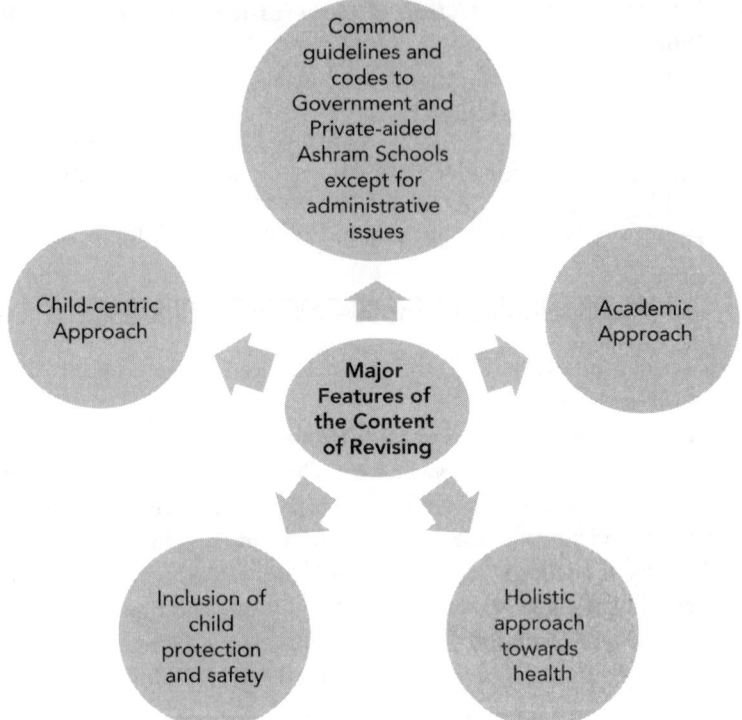

Figure 11.3 *Major Features of the Content of the Codebook*

Source: Ashram School Codebook, TDD, Government of Maharashtra, 2014.

4. *The inclusion of child protection and safety:* The aspect of child protection and safety was totally missing in the earlier Codebook. The revised version of Codebook includes a chapter on the above subject, which covers objectives, responsibilities of each cadre to ensure child protection and safety, code of conduct to ensure child safety, code of conduct in case of exploitation of a child, guidelines to ensure a healthy environment in terms of child safety and protection.

5. *Positive monitoring:* The codes regarding monitoring of ashram schools which were scattered in the old book have been organized in a single chapter in the revised Codebook. A drastic change is in the approach of monitoring, which emphasizes that a monitoring officer should play the role of a mentor rather than the inspector. The ultimate objective of monitoring should be identifying gaps

and finding out solutions to improve quality. Codes, in this section, are written in light of this ultimate objective.

6. *Child-centric approach:* Last but not the least, the entire document of the revised Codebook reflects the child-centric approach. Well-being and development of tribal children in a healthy, non-fearing environment have remained the guiding principle for all sections and all chapters written in the Codebook. Unlike the old Codebook, it has eliminated the sense of distrust in children, but on the other hand, acknowledges the inherent capabilities of children and emphasizes their involvement in the management of school and hostel through a structure of *mantri mandal* (Board of Ministers).

PLAN FOR INSTITUTIONALIZING CODEBOOK

The process of revision of Codebook does not end with redrafting. In order to ensure that the Codebook is referred to as a guide to improve the quality of ashram schools, the department is planning to establish it in the following way is described in the figure 11.4:

CODEBOOK: A FRAMEWORK FOR VISUALIZED CHANGE

The Codebook defines the quality in terms of infrastructural facilities, health, security and education. The department perceives it as a

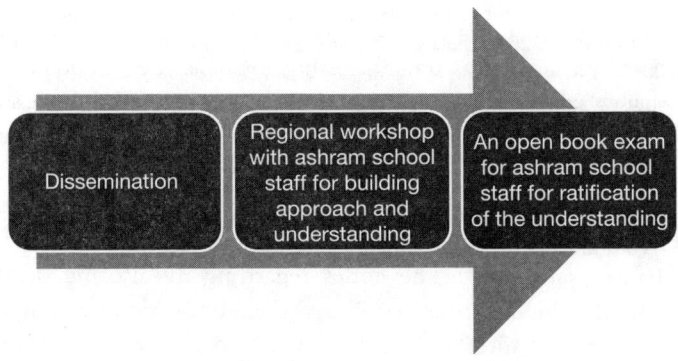

Figure 11.4 *Plan for Institutionalizing Codebook*

Source: Ashram School Codebook, TDD, Government of Maharashtra, 2014.

reference point for final expected output in both physical output and quality output. The following are the programmes and policies:

- *Kayapalat:* A movement led and implemented by TDD for improvement in infrastructural facilities and basic amenities.
- *Atal Arogya Vahini:* A mobile van providing health facilities to ASs.
- *Ekalavya Science Teaching Programme:* Focussing on capacity building of science teachers to conduct practical-based science classes.
- *Karadi Path English Teaching Programme:* Focussing on capacity building of teachers to enable them to improve English conversation of students.
- *Multilingual teaching:* Translation of elementary-level textbooks in 11 tribal languages and development of a kit of 25 bilingual books for supportive reading for children in primary classes.
- *Strengthening education cell:* Strengthen the capacities of the members of education cell to enable them for quality monitoring of educational and administrative functioning of ashram schools and mentoring of teachers.

REFERENCES

Government of Maharashtra. 2013. *'Report of the High Level Committee on Balanced Regional Development Issues in Maharashtra'*. Government of Maharashtra: Planning Department.

Government of Maharashtra. 2016. *'In Search of Hope: Report of Technical Committee for Prevention of Deaths of Students in Ashram Schools'*. Salunkhe Committee Report.Government of Maharashtra: Tribal Development Department

Kelkar Committee. 2014. *Balanced Regional Development*.

TISS. 2015. *A Report on Status of Government and Aided Ashram Schools in Maharashtra*. Unpublished report. Mumbai: TISS.

Tribal Development Department. 2005. Preface. *Ashram School Codebook*. Maharashtra: Tribal Development Department.

UNICEF–CBPS. 2017.

YASHADA. 2006. *Functional Review of Maharashtra State Departments: Detailed Report*. Pune: Tribal Development Department.

Chapter 12

Centralized Kitchen
Providing Nutritious and Hygienic Meals to Tribal Students

Saurabh Katiyar

INTRODUCTION

Centralized kitchen was conceptualized in collaboration of Tribal Development Department of Maharashtra government and Tata Trust. Central kitchen is situated in Kambalgaon area in Dahanu Project of Palghar district. Currently, it covers 27 tribal residential schools within a radius of 65 km. It provides not just midday meal, but it also provides meals four times a day by working 24 × 7. The central kitchen provides nutritious and hygienic food to around 12,000 students daily. It makes central kitchen one of the largest kitchens in Maharashtra.

OBJECTIVE OF CENTRAL KITCHEN

The majority population in Dahanu Project is tribal. Malnutrition, anaemia as well as instances of micronutrients deficiency are rampant in tribal pockets, especially among children. Before this project of central kitchen, in each tribal school, a contractor was selected via e-tendering to supply raw material and a local self-help group was given the job of cooking the food in schools. Due to lack of oversight, it led to the supply of sub-optimal raw material and focus on nutrition

Figure 12.1 *Kitchen in a Tribal School Which Is Not Covered by Central Kitchen*

and hygiene was minimal at the local level as shown in figure 12.1. Hence, the project of central kitchen was conceptualized to achieve both these objectives:

1. To provide nutritious and hygienic food to tribal schools.
2. To break the nexus of corruption involved in the supply of food grains at the local level.

DEVELOPMENT OF CENTRAL KITCHEN

As shown in figure: 12.2, initially, the central kitchen made a humble beginning with a pilot project by covering a school of 400 students. Over time, a lot of innovation was done by improving the operations via automation, improving the machinery, increasing the capacity of RO plant as well as storage capacity, etc. Gradually, the capacity of kitchen was increased and now it covers 27 schools with 12,000 students. The future plan is to expand the coverage in the remaining 11 schools of Dahanu Project in a stepwise manner by:

1. Increasing capacity
2. Reducing food wastage in schools by counselling teachers and then students
3. Optimization of operations

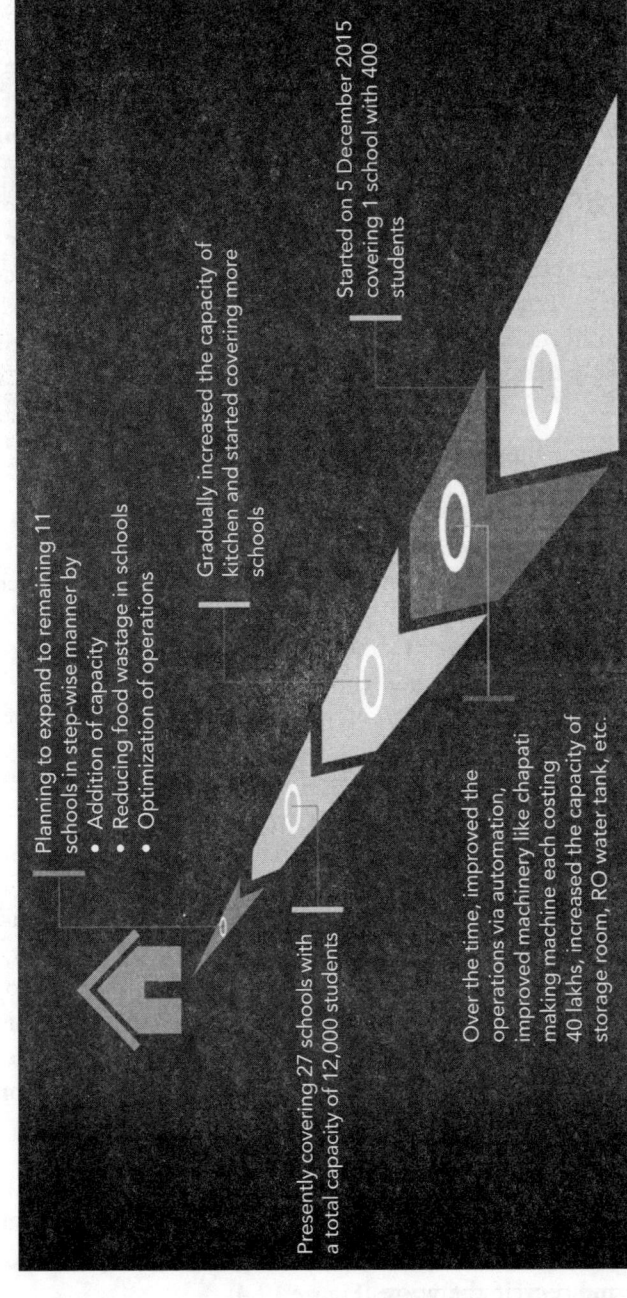

Figure 12.2 *Development of Central Kitchen*

OPERATIONS OF CENTRAL KITCHEN

Central kitchen is run jointly by Tata Trust and Tribal Development Department. Tata Trust mainly looks after the quality control of food. The operational part of kitchen is run by the Tribal Development Department. It serves as the perfect example of a public–private partnership. For the supply of raw material, a centralized supplier is selected via e-tendering. Tata Trust ensures that the supply of the contractor is as per the quality standard. Tata Trust maintains the same quality standard as available in Tata group of hotels. Being a centralized location, it is easier and convenient for the Tribal Department to monitor and run the kitchen, rather than monitoring at 27 different locations in remote areas.

Quality Assurance of Raw Material

1. The supplier of materials is selected by an open tender based on parameters of quality, rating, costing, etc.
2. An executive checks the supply before receiving that the stores are in ambient condition.
3. The quality inspection is followed by standard operating procedure which is adapted from food safety standard.

Purchase and Storage

Fresh vegetables are purchased every two days. Rice and raw food materials are supplied by a standard vendor and stock for minimum seven days is maintained.

Machinery

Central kitchen uses modern machinery for optimal utilization of raw material and manpower. Recently, chapati making machine costing 40 lakh was added which cooks better quality of chapatis. Some of the machinery used in central kitchen is shown in Figure 12.3.

Sewage Treatment Plant

Central Kitchen Project also includes a sewage treatment plant in order to reduce and recycle the waste (Figure 12.4).

Machineries

Roasting Machine

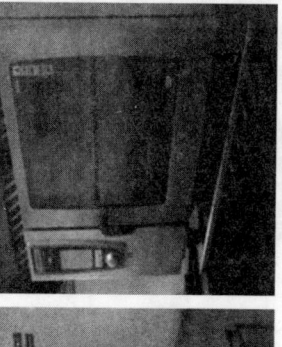

Chapati Machine

Egg's Boiling Machine

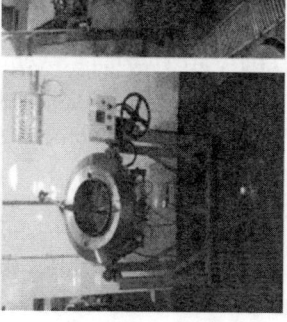

Kitchen Grinder

Dal and Sabzi Cauldron

Rice Cauldron

Idli Steamer

Figure 12.3 *Machinery Used in Central Kitchen*

Figure 12.4 *Sewage Treatment Plant*

Personal Hygiene

Contaminated hands spread bacteria around the kitchen very quickly. To prevent the contamination of food, it is essential to wash hands frequently before handling food. Good hygiene is about having better health for staff and students. Personal hygiene and food safety training is provided to all the staff of central kitchen (Figure 12.5).

Transportation

Food vessels are distributed by vehicles. There are in total 18 vehicles which transport food in batches and groups. Those vehicles are covered and protected by a locking system (Figure 12.6).

CHANGES IN THE PUBLIC DELIVERY SYSTEM

Majority of the tribal schools are in remote pockets. It raises three problems. One, there is a lack of competitive market in such areas which makes it difficult to find a competent supplier of raw material

Figure 12.5 *Personal Hygiene and Food Safety Practices at Central Kitchen*

Figure 12.6 *Transportation Facilities*

for food. Second, there is nexus of systemic corruption at the local level in the supply of raw material. Third, focus on hygiene is minimal at local level leading to instances of food poisoning, anaemia, etc. Because of the scattered location of schools and shortage of staff, it was difficult to have oversight over all schools. Central Kitchen Project solved all three problems. Central kitchen helped in the following ways:

1. The project brought accountability and transparency in the system, hence breaking the local nexus of corruption involved in the food supply.
2. Easy to supervise and monitor due to centralized operation.
3. Strict adherence to quality controls and hygiene.
4. Use of automation leading to optimal utilization of raw material and manpower.

IMPACT EVALUATION

Central Kitchen Project has two major impacts:

1. Malnutrition, anaemia as well as instances of micronutrients deficiency are rampant in tribal pockets, especially among children. Providing nutritious and hygienic food to children is the major

impact of central kitchen. After the Central Kitchen Project, results of Comprehensive Baseline Survey show:

a. Substantial reduction in anaemia levels, especially among girl children (11% reduction)

b. Underweight prevalence reduced by 9 per cent, especially among children <10 years

c. Doctors have also indicated that the number of visits by children to health centres has drastically reduced.

2. School principals are relieved of the cumbersome administrative work involved with decentralized cooking and ensuring four meals a day. Now teachers can focus solely on education.

CONCLUSION

In this project, the main stakeholders are the tribal students. Their basic requirement is a nutritious and wholesome meal. Malnutrition, anaemia as well as instances of micronutrients deficiency are rampant in tribal pockets, especially among children. To counter this problem, central kitchen focused on two aspects—hygiene and nutrition. The quality standards in central kitchen are the same as available in Tata group of hotels. Weekly and monthly timetable for food is prepared in the kitchen keeping in mind the vitamin and micronutrient requirements of the tribal students. Milk is provided daily, eggs once a week and meat twice a month. Providing a hygienic, nutritious and wholesome meal to the tribal students is the biggest achievement of central kitchen.

Chapter 13

Indira Gandhi Memorial Model Residential School (IGMMRS) in Malappuram, Kerala
A Case Study

Muhammed Shafi C. T. and R. R. Patil

INTRODUCTION

Kerala is home for 35 Scheduled Tribes (STs) of which 5 are Particularly Vulnerable Tribal Groups (PVTGs), who have identified declining population, educational and economic backwardness, pre-agricultural occupation, outdated technology, malnutrition, poverty, deprivation of basic amenities, lack of healthcare facilities, etc. The literacy rate of tribes in Kerala is 75.8 per cent, according to the 2011 Census, with a gap of 18.2 per cent in state literacy rate, while the national literacy gap is 14 per cent. The literacy of PVTGs in Kerala is far below the tribal literacy rate. The five PVTGs in the state are Cholanaikkar, Kattunaikkar, Kurumbas, Kadar and Koragas.

Kerala, the most literate state, has a paradox of incorporating one of the most illiterate tribal groups in India, the Cholanaikkar. The tribe has 15.3 per cent literacy rate and Kattunaikkar has 48.9 per cent as per 2011 Census. Both the central and state governments have come up with a number of schemes to boost the educational position of tribes, in general, and PVTGs, in particular. One of such schemes is model residential school (MRS).

Ashram schools are established to provide quality education with residential facilities of all kinds to the members of PVTGs. Out of the 25 Eklavya Model Residential Schools (EMRSs), there are three ashram schools, exclusively for PVTGs. The ashram schools in Kerala are distributed in PVTG-dominant districts of the state—Wayanad, Malappuram and Palakkad. These schools are provided with all the facilities required for leading a decent student life at par with government schools as well as aided and unaided private schools. Ashram schools in Kerala have a normal capacity of accommodating 350 students in classes 1–10 plus 70 students in higher secondary classes.

The ashram school in Malappuram district, Indira Gandhi Memorial Model Residential School (IGMMRS), is located in Nilambur, the forest of which is inhabited by the most vulnerable PVTGs in Kerala, Cholanaikkar and Kattunaikkar. Governed by both Ministry of Tribal Affairs and Ministry of Education of Kerala, IGMMRS is an ideal modern school, equipped with all amenities to provide the students from PVTGs with education and other life skills. The school accommodates 508 students, mainly from Cholanaikkar and Kattunaikkar, above its capacity of 420 students. The school has made remarkable changes in the educational level of Cholanaikkar and Kattunaikkar PVTGs whose literacy rate, as per 2011 Census, was 15.3 per cent and 48.9 per cent, respectively.

The school performs well in multidimensional aspects of curricular and extracurricular and the authorities and teaching and non-teaching staffs are very committed to the holistic development of the students. The students are encouraged to participate in various competitions held at district and state levels. The teachers take the helm in leading their students to good standard education and are very sincere towards their professions. Some of them have been working in the school for 14–15 years, even when they can apply for transfer and be appointed in other schools after three years of appointment. The school is very successful in creating awareness among the tribes about the importance of education and its role in the modern world. There is a change of mindset among the tribes towards education. The education has also enabled them to understand the exploitation by others, their civil rights as well as the welfare schemes of government for their betterment.

Although the students get access to the formal educational system, they are isolated from mainstream society and students. Here, students from PVTGs do not have chances to mingle with students of other tribes and outsiders. Presently, the dropout rate is near zero. The students, enrolling with little knowledge of Malayalam and English, have to struggle tirelessly to reach at par with the standard of others and in this effort, only some students succeed. Others, after their 12 years in IGMMR, go back to their caves and dwelling units in tribal colonies and make no use of their knowledge, ending their life eventually in drugs and alcohol. There is no comprehensive plan to recruit these passed out students after their 12 years into suitable jobs and enable them to find out their own livelihood.

The headmistress (HM) of IGMMRS has submitted a plan to the ministry with regards to utilizing the passed out students for various schemes of tribal development and the ministry has issued some guidelines on this recommendation. There should be a comprehensive plan to prevent the students from going back to their erroneous habits, which is possible only if an inclusive strategy is prepared to make use of their hard-earned education for their own development. Still, the IGMMRS play a vital role in the overall upliftment of PVTGs, especially in Malappuram district.

Both the government and civil society should make strenuous efforts to make PVTGs in the state mingle with the mainstream and enable them to cope with challenges of the modern world by providing them with modern education and making them qualified for appointment in government jobs. Mixed schools, students exchange programmes, generation of awareness about competitive exams, the appointment of highly qualified teachers with special service conditions and the appointment of passed out students in appropriate public and private jobs are some suggestions to figure out an enlightened educated tribal society.

REVIEW OF LITERATURE

As the study mainly relies upon the primary source and secondary sources are least found, review of literature is confined to the study of Bourdieu and Kakkoth.

Bourdieu (1986) in the article 'The Forms of Capital' explained three forms of capital and how these capitals are accountable for structure building and maintaining the status quo in society. These capitals help certain advantaged sections to enjoy the higher status and keep others at lower ranks. According to Bourdieu, each of these capitals can be converted into monetary value. The marginalized sections of society do not possess the cultural capital of the dominant society; hence they are deprived of all economic and social benefits. These benefits are enjoyed by a minority of people at the expense of the disadvantaged majority. Bordieu also explains the role of different capital forms in suppressing the weaker sections of the society, especially the tribal communities.

Kakkoth (2012) in 'Unheard Voices: A Study on the Perceptions of Tribal School Drop-outs in Kerala' examined the various viewpoints for the high dropout and low literacy rates among the tribes in Kerala. The methodology the author opted for conducting this research was fieldwork and in-depth interviews of the students, their parents and the teachers. One of the important findings of this research is that the tribal students are not comfortable with a freedom-less residential school environment.

Further, the study also depended upon newspapers to elicit the location of the schools, a number of ashram schools and recent reports on achievements of the school.

RATIONALE OF THE STUDY

In the last six years, the educational scenario of tribes, especially PVTGs in Kerala has witnessed a significant momentum through a chain of MRSs and ashram schools. IGMMRS presently is a home for 508 PVTG students where they study, eat and stay. This school has become a silver lining in their life by providing them with proper education, nutritious food and medical care. A bunch of dedicated teachers and other staff has assumed the role of parental care in these schools. Hence, this study aims to find out the recent developments in the curricular and extracurricular status of Cholanaikkar and Kattunaikkar students brought about by IGMMRS.

CULTURAL CAPITAL OF TRIBES VERSUS CULTURAL CAPITAL OF DIKUS

Until the dawn of the 21st century, the tribes were denied their civil rights and basic education due to lack of cultural capital. The capital they possess in terms of language and knowledge had little value in the society dominated by others. The culture of dominant society was given worth as capital and the tribal culture is altogether different from it. According to Pierre Bourdieu, the cultural capital brings financial and social capital and these three capitals are reinforcing each other. As the tribes lack these three capitals, they are considered inferior in society and perpetually suppressed.

OBJECTIVES

The objectives of the study are as follows:

1. To understand the role of IGMMRS in the educational development of Cholanaikkar and Kattunaikkar students in Kerala and the changes thereof.
2. To analyse the motivational energy created by IGMMRS among the students of Cholanaikkar and Kattunaikkar in Kerala.
3. To present the salient features of a model ashram school, thus to be replicated in Kerala and other states.

METHODOLOGY

The chapter is based on case study of IGMMRS in Malappuram district. The purposive sampling method was applied in the selection of the school for the study. As the secondary sources are few, the study primarily relies upon survey and interview of HM, interview of superintendent of school (SS) and representatives of students. The study used a comprehensive interview schedule and questionnaire to interview and survey HM. The representatives of students from Classes 12, 10, 8 and 5 and SS were given a chance to share their opinions about the school, its present system of education, infrastructure, teacher–student relations, accommodation and food, extracurricular activities, educational standard, teaching–learning facilities, achievements of school and appointment of teachers. Discourse and content analyses were used for interpretation and analysis of data. Some reports from newspapers are used as a secondary source.

ROLE OF IGMMRS IN EDUCATIONAL DEVELOPMENT OF PVTGs IN KERALA AND ITS SALIENT FEATURES

IGMMRS is a successful movement for the upliftment of Cholanaikkar and Kattunaikkar PVTGs in a gamut of aspects of their life, particularly education. IGMMRS provided one of the most expedient environments to the children from Cholanaikkar and Kattunaikkar to make advances in educational attainment. The school radiates some salient features, which deserve to be introduced in other EMMRs. The best features are explained below.

The Commitment of Government and Teachers

The school accommodates 508 students spanning in 12 classes, which is more than its accommodative capacity. These students are mainly from Cholanaikkar and Kattunaikkar, dwelling in caves, locally known as Alakal. The caves are far inside the forests of Nilambur. Initially, the authorities had to make concerted efforts to enrol the students. They had to walk more than 8 km to influence the parents and children to enrol. In addition, they had to struggle to evade the attacks of wild animals. However, when the tribes became aware of the importance of education, they started sending their children to schools without much hesitation. Vinod, the first Cholanaikkar to clear 12th standard, a degree from University of Calicut and postgraduation from Cochin

University of Science and Technology, created a much-needed awareness about the necessity of education among PVTGs in Kerala. HM calls the students as 'my children' and added,

> Their parents are illiterate, they don't know the mainstream language Malayalam; they don't have contact with others. The students speak their tribal language. When they attain 5 years of age, they are taken to school and enrolled in the first standard. They are provided the opportunity to study up to 12th standard.

These students are denied the rights enjoyed by mainstream students. They are deprived of many developmental resources ranging from all kinds of formal education to decent livelihoods and their rights over forest produce. They are treated as inferior for lacking the so-called cultural capital. In this backdrop, the state government took a bold step to cater to the PVTG students all the amenities required to bring them at par with the mainstream community.

Considering their backwardness and the circumstances they used to live in, IGMMR upholds a sublime goal of all-round betterment of PVTG students, thereby bringing about the development of PVTGs. The government provides them all opportunities to mingle with others and the students participate in school fete, science fairs, agricultural festivals, etc. The government takes those students who score high marks in 10th class to all India tour, Bharat Darshan.

Teachers' Appointment in IGMMRS

In IGMMRS, teachers are appointed considering the special needs of the students. Present pupil–teacher ratio) is 1:35. State Public Service Commission) carries out the appointments. Lower primary school assistants) are appointed for 1–4 standards and high school assistants (HSAs) are appointed for classes 5–12. There is no appointment of upper primary school assistants for classes 5–7, instead, they are taught by HSAs. This is the normal pattern followed in MRSs in the state.

A permanent appointee has to take a claim of not leaving the school for three years and deposit a bond, which will be confiscated in case of violation of the claim. However, there are some teachers serving the school for 12–15 years, and they are aware of their commitment to the service to the society, primarily the weaker sections. Only Sundays are off classes and there are only 10 casual leaves in a year. Some teachers are even not taking these 10. This commitment and services of teachers are reflected in various achievements of school and accomplishments of students and above all in generating a motivational mindset among them.

School Infrastructure

The infrastructure includes school buildings, hostel facilities, books, library, computer and science labs, smart and sophisticated classrooms, mess, stadium, stage, etc.

Buildings, Computers, Library and Labs

The school has its own infrastructure, consisting of two school buildings, containing 17 classes, two hostels and mess halls separately each for boys and girls. The school has its own library containing more than 1,500 books. The computer lab has 30 computers where students spend at least half an hour a day regularly. The school is also attached with well-equipped separate labs for physics, chemistry and biology.

Smart Classrooms with LCD

Six classrooms—two higher secondary and four lower primary and upper primary classrooms—are smart classes in an interactive mode set up by IT@School, a project of Kerala government to spread IT-enabled education in the state. One school building has a tiled floor as IT@ School stresses on tiled floors to implement its plan. In addition to it, the Department of Education has set up two smart rooms to improve the school. One classroom, which is fitted with LCD, is air-conditioned as part of this initiative.

Normal Classrooms Furnished with Sophisticated Equipment

All classrooms are furnished with all teaching–learning materials ranging from a sufficient number of benches and desks, to attached blackboards, notice boards, table and chair for teachers, etc. The school premises are under surveillance of about 10 CCTVs. It has its own separate electricity facility, first-aid boxes, about 10 DVD/CD players, 4 LCD projectors and television. There are three sources of fresh water—well, borewell and piped water supply by government–to fulfil requirements of school and all its occupants.

Multipurpose Stadium, Upraised Stage and Seminar Hall

A multipurpose stadium was constructed with sophisticated facilities to allow the students to engage their evenings in various sports activities such as football and cricket. The school has an upraised stage, besides the hostel and a seminar hall to help students utilize their extracurricular capabilities.

Accommodation, Nutritious Food and Study Materials

In IGMMRS, the students are provided all the facilities for their holistic development. The school assumes for itself the responsibility of the education and protection of tribal students and bringing them to the mainstream. They are provided education, food, accommodation, clothes, uniforms, study materials, footwear, playground, etc. free of cost. Their dresses are washed in the laundry. The special needs of girls are taken care of by the school. The medical camp is held each month and the students are provided free medical treatment from nearby district hospital and medical college. The food menu is prepared in accordance with the instructions of health inspectors. The menu includes all sources of protein such as milk, meat, eggs, vegetables, rice and wheat.

Curriculum in IGMMRS

IGMMRS has adopted the curriculum prepared by Kerala State Council of Educational Research and Training, which is a replication of National Council of Educational Research and Training syllabus but in the Malayalam language to suit their convenience and make them acquainted with the mother tongue of the state. IGMMRS still keeps pace with private schools and other government schools and bags awards in fairs, art fetes and other competitions.

Enrolment of Students

The school has scrapped the limitation of enrolment due to the exodus of students. Each year, the number of students is shooting up. In 2013, there were 329 students. After that, the students reached 525 in 2016, 516 in 2017 and 508 in 2018, mainly with the launch of higher secondary classes, instead of the actual capacity of 350.

Teacher-Student Relations

The teachers consider the students as their children and take care of their educational, medical and welfare needs. These students are with teachers from 1st standard to 12th. The students spend more time with teachers than their parents during this period. The vital force behind the success of IGMMRS is the dedicated force of teachers who, after their official duty hours, spend a couple of hours with weak students and teach them the difficult subjects.

Routine in School

The students have to wake up early morning by 5:30 AM and perform their fundamental routine deeds. After having tea and snack, they appear in the classes by 7:00 AM and engage in revising previous classes. During this time, they can make use of the library, computer library and science labs. By 8:30 AM, periods start and last until 3:30 PM. In between, there are 7 periods of 45 minutes. At 12:45 PM, after 5 periods, they get lunch break until 2:00 PM, after which there are two other periods. After formal school hours of the day, the students spend their time in various kinds of games and play for two hours until 5:30 PM. Then, after their bath and evening prayer, they come back to classrooms for revision of classes and night classes. By 8:00 PM, they have their dinner. Then they engage in their own activities of study, preparation of notes and extracurricular activities.

Achievements of IGMMR

In the present situation, IGMMR is considered as one of the best EMRS in Kerala. In a period of 25 years, especially in the last 5 years, the school has made remarkable changes in the educational status of tribes and enabled the students to bag many trophies in various competitions including state-level art fetes and fairs.

100 Per Cent Success in Secondary School Leaving Certificate

In the last six years, the school has accomplished 100 per cent pass rate in secondary school leaving certificate (SSLC) examination. When compared to its performance in previous years, this was a golden feather in their cap and the school undertook strenuous efforts to maintain the achievement.

Better Performance in Higher Secondary

In higher secondary category, started in 2014, the school achieved the pass rate of 65 per cent, 70 per cent and 74 per cent in the ensuing years, adding another achievement.

Comprehension of Language

After two years in school, the students start speaking Malayalam well, and spoken English sessions are arranged to train the students in English.

89 Students Qualified for National Means Cum-Merit Scholarship Scheme

What deserves a special mention here is that during the period of 2011–2017, 89 students from IGMMRS qualified for National Means Cum-Merit Scholarship Scheme managed by NCERT at the national level.

Sports and Athletics

Some students are very good at sports and even girls exude good potential in sports. Some students were selected to compete in sub-district, district and state-level athletics and sports competitions.

Third Prize in Science Fete

In a science fete, IGMMR was awarded the third prize in 2017, sub-district level, among 64 schools.

Awards in Organic Farming

Organic farming is practised by the agricultural club of school, supervised by a teacher in one and quarter acres of land. The club cultivates a variety of vegetables, which are more than sufficient to meet the requirements of the school. This scientific organic farming enabled the school to bag first prize in district and second in state in an agricultural fair. Anil Kumar, the teacher-member of the club, was conferred the award for the best agricultural teacher in the state. This not-for-profit farming also got them the award of the Seed Project of Mathrubhumi. In *Haritha Vidyalayam* reality show conducted by Doordarshan, IGMMR was one of the 100 schools selected by the show out of a total of 400 schools competing in the state.

Progress of Students

The Headmistress (HM) looked very proud when explaining about the improvement among students of Cholanaikkar tribe. Out of the total 250 in Cholanaikkar population, 91 students study in IGMMRS; they wake up early in the morning and take a bath. After their 12th, the students go for higher studies and some are appointed in government jobs. Six IGMMR students were recruited to Kerala police from Kattunaikkar.

District collector of Malappuram, chairperson of executive committee, is very satisfied with the achievements and proposed new roadmap to further the progress. This helped to create a feeling among students that the government and teachers are with them.

The Words of SS about the School

SS explained the tireless endeavours of tribal and educational ministries and was proud of the selfless efforts of school authorities, teachers and other staff in leading the students in their way to educational attainment. SS eagerly spoke of achievements of the school.

Teachers are appointed irrespective of their social background. Priority is given to STs or Scheduled Castes in case of a vacancy. There are 42 teaching and non-teaching staffs, for whom dormitory facility is given. No dropout has been reported in recent years. Motivation classes are given occasionally to inspire the students to carry on their study after +2 in either professional courses or humanities according to their taste. Various kinds of training camps are organized. On Saturdays, a special programme of two hours is conducted to do away with their stage fear. Most of the Malayalam and some English newspapers and magazines are made available to students. Some NIT students who visited the school told the SS that such facilities are not available even to them.

The Words of Students about the School

They were very happy in highlighting that no punishments are imposed upon them, while each teacher motivates them to study and perform well. They also repeated the achievements of the school. Food is of high quality which includes biryani and other nutritious foods. On every Saturdays and Sundays, their parents can visit them.

SUGGESTIONS

To improve further the standard of IGMMRS so that it can be replicated by other MRSs in the state and outside, the study moots some suggestions to revitalize the educational empowerment of tribes.

Foremost, the tribal students should be provided the opportunities to mingle with outside students to integrate with mainstream society and develop their abilities. Mingling with outsiders will instil in them the qualities of interacting with others, absorbing the merits of other students and enrich their own with the world view of outsiders without compromising their unique elements. To attain this goal, after lower primary education, the department should provide them with opportunities to enrol in other schools with sophisticated facilities if they are interested. A couple of mixed schools of high quality can also be established, where equal proportions of tribal and other students are enrolled. The exchange of students between normal and tribal schools can be experimented on a pilot basis to provide more opportunities for tribal students to be familiar with mainstream students and their range of education.

Second, apart from humanities stream in higher secondary, science and commerce streams should be provided to empower the students to compete for medical and engineering admission in institutions of excellence along with enabling them to take admission in colleges, universities, and institutions of higher education. The existing stream of humanities can be upgraded to make it compatible with the admission qualifications of central and state universities. The PVTG students should be provided a special reservation in education and jobs. The appointment of dedicated professional teachers of high quality is one good option to iron out the divide with outside students. To attract teachers of high quality, relatively higher salary and favourable service conditions can be extended.

Further, the teachers and authorities should adopt all the measures to generate awareness among the students about various competitive exams conducted by UPSC, State PSCs and other public and private recruiting agencies. It will increase their proportion in various government and private jobs, thereby helping them to prop up their families and enhancing their living standard, in particular, and of the whole tribe, in general. Post-matric hostels should be built to help students seeking higher studies.

The government and civil society should adopt measures to generate awareness among the parents about various projects for the welfare of tribes and detailed instructions about the procedures to be followed to avail the benefits of these schemes should be exchanged in understandable language. The authorities of school and teachers can create awareness first among their students who can then convey the messages to their parents. If implemented in a time-bound manner, the lacunae between the indigenous tribes and the outsiders can be reduced gradually until it is completely eliminated.

CONCLUSION

The educational development of tribes was a challenging concern for both central and state governments in India since independence. The tribes, especially PVTGs, were one of the most marginalized sections in the country. The governments implemented a score of schemes with huge amounts of public money to improve the educational conditions of the tribes. However, the viability of many of these schemes was not to the desired level. MRSs are exclusive schools for educational development of the tribal population in India, which helped create ripples of success in educational betterment among the tribes.

In Kerala too, MRS project, along with other schemes, improved the educational status of tribes to an extent. Among these MRSs, there are three ashram schools, specially engineered for PVTGs. IGMMR School, one of the ashram schools, located in Malappuram, has made a huge impact in educational upliftment of Cholanaikkar and Kattunaikkar PVTGs. The school has achieved a 100 per cent pass rate for the last five years in SSLC and gradually it witnessed an increase in the pass percentage in higher secondary. In 2017, it achieved 74 per cent success rate within three years of commencement of higher secondary courses in 2014.

IGMMR school presents an ideal picture of an ashram school with all the sophisticated facilities for educational development of students including its building infrastructure, 16 classrooms, 6 smart classrooms, computer and science labs with state-of-the-art instruments, multipurpose stadium, upraised platform stage, three sources of pure water. The school also shines in its curricular and extracurricular activities. So far, the school has been awarded the third prize in science fair and first in district and second in state in agricultural fair.

The ashram schools prove to be fulfilling the requirements of PVTGs for their educational development. IGMMR made significant changes in the attitude of tribal students and their parents towards education. PVTGs in Nilambur now want the government to leave no stone unturned to integrate them with the mainstream society without adversely affecting their unique elements of culture. So far, governments were trying to isolate them from the mainstream on the pretext of safeguarding their cultural and linguistic elements. Now they demand a radical change in the approach of the government towards them and push the government at all tiers as well as civil society to adopt effective measures to take them into the domain of multi-social relations and help them enjoy their rights and perform their duties towards the nation and the fellow citizens.

The need of the hour is a transformative change in the mindset of civil society and the government. The civil society should learn to perceive the tribes as equal to them and help them to attain the various developmental aspects at par with them, instead of keeping them at bay. The energy and human resources among the tribes should be effectively utilized for multi-sectoral development of the nation. This is possible only through proper education, healthcare and nutritious food.

REFERENCES

Bourdieu, P. 1986. *The Forms of Capital*. Westfort, CT: Greenwood.
Kakkoth, S. 2012. Unheard Voices: A Study on the Perception of Tribal School Dropouts in Kerala. *Child Rights and You*, 8–13.

PART III

Rethinking Policy and Planning for Tribal Education

Chapter 14

Revisiting Policies and Need for Reform in Tribal Education

Sonal Shivagunde

INTRODUCTION

India is home to the single largest tribal population in the world. The 834 tribal communities[1] form 8.6 per cent, that is, 10.3 crores of the total population (Census 2011). The Scheduled Tribe (ST) population represents one of the most marginalized, economically impoverished and educationally backward groups in India. For ameliorating the situation of the ST, education, among others, is the key driving factor. Issues and prospects of their education are embedded in the larger socio-economic, psycho-social and cultural factors and hence cannot be analysed in isolation. As a result, although policy initiatives and programmes, including setting up of ashram schools in tribal habitations have been undertaken since 1956, the overall educational development has lagged behind when compared to the mainstream population. The ashram school programme, implemented since 1975, has significantly contributed to this positive trend in literacy level among STs since these were the only schools accessible to the tribal population until the 1990s (8.53% in 1961 to 58.96% in 2011, as per Census). Access to other schools increased after the universalization of primary and elementary education was achieved post–2001. Regarding school education, currently, a total of 251,309,665 students are enrolled from Class 1 to 12 in 1,535,610 schools across the country. Among these, 32,632 (3.03%) schools are managed by Department of Tribal/Social Welfare, and 4,815,284 ST students (19% of total enrolment) are enrolled across different schooling systems, and 48 per cent among them are females. Exact data is not available regarding the total number of ashram schools and enrolment. The trends in key indicators over the last few years reflect gradual improvement in terms of improved access, increased enrolment, reduced dropout rate and higher transition rate among STs. The learning outcomes, measured through National Achievement Survey) by the National Council for Education Research and Training also indicate improvement in achievement levels of the STs. However, the gap in indicators between the STs and national average reflects that there is much to be done at both policy and implementation level for improving school education of STs, with a special focus on ashram schools (see Tables 14.1 and 14.2).

Table 14.1 *Key Educational Indicators, 2016–17*

Key Indicators		ST	All
Gross Enrollment Ratio	Elementary	99.57	93.55
	Secondary	73.48	79.35
	Higher Secondary	42.67	55.4
Transition Rate	Primary to upper primary	86.65	88.56
	Elementary to Secondary	83.29	90.32
	Secondary to Higher Secondary	57.47	66.42
Dropout Rate	Primary	8.54	6.35
	Upper Primary	9.58	5.67
	Elementary	8.88	6.12
	Secondary	26.51	19.89
	Higher Secondary	8.43	5.95

Source: DISE, 2016–17.

Table 14.2 *National Achievement Survey, 2017*

Class	Subject	ST	National
Class 3	EVS	63	65
	Language	66	68
	Mathematics	62	64
Class 5	EVS	55	57
	Language	55	58
	Mathematics	51	53
Class 8	Language	53	57
	Mathematics	40	42
	Science	43	44
	Social Science	43	44

Source: NCERT, 2017.

POLICIES, PROGRAMMES AND APPROACHES FOR OVERALL DEVELOPMENT AND SCHOOL EDUCATION OF STs

The major challenges in the overall development of STs with reference to school education are rooted in several chronic and historical issues which need to be addressed. Traditional inhabitation of STs in remote areas due to need for proximity to forests and natural resources is a key reason for excluding STs from the mainstream population, resultantly depriving them of resources and opportunities for development in various spheres. This is worsened by increasing exploitation of natural resources leading to encroachment in the natural habitats and land alienation, which is a threat to the agro-based livelihood of the majority of tribals. The resultant displacement, poverty and heightened levels of exploitation through a system of bonded labour further trap them in the downward spiral of exclusion (Subramaniam 2005; Sujatha 2002). Since survival itself is at stake, naturally, education cannot be a priority for STs, when considered from the perspective of demand for education. Hence, even if education delivery, that is, supply has expanded, low uptake, low retention and high dropout at the school level are persistent. Unless all these key issues are dealt with, expansion of education delivery alone may not lead to the desired impact and result.

Post-1950, several constitutional, policy and programmatic measures were undertaken by the Government of India for holistic development of the tribal communities. Although no specific policy was developed for the education of STs, all key policies, regulations and programmes related to education have incorporated specific provisions for the educational advancement of the STs. The Directive Principle under Article 45 of the Constitution of India seeks to provide free and compulsory education for all children up to the age of 14 years. Article 350(A) directs every state/local authority to provide adequate facilities for instruction in the mother tongue at the primary level for children from linguistic minority groups. The 86th Constitutional Amendment Act of 2002, under Article 21A recognized 'education' as a fundamental right. Education commissions such as Secondary Education Commission, 1952–1953; Kothari Commission, 1964–1966; National Education Policy (NEP), 1956 and 1986; Programme of Action, 1992; National Curriculum Framework, 2005, and the most recent Draft NEP, 2016, have made specific recommendations for education delivery for STs and its modalities with due consideration to challenges in doing so (MHRD 1968, 1986; MoTA 2007; NCERT 2005).

The directives and recommendations of these policies have been reflected in the subsequent national- and state-level programmes and initiatives designed and implemented over a time period. Among the ongoing ones, Ashram School Programme and Eklavya Model Residential Schools (EMRS) supported by the Ministry of Tribal Affairs (MoTA) are exclusively meant for the STs. Other programmes accommodating STs comprise Samagra Shiksha Abhiyan (erstwhile Sarva Shiksha Abhiyan and Rashtriya Madhyamik Shiksha Abhiyan); Kasturba Gandhi Balika Vidyalaya; the National Programme for Education of Girls at Elementary Level) by Ministry of Human Resource Development (MHRD) and Mahila Shiksha Kendra under Mahila Samakhya Programme by Ministry of Women and Child Development (MHRD 2016; Planning Commission 2010).

Among these, it was envisaged that the Ashram School Programme, designed with due consideration to the challenges and limitations, would be most effective in the educational development of the STs. The concept has been derived from the traditional Indian *gurukuls* and the Gandhian philosophy of basic education in which the teacher and the taught live together and have close interactions for the purpose of helping the students in the development of a complete personality and in honing their capacities. In the 1960s, ashram schools were started on an experimental basis in Gujarat and Maharashtra and scaled up subsequently across the country.

ASHRAM SCHOOL PROGRAMME: GENESIS, DESIGN AND VARIATIONS IN IMPLEMENTATION MODALITIES

Ashram schools were introduced as an exclusive programme for tribals by Government of India in 1974, and since 1990–1991, they are being established under the Tribal Sub-Plan Areas as a 50–100 per cent centrally sponsored scheme (as based on composition or geographical region, funding varies between 50 and 100) to improve literacy rates and provide a conducive learning environment and residential facilities to tribal students, including those from primitive vulnerable tribal groups. Ashram schools target remote rural areas and serve as a means to check the problems affecting tribal education and gradually facilitate mainstreaming. The programme design itself is based on recommendations of several committees (such as Renuka Ray Committee, 1959; Elwin Committee, 1960; Dhebar Commission, 1962).

By virtue of being established in remote areas, ashram schools are well placed to develop local educational resources and promote enrolment and retention. The residential nature of the schools enables students to get uninterrupted access to education. The curriculum and pedagogy are required to be aligned with the needs of tribal learners. The programme design comprises life skill education, vocational education and extracurricular activities such as sports, art and cultural activities. Initially, the intent was to provide 'relevant' elementary education to the STs in consonance with their life and culture which later scaled up to Class 12.

The MoTA guideline for Ashram School Programme provides flexibility to state governments for adopting the most suitable operational mechanisms leading to the state-to-state variation in the pattern of implementation. For example, in the case of states such as Maharashtra, Rajasthan, Jharkhand and north-eastern states, the programme is implemented directly by the Tribal Development Department (TDD) of the state. Some schools are also managed through voluntary organizations under the scheme 'grant-in-aid to voluntary organizations for running ashram schools'. While in Gujarat, Odisha, Andhra Pradesh, Telangana and Karnataka, autonomous societies have been formed by TDD. The respective societies manage 20–250 ashram schools (in addition to EMRS and hostels), undertake staffing, monitoring, teacher training and co-curricular activities. In addition to these two modalities, Gujarat also has a public–private partnership model for either adopting entire school or sponsoring specific interventions across schools (such as meals or teacher training). Madhya Pradesh, Chhattisgarh and West Bengal have adopted a mixed model, wherein the schools are established and funded by TDD, but the overall management and administration are entrusted to the Department of School Education (Annual Reports of respective states for the year 2016–2017 and 2017–2018).

KEY ISSUES AND CHALLENGES IN IMPLEMENTATION OF ASHRAM SCHOOL PROGRAMME

Considering the fact that Ashram School Programme has not been able to deliver results as expected, it is imperative to revisit the programme design and relevant policies and regulations that have contributed to the original programme and subsequent modifications therein over a period. From the programme delivery perspective, adequacy of funding, planning, management and administration at all levels, monitoring mechanisms and systems and processes adopted for implementation also need to be reviewed.

An in-depth study of ashram schools in the central tribal belt (Sharma and Sujatha 1983) shows differential utilization of ashram school facilities by different tribal groups. The Tribal communities with higher literacy level and social hierarchy utilize the facilities better while the primitive tribes tend to have much lesser access to education in any form. Sample surveys have reported weak infrastructure. Classrooms are not adequately lit and desks are inadequate. In the majority of schools, desks are not provided at the primary level. Leakage in roofs and seepage in walls during monsoon are evident. Adequate bedding is not available and many times, woollens are not provided during the winter season. Learning facilities such as computer lab, science lab and library are not available in majority schools (Bagai and Nundy 2009). Toilets and bathrooms are not maintained well, and students continue open defecation, partly due to lack of maintenance of toilets and partly due to behavioural issues. This also has implications on safety, since open defecation leads to instances of snake and scorpion bites, some of which tend to be fatal. The overall safety of the students, especially girl students, is also being questioned repeatedly after cases of molestation and exploitation began getting exposed and intensified in the last 5–7 years. Maharashtra has reported 1,200 deaths since 2001 (TDD 2017).

Similarly, health and nutritional status is also a matter of concern. The menu and time of meals are standardized at the state level and the local and indigenous food items are also incorporated in the menu. However, implementation at the school level is grossly compromised. This is indicated by serving an inadequate quantity of food, lack of quality in meals and having meals in unhygienic conditions due to non-availability of dining spaces which has repercussions on overall nutritional status and health of the students (Sujatha 2016). This is reflected in the nutritional deficiencies (Vitamin A and D3, proteins, iron). Resultantly, malnutrition, anaemia and problems related to eyesight are common. Tribal students also have a low level of awareness regarding personal care and hygiene. Coupled with the absence of initiatives in schools for behavioural change, the prevalence of communicable diseases and gynaecological disorders among adolescent girls is very high. The problems are exacerbated as medical care is not available on time, both due to the negligence of school and lack of practitioners or functional dispensaries in remote areas.

Review of overall Ashram School Programme reflects that education delivery through the schools is not aligned to the needs of tribal learners, although policy directives have recommended these from time to time (Sedwal and Kamat 2008). The curriculum and content are the same as those of general schools and not contextualized. Multilingual education is rarely practised in 5 out of 19 states. Life skill education, orientation for WASH (water, sanitation and hygiene), etc. are not integrated with the curriculum. Except for Andhra Pradesh and Telangana, vocational training is not being conducted. Promotion of tribal art, craft and culture through schools is lacking. Tribal students have inherent agility, strength and skills suitable for sports such as athletics, football, hockey, archery and swimming. These are being promoted actively through EMRS, but ashram schools seem to lag on this front, although the school campuses are generally large enough to accommodate facilities and space for training in sports. Thus, apart from regular classes and extra classes or self-study, students do not have scope for edutainment or co-curricular activities. Lack of qualified teachers with a tribal background, high absenteeism among teachers, low motivational levels due to isolation and inadequate facilities, dissatisfaction regarding salary, etc. are some of the persistent teacher-related challenges.

The low quality of education does not prepare ST learners to succeed at higher levels of education or compete for jobs, thereby demoralizing young people. School education has failed to acknowledge the issues of self-worth and dignity. This also results in dropout or low performance in examinations, undermining opportunities to progress to higher levels of education.

Overall mismanagement of ashram school and its funding across the states was highlighted by the Prime Minister's Office itself (Sharma 2015). Inflated enrolment numbers, especially by non-governmental organizations managing the ashram schools (for claiming a higher amount of funds) is common. This is attributed to weak monitoring mechanisms and lack of governance and the absence of an appropriate regulatory mechanism. There is an absence of community and parental participation in overseeing school functioning. It is difficult to obtain evidence and take appropriate measures to contain the incidences of mismanagement. Lack of centralized and real-time data capturing for all the relevant key indicators creates a lacuna in the overall system of Ashram School Programme. The District Information System for Education (DISE) captures data of over one million schools, including ashram schools, but it is clubbed with all other categories of residential schools under the head 'Tribal/Social Welfare Department'. A closer examination of parameters and indicators captured in DISE reveals that the aspects related to residential infrastructure and safety are not captured. Several schools do not respond to the requirement for submission of data in the requisite format for DISE and are thus left out of the database. At present, there is no single source in public domain providing data on key indicators of ashram schools. This makes it challenging to monitor the overall programme or take policy decisions.

At the policy and regulatory level, the absence of a single integrated policy for tribal education, lack of detailed guidelines for management of ashram schools and non-availability of designated regulatory authority to monitor and examine critical issues related to ashram schools are the major lacunae. At the national level, the National Council for Protection of Child Rights and its state subsidiaries are authorized to enquire into matters regarding violation of child rights and the judiciary is empowered to examine and take corrective actions or make recommendations from case-to-case basis. High-powered committees are also appointed from time to time by the Government of India. But there is no specific, consistent and continued focus on matters and issues related to ashram schools (except for the committees constituted for the purpose). The Right to Education Act, 2009, does not cover aspects specific to residential schools. While improvement of governance (and quality of education, to a certain extent) in the school education system is being attributed to the implementation of the Act, at ground level, there is no such comparable evidence available in case of residential schools, including ashram schools.

While the overall situation of the ashram schools and education delivery therein reveal several lacunae, some initiatives of government and non-profit organizations need to be highlighted, since these serve as illustrations to address the challenges to a significant extent. Review of literature and consultations with relevant officials from TDD and societies across six states reflects that the schools managed by the independent societies governed by TDD are performing better. These are characterized by better infrastructure, higher quality of teaching and consistent capacity building of teachers. Pedagogy involves contextualization of the content, multilingual classroom transaction and activity-based learning. Multilingual teaching is adopted up to Class 2, after which, generally, language transition of the students takes place to the regional language of instruction. Life skill education is integrated into the curriculum. Information and communications technology (ICT) is used as required, especially for interactive teaching and learning English—the subject as well as the language which is generally found to be the toughest by the tribal learners. Sports are actively promoted through the schools, with several candidates making it to the state-level teams. The monitoring cell of the societies has systematic online and offline mechanisms to monitor the performance of the schools and the overall well-being of the students. As a result, the quality is maintained and appropriate measures are taken in case of deviations.

The departments of school education of few states have taken pro-active measures in favour of students attending schools established by the department in tribal areas. Assam, Odisha and Chhattisgarh have adopted multilingual education up to Class 4. In the case of Jharkhand, multilingual textbooks have been developed during 2016–2017 with the support of UNICEF and have been adopted from the academic year 2017–2018. TDD, Madhya Pradesh, is in the process of setting up 23 centres of excellence in sports, specifically for the tribals. Among these, 11 have already been set up and are functional, providing both education and sports training to the students.

Large-scale programmes implemented by MHRD through respective department of school education also incorporated specific interventions for tribal learners and proved to be successful to a significant extent. The World Bank supported District Primary Education Programme) had a significant focus on reforming teacher education, improving pedagogy and consistently orienting the teachers to adapt their pedagogy and align with the needs of their students. They were trained and encouraged to prepare their own contextualized teaching–learning material and apply activity-based learning methods. This led to encouraging results in the tribal blocks also (Pandey 2000). The erstwhile Sarva Shiksha Abhiyan (now Samagra Shiksha Abhiyan) had also demonstrated similar initiatives, comprising development of contextualised curriculum content in tribal dialects and bilingual dictionaries in tribal dialects in Maharashtra, Andhra Pradesh and Madhya Pradesh (Planning Commission 2010).

Among the ongoing successful programmes/interventions by non-profit organizations, two initiatives have made a significant impact over a period. Kalinga Institute of Social Sciences, Odisha, providing education to 38,000 tribal students from kindergarten to postgraduation in single campus since last 27 years, stands out as a striking example of quality education delivery specific to tribal context and subsequent integration of students with the mainstream, through higher education and placement as well as skill development for livelihood generation (Kalinga Institute of Social Service 2018). The School Transformation Programme, designed and implemented for tribal students in Jharkhand by Collectives for Livelihood Initiatives and Tata Trust also serves as a concrete reference. Launched in 2012, the programme has already proven its efficacy, relevance and responsiveness for education and empowerment of approximately 69,000 tribal learners. Other initiatives such as Janashala Project (1998–2004) supported by five UN agencies and implemented in Uttar Pradesh, Jharkhand and Bihar; Shikshan MITTRA by BAIF–MITTRA in Maharashtra (2003–2008) were also commendable in this context.

RECOMMENDATIONS FOR STRENGTHENING ASHRAM SCHOOL PROGRAMME AND INTRODUCING SYSTEMIC REFORMS IN TRIBAL EDUCATION

In light of the above challenges and considering the developmental trends in larger social context, it is imperative to revisit the policies and regulations pertaining to tribal education. It also calls for concrete measures at the systemic level and radical and pragmatic reforms for strengthening the Ashram School Programme. The recommendations for the purpose are further elaborated.

- An exclusive policy for the education of STs needs to be developed, providing clear direction for addressing the key issues pertaining to the education of STs. It should cover entire continuum of lifelong education, with specific reference to the school, general higher education, technical and vocational education. A single but holistic, inclusive and flexible model for education delivery of the STs could be recommended for all states to follow, incorporating learning from best practices. The policy needs to pave way for introducing reforms and creating an enabling environment, by harmonizing initiatives and facilitating convergence with relevant ministries at the central level and departments at the state level.

- At the central level, a central entity could be formed, subsuming the EMRS society with state-level subsidiaries, covering all residential institutions for the STs, including EMRS, ashram schools, residential schools set up by the state and hostels. While the national-level entity would have a broad mandate for management, governance, policy formation with regulatory functions, the state-level subsidiaries could be entrusted with the administration and monitoring of the institutions as well as undertake appropriate projects for the institutions suitable to the local context. The state-level societies could work in close coordination with the Tribal Research Institutes, relevant departments (such as school education, higher education, sports and culture, and planning), international development agencies and civil societies. These entities could have both academic and non-academic mandate, comprising administration, governance, convergence, monitoring, staffing, developing contextualized content, infrastructure upgradation, ICT enablement, training, research, organizing competitions and programmes, etc.

- A pan-India rapid survey of all residential institutions should be undertaken, collating data related to all key indicators for the assessment of the current situation of the infrastructure, human resources, quality of education and key local issues. The findings can be further utilized at the policy and implementation level and designing specific, localized interventions for both course corrections and systemic strengthening of education for STs. Such surveys need to be taken periodically to monitor and evaluate the overall progress of the revamped programme for education of STs and take measures for further strengthening.

- The DISE system should be revisited and parameters and indicators for residential institutions should be introduced. Features should be made available to extract segregated data. Also, a single management information system (MIS) needs to be developed and deployed across all educational institutions for STs in the country. Web-based and geographical information system-based technology is recommended for this purpose, with the facility of both online and offline data entry and dashboard. MIS also needs to be synchronized with DISE. This would resolve the issues related to data availability. Some states such as Jharkhand and Madhya Pradesh have already developed MIS with above features. These are operational at a smaller scale. Possibilities of adapting and scaling up these may be considered, instead of developing a new system.

- A large number of ashram schools are located in extremely remote locations. This results in exclusion and isolation of students, pose challenges in administration and monitoring and meeting shortage of teachers (and reducing their absenteeism). Hence, all ashram schools in a tribal block should be converted into ashram school complex at block or district level as feasible (depending on the number of schools and enrolment). The complexes should include facilities for sports, promotion of tribal art and culture and host programmes, competitions and festivals of STs and non-tribals. This will also help in resolving issues related to the shortage of qualified teachers and reducing absenteeism of teachers.

- Currently, the majority of ashram schools enrol students from Class 1 onwards. Instead, the students from Class 1 to 5 may be enrolled in the schools under Department of School Education (since universalization of primary education has already been achieved and schools are available within 1 km radius of the villages). Ashram schools could provide education from class 6 to 12. Also, they could have a provision of accommodating 25 per cent of non-tribal students instead of enrolling all ST students. This will help in cross-learning and acculturation of STs with the non-tribal population and facilitate mainstreaming and integration of STs with the non-tribal population at a later stage. This is also to create an enabling environment for the STs to reduce dropout and continue higher education in institutions wherein majority of students are from the non-tribal background.

REFERENCES

Bagai, S., and Nundy, N. 2009. *Tribal Education: A Fine Balance*. Mumbai: Dasra.

Census of India. 2011. 'PCA Maharashtra 2011'. Director of Census Operation, Maharashtra, Retrieved from http://pibmumbai.gov.in/English/PDF/E2013_PR798.PDF

Kalinga Institute of Social Service. 2018. *Annual Report, 2017–18*. Bhubaneswar: Kalinga Institute of Social Service.

MHRD. 1968. *National Policy on Education, 1968*. New Delhi: Government of India.

———. 1986. *National Policy on Education, 1986*. New Delhi: Government of India.

———. 2016, April 30. 'Report of the Committee for Evolution of New Education Policy'. New Delhi: Ministry of Human Resource Development, Government of India.

MoTA. 2007. *Draft National Policy on Tribals*. New Delhi: Government of India.

NCERT. 2005. *National Curriculum Framework*. New Delhi: NCERT.

Pandey, R. 2000. 'Going to Scale with Education Reform'. *Country Series, Education Reform and Management Publication Series* 1.

Planning Commission. 2010. *Evaluation Report on Sarva Shiksha Abhiyan*. New Delhi: Government of India.

Sedwal, Mona, and Sangeeta Kamat. 2008. *Education and Social Equity with a Special Focus on Scheduled Castes and Scheduled Tribes in Elementary Education*. New Delhi: CREATE and NEUPA.

Sharma, G. D., and Sujatha, K. 1983. *Educating Tribals—an In Depth Analysis of Ashram Schools*. New Delhi: NIEPA.

Sharma, N. 2015, September 2. 'PMO forces Rethink on Ashram Schools for Tribal Students'. *Economic Times*.

Subramaniam, R. 2005. 'Education, Exclusion and the Development State'. In Chopra, R., and P. Jeffery, (eds.). *Educational Regimes in Contemporary India*. New Delhi: SAGE Publications.

Sujatha. K. 2002. 'Education among Scheduled Tribes'. In *India Education Report: A Profile of Basic Education*, edited by R. Govinda. New Delhi: Oxford University Press.

———. 2016. *Assessment of Available Facilities for Primary and Upper Primary Education in Predominantly Tribal Areas in Nine States*. New Delhi: NUEPA.

TDD. 2017. *Report on Deaths in Ashram Schools*. Maharashtra: TDD.

Chapter 15

Rethinking Policy Design and Reforms for Tribal Education in India

Naresh Kumar

INTRODUCTION

The tribal population has always remained at the margins of mainstream society. However, some efforts have been made to improve their situation and as a result, recent decades have witnessed initiatives from the government to bring them into the fold of the development processes. Most of the development initiatives have remained controversial as they supposedly disturbed tribals' relation with nature. One of the major concerns which the policymakers are addressing is their educational development and this has remained staggered.

The chapter takes a relook into the status of tribal education in India with a socio-anthropological perspective to argue that development initiatives[1] have seriously undermined the essence of their culture and therefore failed to address the core issues of tribal education. Tribals

---

[1] The development has been understood in terms establishing formal schooling for tribal children and initiatives taken in this dimension.

being the marginalized group undergo huge dropout, especially the tribal girls. Their underperformance in the educational field results in different marginalities. Governments from time to time have acknowledged the poor educational performance of tribals. Apart from mainstream schooling, alternative school provisions have facilitated their educational growth. For example, programmes such as Eklavya and ashram schools, which are running in a few states, have remained limitedly successful as against the policy objectives. Even the promotion of tribal non-residential schools has failed to perform. The chapter is based on the secondary sources and intensive review of the relevant studies and government documents. It strongly urges that the policy initiatives have undermined the socio-anthropological perspectives for planning the education of tribal children. There is a need to look into their development through sociological perspectives rather than purely development steered by economic agenda.

There are several studies which are being conducted by researchers regarding the functioning of ashram school. Most of the studies are dealing primarily with the existing functioning and practices in ashram schools. Either the researchers valourize ashram school for building the capacity of the tribal children or take a critical strand for its negligence and poor infrastructure. Thadathil and Danane (2017: 26) points out that deprivation in these schools is quite pervasive and its impact on students' well-being is significant because many of them are first-generation learners. School-wise remedial measures seem to be missing in the management of *ashramshalas*. Neither the tribal department nor the school management are working towards filling vacant posts with temporary staff. Initiatives that solve such issues would probably enhance the perception and reality of children's security at these schools.

There is hardly any study which questions the idea of ashram schools: Why ashram school for tribal children is required? Are ashram schools really necessary for the education of the tribal children? There is hardly any theory which engages with these questions. The institution of schooling could be seen in a variety of ways and there exists immense literature dealing with these questions. The school could be functional as well as reproductive of the tribal culture (Bourdieu and Passeron 1977; Durkheim 1956; Willis 1977). The school could also be considered as a transformational agent depending upon its objectives.

Political philosophers though doubt its potential and would argue that a school does not possess any culture. Whatever school possesses are cultural values of the pupils solely, thus school culture depends upon preschool cultural resources coming directly from society. This makes it important for a researcher to examine what objectives ashram schools are fulfilling and directing their functioning.

ADMINISTRATION OF ASHRAM SCHOOLS

Ashram schools have been viewed as effective institutions to meet the educational needs of Tribal living in the interior, most backward and scattered habitations where opening up of normal schools is not viable. The concept of Ashram school stems from the objective of providing an atmosphere in which the inmates are offered full opportunities for total personality development. Ashram schools are residential schools in which free boarding and lodging along with other facilities and incentives are offered to the inmates. One of the major thrusts of Ashram school is: imparting skills in crafts, vocations, apart from providing general education. (Sujatha 1990).

Mishra and Dhir (2005: 5) argue that the establishment of ashram schools was envisioned as a direct intervention to tackle the socio-economic and geographic inequalities of the tribal population, particularly sparsely populated areas by providing educational opportunities. Sujatha (1990) summarizes the objectives as envisaged by the committees and commissions on ashram schools in India as follows:

1. Children should be weaned away from an atmosphere which is generally not conducive for the development of their personality and outlook—cultural backwardness theory.
2. Ashram schools should be inter-village schools.
3. Ashram schools should be opened in such areas where normal schools cannot be opened, and most backward tribal groups should be covered.

These are just a few objectives which have been guiding the working of Ass, whereas there are various other objectives giving primary attention to the 'learning activities' in the ashram. A very interesting fact which needs to be reminded is that ashram schools should not be considered as 'alternative schooling', rather the attempt to replace/or fill the gap of normal schooling and opened in an area not having a normal school. The absence/lack of normal schools led to the upcoming of ashram schools, rather than the teaching and pedagogical innovation to promote the education of the tribal children. Therefore, it is grossly mistaken to consider ashram schools as the alternative schooling.

Studies pointed out that either there is no infrastructure in ashram schools or underutilization of the existing resources and infrastructure. It points to the fact that there is an absence of an alternative strategy to make it as alternative schooling. Recent decades have also witnessed the initiatives to extend healthcare facilities to the tribal schools, thereby extending functions and utility of these schools, though resource support is mainly provided by the government schools. Most of the facilities are provided in the form of project mode/programmes which are usually executed on a large-scale population. This has substantially increased the resource demand by ashram schools for various purposes.

PARADOXES OF THE ALTERNATIVE SCHOOLING FOR TRIBALS

The fact cannot be undermined that ashram schools have eventually evolved on the model of alternative schooling under the different initiatives by the stakeholders including non-governmental organizations and government. The educational development of the marginalized communities has always captured the imagination of the policymakers in India. Scholarly debates have brought these issues to the centre of the policy discourse and public scrutiny time and again. The history of educational development has witnessed many interventions for the upliftment of tribal education (as mentioned in Table 15.1). Most prominently among these initiatives include the steps to improve tribal school accessibility provisions. These provisions were followed by attempts to reduce dropouts and increase their completion rates. Needless to point that a number of policies from the Kothari Commission to Right to Education have attempted to address these provisions. The policy initiatives did result in some positive implications, though the problem still persists. The policy obsession to bring tribal children to the school could be justified while keeping in context their lowest enrollment and highest dropout rates when compared with other caste/social groups.

Table 15.1 *Central Schemes for the Educational Development of the Tribals*

S. No.	Educational Programme	The Specific Focus of the Programme
1.	Pre-matric scholarship	1. Given to ST students studying in Class 9 and 10. 2. Covers all ST students whose parents' annual income is below ₹2 lakh. 3. Scholarship of ₹150 per month for day scholars and ₹350 per month for hostellers is given for a period of 10 months in a year.
2.	Post-matric scholarship	4. Open to all ST students and is given to enable them to pursue higher studies at post-matriculation level including technical and professional studies. 5. Covers all ST students whose parents' annual income is below ₹2,50,000. 6. Compulsory fees charged by the educational institutions is reimbursed and scholarship amount of ₹230 per month to ₹1,200 per month is given depending on the courses of study.
3.	Vocational training centres	7. Aimed at upgrading the skills of the tribal youth in various traditional/modern vocations depending upon their educational qualification, present economic trends and the market potential. 8. Grants will be available for organizing vocational training in recognized institutes or in vocational training centres.
4.	Establishment of hostels for ST boys and girls	9. Aims to supplement the efforts of the state governments for creating a congenial study atmosphere free from the shackles of domestic shores, so as to encourage students belonging to the target groups to pursue their educational career without dropping out. Such hostels are immensely beneficial to the students of the ST community hailing from rural and remote areas.

(Table 15.1 Continued)

(*Table 15.1 Continued*)

S. No.	Educational Programme	The Specific Focus of the Programme
5.	Establishment of ashram schools	10. The objective of the scheme is to provide residential schools for STs in an environment conducive to learning to increase the literacy rate among the tribal students.
6.	Top-class education	11. Given to ST students for pursuing studies at degree and postgraduate level in any of the 213 identified institutions of excellence such as IITs, NITs and IIMs. 12. Scholarships are given every year to meritorious students whose family income does not exceed ₹4.5 lakhs per year. 13. Scholarship amount includes tuition fees, living expenses and allowances for books and computer, etc.
7.	National fellowship	14. Fellowship to ST students each year for pursuing higher studies of MPhil and PhD in India. 15. Fellowship amount varies from ₹16,000 to ₹20,000 per month for a period of 2–5 years.
8.	National overseas scholarship for ST students	16. Provides financial assistance to selected students to pursue postgraduation, PhD and post-doctoral study abroad. 17. There are 17 awards for ST students and 3 awards for students belonging to particularly vulnerable tribal groups. 18. The selected students are given tuition and other educational fees charged by foreign universities, maintenance and other grants along with travel expenses. 19. Given to the students whose total annual income along with the income of the parents does not exceed ₹6 lakhs.

Source: Dubbudu (2015).

The chapter juxtaposes two paradoxical theoretical frames which are being prominently used by the policymakers and government agencies for the upliftment of tribals' educational status. It draws attention towards the inconsistencies prevailing in the policy discourse. The dominant discourse never paid attention to the irregularities, and rather sided with one or the other approach. In the context of improving educational status, the case of tribal residential schooling has been discussed. The role and function of the tribal residential schooling popularly called ashram schools assume a significant place as their working remained far more contentious in spite of their normal projections[2] in the policy documents.

1. The first assumption which has been guiding the tribal educational programmes is the idea of their cultural underdevelopment and the associated beliefs that their culture acts as an inhibitor. There are sets of scholars who believe that there lies inherent backwardness in the cultural life of the tribal children which consequently inhibits their educational mobility. 'Tribal cultural arbitrarily' unsuitable to the 'formal schooling' could be factored as a major obstacle to the government initiatives. The cultural backwardness theory has also remained one of the major theoretical explanations so far, for the researchers and policymakers. The cultural backwardness thesis has steered many educational initiatives so far undertaken by the Government of India. Enhancing their school enrolment and completion, school accessibility, modern teaching–learning tools, etc. are some of the interventions.

2. The establishment of ashram schools in some of the states of India is a phenomenon which probably could be seen as a departure from the theory of cultural backwardness to protecting their indigenous culture. One of the leading objectives which possibly underlie the objectives of establishing ashram schools is to protect the legacy of tribal tradition, culture and heritage. It is believed that separating tribal conglomeration from other social groups could possibly reduce the sense of discrimination against them as well as insulate their traditional values. Tribal children living and studying in a school together would develop a sense of 'we feeling' and prepare them as community leaders.

---

[2] We can discuss different theories of tribal development.

The thesis of isolated schooling of tribal children in ashram schools has come up very strongly in some of the states, as an alternative form. It is important to note that both the principles mentioned above from cultural backwardness to protecting cultural values juxtapose the idea of tribal development. Somehow this has also misled the policy discourse for the education of the tribal children. The prominent theories of cultural diversities have proved that cultural diversity in educational institutions promotes the learning level of the children. It also enhances intercultural learning. One of the studies conducted by Jojo (2013) in Maharashtra informs that many tribal teachers from ashram schools objected to the establishment of ashram schools, as it inhibits the possibility of diverse cultural learning of the tribal students. The tribal teachers consider ashram schools as ghettos. Field insight raises an important issue which probably most of the policy discourses have undermined until now. These include the stakeholder's perspective into the development initiatives.

The issue of tribal education has been subjected to many experiments without having many fruitful results. The retention and completion rates are relatively very high among the community and several cases of harassment, sexual abuse, deaths, etc. have been reported due to different reasons, primarily the unavailability of basic provisions. Meagre resources and lack of attention has caused much harm to the indigenous people. What has remained starkly absent in the policy discourse is the role of community members. They are still considered at the receiving end without having much wisdom in the policymaking processes. Research studies conducted on the tribal issues remained highly quantitative and subjectively biased against them. There exists plethora of literature which is reproducing the kind of knowledge which has already existed. The issue of the participatory process has been undermined relatively in the tribal studies which needs to be acknowledged.

HOW TO APPROACH THE ISSUE OF TRIBAL SCHOOLING?

Ashram schools could also be seen as a colonial model for civilizing tribals by considering them backward. This approach has led to the complete decline of their indigenous knowledge system. In the hierarchy of the schools, ashram schools belong to the bottom of the hierarchy. There is a need to initiate context-specific research studies. Could it be assumed that the policy framework on the educational changes in India has some inherent drawbacks that it is unable to locate the issues in proper perspective and in the appropriate context? That understanding and acceptance of the fact like multiculturalism and multilingualism in India have prompted policymakers to do experimentation on the issues of pedagogy, curriculum and several other dimensions of schooling, which more or less make the process of schooling complicated, give scope for the introduction of different policies. At the same time, the perception of schooling and education among different communities vary because of their distinct aspirations and sense of mobility. The marginal sections of the Indian society have witnessed much policy experimentation as far as education and school-ing are concerned. The purpose of schooling could differ from the state perspective and the tribal perspective. For the state, education could be an instrument of integration in the mainstream society, whereas trib-als can consider it as a means of accessibility for resources and upward mobility. Even we need to relook at the idea of education and social mobility among the tribals of India. It will be interesting and kind of path-breaking work if we could have some narratives from the tribal population about experimentation and implementation of recent poli-cies and if they have contributed significantly in the tribal way of life. The continuous changes from state and its welfare perspective about the tribal education itself raise several questions about the understandings of specificities and peculiarities of tribal life and policy implementation and its performance in the tribal areas. There is a need to relook into the idea of ashram schools in a changing time—old ashram schools to new ashram schools.

REFERENCES

Bourdieu, Pierre., and Passeron, Jean-Claude. 1977. *Reproduction in Education, Society and Culture*. London: SAGE Publications.

Dubbudu, R. 2015. 'The Eight (8) Central Sector Schemes for the Education of Tribal Students'. Available at https://factly.in/the-eight-8-central-sector-schemes-for-the-education-of-tribal-students/ (accessed on 20 June)

Durkheim, Emile. 1956. *Education and Sociology*. New York, NY: The Free Press.

Jojo, Bipin. 2013. 'Decline of Ashram Schools in Central and Eastern India: Impact on Education of ST Children'. *Social Change* 43 (3): 377–395.

Mishra, B. C., and Dhir, A. 2005. *Ashram School in India: Problems and Prospects*. New Delhi: Discovery Publishing House.

Sujatha, K. 1990. 'Education in Ashram Schools: A Case of Andhra Pradesh'. NIEPA Occasional Paper 18. New Delhi: National Institute of Educational Planning and Administration.

Thadathil, Abhilash., and Rajesh Dinkar Danane. 2017. 'Ashram Schools: Need for a New Approach'. *Economic & Political Weekly* LII (49): 25–28.

Willis, Paul. 1977. *Learning to Labour: How Working Class Kids Get Working Class Jobs*. Farnborough: Saxon House.

Chapter 16

Inclusive Education Policy for Tribal Ashram Schools in Odisha

Bibekananda Nayak

INTRODUCTION

Education is the basic input for the socio-economic development of the country. It was low at the time of independence. As per Education Development Index developed by National University of Educational Planning and Administration (Department of Educational Management Information System 2009), Odisha occupies 28th position among the states and union territories of the country, which puts it as an educationally backward state. Tribal education is mostly marginalized compared to other communities. Post independence of India, the Government of Odisha opened various formal schools for the tribal children with the provision of several facilities such as free boarding, lodging, books, dress and pocket money/stipend/scholarship, for attracting the tribal children to the fold of formal education. With these efforts, and with many more facilities added over a period of time, the rate of tribal literacy has gone up faster than that of the general population over the last six decades, and yet the achievements made so far do not match with the efforts put in. This study attempts to identify the constraints and impediments for achieving this goal with respect to the state of Odisha and suggests remedies by analysing the case studies for tribal students.

There are several factors responsible for low or inconsistence performance of ST and SC Development (SSD) Department schools. Unwanted posting and arbitrary transfer, lack of cordial relationship with the parents, the burden of non-teaching activities, non-completion of course due to the late supply of books, strenuous teaching for long hours due to a shortage of staff and the inadequacy of accommodation are some of the major problems faced by the teachers in tribal areas. The teacher–pupil ratio is found to be very high in government high schools where the ratio varies between 50 and 80. It is found that the posts of teachers in different streams are vacant in all of the 25 studied schools. Some sample schools are not provided with an adequate number of teachers. Besides, in 35 per cent of sample schools, the posts of science and mathematics teachers are vacant. Absence of qualified teachers to teach at the secondary level puts extra workload on the subject teachers, requiring him or her to teach lessons in about six to seven periods in a day, thus taking away the opportunity for him or her to take extra coaching classes for students of Classes 9 and 10 who deserve special attention. It is observed that none of the schools has a clerk in their establishment except that of the Kandhamal district. Due to unavailability of the clerk, a competent teacher generally performs the work of the assistant or clerk in the high school, such as maintenance of several registers and records, cashbook accounts, correspondences and sending reports to various quarters, which consumes most of his/her working hours. Further, the number of non-teaching staff is also found to be less in these schools. It is also found out that in some of the girls' high schools, the number of male teachers posted is more in comparison to female teachers except in one girls' high school which is located nearer. Also, teachers having higher secondary certificate (HSC) qualification are also taking higher classes where the vacancy of teachers exists for a longer period. This may be one of the reasons for low performance in high school examinations. In some schools, the school atmosphere is not conducive for studying. The boys' and girls' hostels are located in one boundary and in close proximity which disturbs the study atmosphere.

AREA OF STUDY

Tribal communities in the study area constitute 54 per cent of the total population of the district. As per an estimate, 74 per cent of people in those sample districts are below poverty line (BPL). Their literacy reported at 36 per cent is much lower than the state average of 63.08 per cent. The female literacy rate at 24 per cent also compares unfavourably with the state average of 50.51 per cent. There are 62 tribes in Odisha with a population of 8,145,081 (Census of India 2001), which constitute 22.13 per cent of the total population of the state. The Kandhamal district is centrally located in Odisha. It is dominated by the Kondh tribe. The Kandhas, once infamous for their human sacrifice (*meria*) during British colonialism in India, are believed to be from the Proto-Australoid racial stock. They have a distinct language called 'Kui' which has no script. They are forest dwellers as well as plains dwellers exhibiting greater adaptability to the great tradition or modern civilization standards in many ways. Their traditional lifestyle, customary traits of the economy, political organization, norms, values and worldview have drastically changed over a long period of time.

In Kandhamal district, there are 48 Scheduled Caste (SC) and Scheduled Tribe (ST) hostels, out of which there are 20 hostels for boys and the rest 28 are for girls. They are looked after by different government bodies like Integrated Tribal Development Agency (ITDA), which has total 15 high schools hostels, out of which 8 hostels are for boys and 7 hostels are for girls. The Kasturba Gandhi Balika Vidyalaya has eight girls' hostels. The Higher Education Department has a total of 17 hostels, out of which 5 are for boys and 12 for girls (ST & SC Development, Minorities & Backward Classes Welfare Department 2012).

The study has taken 20 ashram schools for the purpose of the study, out of which 10 are boys' schools and 10 are girls' schools.

ODISHA AT A GLANCE

In Odisha, there are a total of 1,599 educational institutions of the SSD Department that are functioning in 28 districts of the state to provide educational facilities to ST and SC children. There are 319 high schools of the SSD Department out of which 143 are girls' high schools (GHSs). Besides, there are eight higher secondary schools for science and commerce in different districts to provide education to the tribal students. During the year 2006–2007, 36 *kanyashrams* functioning under this department have been upgraded to GHSs. Apart from the 1,599 schools, the SSD Department has also established a number of hostels, some of which are attached to its schools and Mass Education Department schools to provide the residential facilitates to ST and SC students. There are total 3,197 hostels, out of which there are 1,548 primary school hostels in different blocks of ITDAs, 646 primary school hostels for ST girls and boys in Kalahandi–Balangir–Koraput districts and 1,003 hostels for ST girls in the state. For promoting education among ST students, the SSD Department has opened 52 GHSs from Class 10 in the tribal blocks of the state. Each school has a strength of 250 girl students. From among the 52 newly established GHSs, 21 GHS have been established in 5 study districts. In order to impart higher education to the children of primitive tribal groups and to reduce the dropout rate, 19 educational complexes have been opened since 2008 in micro project areas.

The average literacy rate in Odisha was 72.87 per cent as against the all-India average literacy of 74.04 per cent during 2011, with male literacy rate being 81.59 per cent and female literacy rate at 64.01 per cent. The ST literacy rate in Odisha is 52.24 per cent, with male literacy rate being 63.70 per cent and female literacy rate at 41.20 per cent. The ST literacy rate is 69.72 per cent, with male literacy rate being 79.21 per cent and female literacy rate at 58.76 per cent. The literacy rate in Kandhamal district is 64.13 per cent, with male literacy rate being 76.93per cent and female literacy rate at 51.94 per cent. The ST literacy rate in the district is 58.34 per cent, with male literacy rate being 72.12 per cent and female literacy rate at 45.58 per cent. The SC literacy rate in the district is 66.12 per cent, with male literacy rate being 78.88 per cent and female literacy rate at 53.90 per cent (ST & SC Development, Minorities & Backward Classes Welfare Department 2011). There is one primary school for every 3.2 sq. km of area.

Mid-day meal (MDM) programme has been operational since July 1995. In 2007–2008, about 42.30 lakh children in 65.528 primary schools and 5.26166 upper primary students in 8.410 upper primary schools were covered under the scheme. There is one upper primary school for each 8.13 km of area in the state. The overall dropout rate at the primary stage was 7.79 per cent, the dropout rate for girls being 7.83 per cent and for boys at 7.76 per cent during 2007–2008. The dropout rate at the primary stage was 12.54 per cent for SCs and 16.89 per cent for STs. The dropout rate at upper primary level has decreased from 59 per cent in 2002–2003 to 13.27 per cent in 2007–2008, for SCs from 47.50 per cent to 18.80 per cent and for STs from 77.70 per cent to 23.83 per cent. This shows that the dropout among the ST students at upper primary level has reduced to a greater extent in comparison to other communities from 2002–2003 to 2007–2008, but in absolute terms, it is found to be high in comparison to other communities.

FACTORS RESPONSIBLE FOR LOW LITERACY AMONG TRIBAL CHILDREN

The level of literacy is low among weaker sections of our society, especially among the tribal population. The sociocultural practices in simple and traditional societies contribute a lot to educational backwardness among tribal children. They depend highly on nature for their survival. From the very childhood, they are engaged in household work, caring for siblings and domestic animals and collection of minor forest produces and boys are engaged in assisting parents in agricultural activities. The tribal parents possess a negative perception towards modern education, as there is a loss of manpower in the family for agricultural activities and also a detachment of children from the family. In the case of girls, one of the fears is that education may lead to cessation of the bride price to parents. Educated children may not contribute labour towards economic activities and may not do any household work. It will also create a gap in acquiring traditional knowledge of their society which helps them to lead a smooth life. Besides poverty, detention, frequent ailments and early marriage act as a barrier to their educational advancement.

Again, poor infrastructure and lack of communication facilities, use of English language as a medium of instruction followed at school, inadequate provision of meals, holiday pattern not in consonance with the rituals and festivals of their society, lack of adequate teaching–learning materials, unsuitable curriculum and syllabus, inadequate teaching staff are some of the major causes for low enrolment which in turn leads to low literacy. It was found that the rate of enrolment is not a problem, but the rate of dropout is a very serious issue which is more among tribals, especially among ST girls because their high demand in the family to perform household chores which keeps them away from their school education.

After independence, several steps and educational schemes were taken up by the union and state governments for promoting education among the people, especially the weaker sections, such as SCs and STs. Gradually, the educational development programmes were broadened, and more schemes got introduced.

Some factors responsible for low literacy levels among tribal children are as follows:

1. Textbooks are not supplied to the schools at the beginning of the academic session either by SSD or by the Text Book Press. This irregularity creates problems both for the teachers and students and becomes one of the reasons for the low performance of the students. Further, stipends are not given in due time which creates a lot of problems to manage the mess and to supply the uniform to the boarders, which are expenses usually met out of the stipend money.

2. Quarters allotted to the teaching staff within the school boundaries are not provided with an adequate supply of water and electricity. The toilets and bathrooms are also defunct. Therefore, the female teachers are not showing interest to stay within the school premises. It is observed that in some of the GHSs, the male teachers are staying in the girls' hostel due to a shortage of staff quarters.

3. Teachers having HSC qualification are teaching in higher classes where the vacancy of teachers exists for a longer period. Out of 20 sample schools, in 5 schools the post of science teachers was vacant and in all sample schools, 26 per cent of teaching posts were vacant at the time of the study. The strength of male teachers is more in number than that of their female counterparts posted in six GHSs located in interior pockets. Currently, many primary

schools are being upgraded to secondary schools, without provision of required teachers, rooms and other pedagogical requirements, which severely compromises the quality of education.

4. From the study it is found that 45 per cent of schools did not have a bench and desk for the students of Class 9, 32 per cent of schools did not have a bench and desk for even students of Class 10, 55 per cent of schools did not have toilet for boy hostellers and 15 per cent schools did not have toilet for girl hostellers, 24 per cent of schools had no storeroom and common room, 45 per cent of schools had no or insufficient drinking water. A total of 22 per cent of schools had an inadequate supply of electricity, 20 per cent had no adequate toilet facility, 22 per cent teaching and 31 per cent non-teaching staff posts were vacant and 22 per cent staff quarters are further required in sample schools to provide accommodation to the teaching staff.

5. The students of higher classes, that is, Classes 9 and 10 are taking meals twice a day, which is not sufficient for them. In some schools, the headmasters on their own manage to cover the students of higher classes with MDM, whereas in some other schools neither they are adjusted with MDM nor they are provided with extra meal/tiffin during the recess break at noon and even during late afternoon when all the classes are over. They have to wait for dinner at 8:30 PM at night. With empty stomach for hours, they are not able to concentrate on studies.

6. The remedial measures suggested by the study are immediate filling up of vacancies of teachers in schools and provision of basic infrastructure facilities for each school, timely disbursement of stipend money, handing over mess management to self-help groups or to any private party, review of examination results of schools every year, taking up some measures such as special coaching, involvement of subject experts for performance development, in-service training to teachers, resolution of teachers' genuine claims and reward to dedicated teachers and meritorious students.

7. Use of information and communications technology should be made more accessible to teachers and students so that each and every student should know its basic and minimal operation. Computer-aided learning also requires training of teachers and other staff in order to make the best use of technology.

8. Proficiency in English is widely perceived as an important avenue for employment and upward mobility. Thus, spoken English classes/remedial coaching may be introduced at high school level so that the students will go for outside exposure with confidence.

9. If the comprehension power, as well as interest of the students, can be created and developed through constant and regular coaching and watching by teachers, and students get enough scope to express all their problems before teachers, it may solve the problem of low performance, though not cent per cent, but to a major extent.

10. The positive association between school facilities and students' achievement is stronger in the educationally backward states. The pupil–teacher ratio also matters; pupil's achievement drops if it exceeds 50. Besides, the teacher's qualification and training have a positive and statistically significant impact on pupils' achievement in some schools (Public Report on Basic Education in India).

11. For the smooth functioning of the schools as well as the hostels, electricity is one of the prime requirements to enable the boarders to concentrate on their studies during evening and night times. But out of the 20 sample schools, only 2 schools have adequate electricity, whereas in the rest 18 schools there is an inadequate supply of electricity. Frequent load shedding and low voltages disrupt the normal functioning of these schools. The classrooms as well as the majority of the hostels which have been constructed under the 100 ST Girls' Hostel scheme do not have fans and so the students have to face the vagaries of hot and humid temperatures which have been grasping the state during the last few years (ST & SC Development, Minorities & Backward Classes Welfare Department 2012).

12. It is found that during the last five years of disbursement of pre-matric stipend in sample schools, the data was not available in most of the schools. In Raikia High School, the sanctioned strength is not mentioned during last four years from 2008–2009 to 2012–2013, whereas in Daringbadi High School, the disbursement amount is not mentioned which obviously shows the irregularity in the record keeping. The record shows that the disbursement of pre-matric stipend is less than the sanctioned amount during the last five years without mentioning the reason thereof. It is inferred that

some of the students have not got the scholarship amount during their course of study or there may be dropout of some students in the mid-session.

REASONS FOR LOW PERFORMANCE OF THE SCHOOL

There are various opinions of different government officials, public representatives and headmasters of schools, summarized in the following lines.

1. *Vacancies of teaching staff:* Posts of teachers, especially for subjects such as science and mathematics, are not being filled up for a longer period which creates problems for completion of courses within the stipulated time. Due to area being malaria prone, both teachers and students suffer from malaria regularly. Therefore, the teachers are not interested to continue in school. Thus, teachers' posts remain vacant regularly. Schools are managed by 7/8 teachers as against the requirement of 12/15 teachers. In a *sevashram* or service center where the actual requirement of teachers is five, the existing teachers are three in number who have to manage the classes from 1 to 5 with great difficulty.

2. *Dualism in government instruction:* Circulars have been issued that if the student remains absent from the school continuously for three months, his name is to be struck out from the school enrolment register. But instructions have been issued at the district level meeting of Sarva Shiksha Abhiyan (SSA), School & Mass Education Department, that all students up to Class 6 will be given promotion even if they do not appear at the annual examination or have not attended the school regularly. Students do not care about their studies as there is no performance testing examination or prevention of promotion to the next higher class.

3. *Negligence of administration:* During the time of final HSC examination, the Chief Invigilator of schools with special squad party (consisting of three members including the CI), go for a surprise visit to examination centres under his/her zone with a video camera. They submit the report regarding the management of the final HSC examination at different centres/schools to the collector of the district that is expected to take steps against the unfavourable

report of CI of the school on the management of examination at different centres. But this is actually not implemented properly.

4. *Engagement of teachers in other activities:* It is reported that many teachers are engaged in other non-teaching activities of the school. Primary teachers are generally involved in the Census work, distribution of BPL cards and such other activities in the area assigned to them by the government from time to time. Teachers at high school level are involved in election duties and other activities provided to them from time to time which creates disturbance in the teaching process. Teachers who are in charge of hostel/keeping up official records have to devote time for maintenance of records. Thus, they do not find time to teach students.

5. *Wrong process in selection:* Students are selected to get admission in the school through the interview. Maximum students having zero percentage are selected for getting admission in the school as no importance is given at primary level for improvement of their performance. So no quality education is found in the school.

6. *Lack of orientation training to teachers:* Orientation training is not imparted to teachers for improvement in their teaching process. If orientation training programme for teachers posted in remote areas will be organized two–three times in a year by inviting experts from the board, that will have a positive impact on improving teaching methods.

7. *No provision of a vehicle to supervising staff:* When the supervising staff, like CI/DI of school visit a school, it is often situated in far-off inaccessible remote villages. The supervising staffs have to take the help/assistance of the teachers/staff of that school to reach the school and also have to accept the lunch/tiffin supplied by them due to the scarcity of basic facilities in the area. Therefore, it is not possible on their part to inform the higher authority against any lacuna/mismanagement found in the school.

8. *Non-sanctioned post:* In some schools, headmaster post is not sanctioned. Teachers that are posted on deputation do not show interest in teaching students regularly. In some tribal schools, not even two posts for teachers are sanctioned at upper primary level.

9. *Appointment of regular teachers:* Regular teachers should be appointed instead of a contractual teacher in the school. Contractual teachers

posted in the school do not show full interest in teaching. Therefore, emphasis may be given for the appointment of regular teachers against the contractual teachers for better performance in the school.

10. *Extension of boarding facilities to all the students:* There is a government circular that students residing within 3 km from the school should not be provided boarding facilities. Thus, all the students of a school are not getting the boarding facilities. It is found that the boarders of the school perform better in studies in comparison to day scholars. So boarding facilities may be extended to all the students for the better performance of the school. Again, as per the instruction of the government, hostel facilities are withdrawn from a failed student. But if the government will consider giving one more chance to the failed student, there may be a possibility that he may work on his/her performance.

PROBLEMS FACED BY TEACHERS

The teachers posted in these schools have been facing several problems. Their grievances have not reached to the competent authority. There are various problems faced by the teachers such as unwanted posting, accommodation, distracting duties, unsupportive management, lack of infrastructure and inadequate staff. These schools have a great role in nation building and a teacher plays a crucial role in this. The problems faced by the teachers are discussed as follows.

Unwanted Posting

Unwanted positing and arbitrary transfer are seen as a constant threat to teachers. Many teachers try to avoid posting in the schools in remote or inaccessible areas. The practical reason is the inconvenience of living in a remote village with poor facilities. There are no incentives to teachers for their posting in schools in the remote area; on the contrary, teachers receive higher living house rent allowances, when they are posted in urban areas. Teachers spend a great deal of time and energy trying to avoid undesirable transfers, lobbying for preferred postings and building up influential connections to play the transfer game. This syndrome has become a major diversion in the teaching profession.

In tribal villages, villagers have virtually no relationship with the teachers. Teachers do not get any accommodation facility in the village, which makes them irregular, which in turn hampers the normal routine of a school. Another reason is alienation from the local residents, who are sometimes squandering their money on liquor and show odd behaviour towards teachers. In some sample schools, it is observed that parents are not cooperative and putting the teachers in trouble.

Distracting Duties

The burden of non-teaching activities is a major reason for not concentrating on teaching. Many teachers are engaged in non-teaching duties such as management of hostels as assistant superintendents, members of the purchase committee in respect of food and other provisions of the hostels and even act as clerks for maintenance of various official records. The teachers are also engaged in election activity. There is no clerical staff in many of the sample schools because of which various records are maintained by the teachers of the schools. The task of maintaining registers puts extra workload due to a shortage of staff.

Unsupportive Management

The school management committee has put extra workload on teachers. The textbooks and scholarships are not provided to the students timely. Therefore, the teachers face the problem of managing the mess in the hostel and distribution of uniform to the students in time as they run out of scholarship money. Again, teachers are unable to complete the course in due time because of the late supply of books. They also have to teach more than 2–3 subjects due to a shortage of staff. Threatening of higher officials for transfer to inaccessible areas, cessation of increment, proceedings against teachers regarding the low performance of the school without listening to their problems also dishearten them.

Inadequate Staff

In most of the sample schools, the teaching and non-teaching staffs are inadequate. It is not possible to control and teach the students of 2–3 classes at a time. Therefore, sometimes, the classes are running without teachers.

School Environment

The atmosphere in residential school is conducive but some schools are not conducive for the study. It needs to promote an inclusive environment. Boys' and girls' hostels in some schools are located in one boundary and close to each other. The surrounding of the campus should be pro-nature and pro-culture.

POLICY RECOMMENDATION FOR EDUCATIONAL INCLUSION OF TRIBALS

The Government of India has been implementing various schemes and programmes for upliftment of marginalized communities such as SSA, National Programme of Education for Girls at Elementary Level, MDM scheme, National Literacy Mission, Non-Formal Education and Mahila Samakhya. The Ministry of Tribal Affairs has some schemes and programmes such as hostel for ST girls, post-matric scholarship, distribution of bicycle to ST girl students and cash award for best ST students. The perception of modern education among the tribes is positive. The literacy rate is increasing every year. There is still a lag in education because of societal factors such as patriarchal, patrilocal and exclusionary approaches.

It was found that the government has various schemes for empowerment of tribal communities. There is an improvement in their status but they are still lagging in some areas. The backdrop area should be improved for inclusive tribal education such as: (a) the teacher–student ratio has to improve, (b) tribal schools have buildings but they require more rooms for separate classes, (c) the school should have more sports and entertainment equipment, (d) no fail system at primary level in schools. It should be based on the grade system to encourage more enrolment (e) there should be more language teachers at the entry level. It will help to communicate properly, (f) the tribal schools should have vehicles for day scholars to drop them at home, (g) the teachers appointed in schools of any department must be well qualified and they should preferably belong to local areas and must be able to explain their subjects fluently in official language as well as in local tribal language, (h) tutorial facility for students with poor academic performance and the teachers engaged in extra classes must be rewarded, (i) vocational courses should be taught at high school levels and (j) the poor parents should get some government initiatives/facilities to send their child to school. It will strengthen the financial as well as psychological matters (Nayak 2016).

CONCLUSION

The traditional institutions of education for tribals, particularly for vulnerable tribal societies were of a different kind. Learning activities in tribal society generally start from childhood through the process of enculturation, socialization and assimilation of knowledge and skills from the family, kin and peer groups. The youth dormitories, which still exist even today in some tribal societies, are the institutions of learning. These dormitories perform various functions including teaching and learning of various skills, such as hunting, fighting, dancing, arts, crafts and other household activities. In the past, such traditional institutions were found more in number and very vibrant in the transmission of learning from the older generation to the younger generation.

It has been observed that the enrolment in SSD Department schools has been increasing year by year, but the infrastructural facilities in the schools although improving, have not been commensurate with the need. This adversely affects the study of students, especially in tribal areas, which is one of the major causes of low performance. The inadequacy of school infrastructure begins with lack of sufficient classrooms, hostel rooms for boys and storerooms. A serious problem is that of poor maintenance and utilization of existing facilities. Congenial school environments, which can be created by utilizing available resources, are not utilized properly. Another concern is the teacher–student ratio in the school, which is found to be highly uneven. Student's achievements reflect both family background (household and parental education) and school characteristics. The critical school characteristics include infrastructure facilities, teacher attributes and the teaching–learning process.

The formal schools entered late in the tribal societies. The schools were established to bring about changes in the life of the tribal people so that they could fit themselves into modern society. Although various incentives are provided, they could not meet fully the goal of educating the target communities effectively. Most of the children attend schools, which promotes learning capacity building and most of them feel the school environments and curriculum help towards nation building.

This study provides a deep insight into the working of the tribal high schools in the context of the tribal social milieu. It also highlights the various problems and limitations, which has hindered the successful functioning of these institutions.

REFERENCES

Census of India. 2001. 'District Total Tribal Population'. https://mahades.maharashtra.gov.in/files/report/CensusReport.pdf (accessed on 3 April 2020).

Department of Educational Management Information System. 2009. 'Educational Development Index'. New Delhi: Department of Educational Management Information System, National University of Educational Planning and Administration.

Nayak, Bibekananda. 2016. 'The Issues and Challenges for Educational Inclusion of Tribes in Modern India'. In *Social Exclusion and Inclusion: A journey from Past to Present*, edited by R. C. Sobti and R. B. Ram, 119. Delhi: Jaya Publishing House.

ST & SC Development, Minorities & Backward Classes Welfare Department. 2011. 'District Wise Literacy Rate, 2011 Census'. Bhubaneswar: ST & SC Development, Minorities & Backward Classes Welfare Department, Government of Odisha.

———. 2012. 'District-wise List of Hostels/Hostel, 2011–12'. Bhubaneswar: ST & SC Development, Minorities & Backward Classes Welfare Department, Government of Odisha.

Chapter 17

Ashram Schools and Education of Tribal Children in India
A Policy Perspective

Mrityunjay K. Singh

INTRODUCTION

The overarching principle of universal free compulsory education enshrined in Articles 45 and 46 of the Constitution of India gives the Indian State the responsibility of taking 'special care' of educational interests of the Scheduled Castes and Scheduled Tribes (STs). At the time of independence, these governing provisions ensured that the educational needs of the tribals were met with. Living in remote terrains and on the periphery of other social groups, the tribals were culturally exclusive. As compared with the non-tribal population, tribals were considered the most backward sections of the society. Except for a few pockets in the northeast and central India, tribal societies were hardly influenced by the modern education system. Available statistics of the time show that tribal participation in formal schooling was marginal. In fact, the literacy rate of the tribals was only 3.46 per cent in 1951.

The early years of independence were the age of a predominant nationalist view that the Indian tribes were 'backward Hindus', as propounded by sociologist G. S. Ghurye. Called *Vanvasi* or *Adimjati*, the tribals were believed to be primitive savages, in dire need of 'civilization' by the agency of the advanced plainsmen. Nehru pleaded that development of the tribals should be 'along the lines of their own genius' and effort should be made not to impose anything on them from outside. Further, he suggested encouragement to tribal traditional arts and culture. Nehru also disapproved of the paternalism of outsiders and wanted to train and build the tribals' capacity to carry out the work of administration and development. The Dhebar Commission formed after independence for tribal education recognized pedagogical ingredients in tribal culture and wanted to make use of tribal language and cultural resources, such as folklore, songs and history in teaching. The Dhebar Commission was aware that such far-reaching intervention required reorientation of teachers, revision of curriculum and development of instructional materials. Recognizing the crucial role of teachers in the whole educational process, the Commission suggested their complete familiarity with tribal life, culture and language, and appealed to the teachers to be the tribals' friend, philosopher and guide. To remove the existing cultural gulf between teachers and students, the Commission recommended the appointment of teachers from the tribal community, opening teacher training centres in the tribal heartlands and raising a separate cadre of teachers for a period of 20 years.

During the First Five-Year Plan period, the government attended to 'pre-matric' and 'post–matric' educational needs of the tribals. Some 4,000 schools were established in the tribal areas. This included 1,000 ashram and sevashram schools and 650 sanskar kendras, balwadis and community centres in the central tribal belt between Odisha in the east and Rajasthan and Maharashtra in the west.

The government, in this initial phase, paid special attention to educational grooming of the tribal children in ashrams, namely hostels and residential schools, segregating them from their homes and habitats. The consideration occasionally was to bring children to the relatively central locality from remote parts where opening school was immediately not possible. But the guiding principle was that the tribal people were savage and wild, who needed to be civilized by the means of education outside the tribal social and cultural life. With this in mind, a step further in the direction of ashram proposition was opening of the 'sanskar kendras' to reorient children in upper-caste Hindu cultural norms. Such importance assigned to residential school concept, led, later on, to the tendency of ashramization of the whole programme of tribal education.

The Sixth Five-Year Plan (1980–1985) estimated that 56 per cent of the tribal children of the country (49% boys and 70% of girls) were yet to receive elementary education. After deliberating on the previous challenges, a National Policy on Education was framed in 1986. Recognizing that the situation of stagnancy at primary school level bore upon overall low participation of disadvantaged sections at upper levels, the Seventh Five-Year Plan (1985–1990) set out to give 'overriding priority' to the universalization of elementary education for the children of age group 6–14 years by 1990 (Planning Commission 1985).

The policy suggests an expansion of residential schools, including ashram schools, anganwadis and adult education centres. For teaching jobs in tribal areas, it seeks to encourage and train tribal youth. Finally, to create awareness of the tribals' rich cultural identity and to promote their enormous creative talent, the policy recommends suitable designing of the curriculum at all stages of education. Adopting 'a warm, welcoming and encouraging approach', it allows learners, especially first-generation learners, to set their own pace of learning. It, therefore, underscored a no-detention policy at the primary stage. At the secondary level, the policy stood for widening the educational access of the weaker sections and promoting vocational education as a distinct stream. Complementing the work of the Ministry of Human Resource Development, the government launched in 1990–1991, under its tribal division, fresh ashram schools from the primary to secondary level in tribal sub-plan areas with an equal fund sharing arrangement between the centre and states. The government revamped the scheme of grant-in-aid to voluntary organizations, especially modifying the rules to provide for 100 per cent assistance, rather than 90 per cent. The government strengthened the education policy through the Constitution (Eighty-Sixth Amendment) Act, 2002, making free and compulsory education of the children of age group, 6–14 years, a fundamental right.

Because of these efforts between 1993–1994 and 2007–2008, the number of tribal households within 1 kilometre of the vicinity of the primary school rose from 77.12 per cent to 88.46 per cent. The rise was discernible more in the rural areas, where it rose from 73.86 per cent to 88 per cent (National Sample Survey 2007–2008).

EDUCATION OF TRIBAL CHILDREN

Along with the shortage of teachers, the quality of teachers, their approach and method of teaching have been a serious issue that engaged the Dhebar Commission half a century back. Recently, the subject has been the concern of the National Curriculum Framework, 2005. Both have underscored the need for familiarity of teachers teaching tribal children with tribal culture and language so that learning is hassle free. For intimate orientation and training of teachers, the Dhebar Commission even insisted on teacher training centres to be located in the tribal areas and wanted the teachers so trained to serve the tribal area for at least 20 years. The crux of this idea was not recognized in the succeeding years. The Programme of Action, 1992, actually came with the idea of raising teachers with 'crash course' to meet the shortage of teachers in the tribal areas. Equally important is the need for production of teaching materials in tribal languages in the interest of a large number of early tribal learners. But the indication is that there is not much effort in developing curricula and devising instructional materials, keeping in mind sociocultural milieu of the tribals. The National Sample Survey data reveals that the tribal languages listed in the Eighth Schedule, namely Bodo, Dogri and Santhali, are educationally used merely by 0.11 per cent, 0.02 per cent and 0.01 per cent of the tribals, respectively (National Sample Survey 2007–2008).

ASHRAM SCHOOLS AND TRIBAL CHILDREN

As a way of providing quality education to the tribals in an efficient manner, the government has been, from the 1950s to the present policy, opening residential schools and hostels for them at central places. Ashram school, Eklavya Model School and Kasturba Gandhi Balika Vidyalaya are leading schemes under this approach. What has come as a standard approach is that it is generally found that there is 'cultural discontinuity' between the school environment and social life of the children back at home. The problem was first pointed out by the Scheduled Castes and Scheduled Tribes Commission in 1987 and later, by the framers of the National Curriculum Framework, 2005. Citing authoritative studies, the latter document claims that in the event of the school environment and functioning being in tune with the tribal cultural life, the performance of the student is better (NCERT 2007). While such coordination is not forthcoming, the tribal residential schools and hostels remain commonplace institutions. They are often in the news for corruption, bad maintenance of facilities and sexual exploitation of resident girls (NCPCR 2013).

The broad policy guidelines for the ashram schools as envisaged by various committees and study groups on tribal welfare programmes are as follows: Such schools should be inter-village schools. They should be opened in such areas where normal schools cannot be opened and most backward tribal groups should be covered. Generally, these schools provide education up to Standard 5 but in many cases, the classes are from 1 to 7 or 4 to 7 or even 1 to 10. The pattern, size and policy of admission to the institutions differ from state to state. In some states such as Gujarat, Maharashtra and Odisha, these schools are of three levels: primary, middle and secondary, whereas in Rajasthan and Andhra Pradesh, they only cover the primary level of education.

Vocational or craft education is strongly envisaged to be implemented in the ashram schools but has not taken roots, except in a few schools in Maharashtra, Gujarat and Odisha. Mostly, ashram schools function like general schools with free boarding and lodging facilities within a highly structured and systemic framework (Mishra and Dhir 2005).

STATUS OF TRIBAL EDUCATION AND ASHRAM SCHOOLS IN JHARKHAND

There are 32 different tribal communities residing in Jharkhand and they constitute 26.3 per cent (6.6 million) of the total population of the state. More than 60 per cent of these tribals are living below the poverty line. The average literacy rate of Jharkhand is 54.13 per cent, but among some tribals, particularly among the female, the literacy rate is as low as 10 per cent. Although the overall literacy rate among the

STs has increased from 27.5 per cent (Government of India 1991) to 57 per cent (Government of India 2011) but despite this improvement, the literacy rate among the tribes is below in comparison to that of all STs at the national level (59%).

There is a high dropout among tribal children in school because the experiences of tribal children range from discrimination to a sense of complete alienation. Students from ST communities encounter a series of obstacles including commuting long distances to school in hostile environmental conditions, abuses and discrimination from teachers and fellow students from non-tribal backgrounds, difficulty in comprehending the language of instruction and negotiating space for themselves which they had been denied historically.

Most teachers in schools in ST areas are non-STs who tend to view tribal language, culture and social practices as inferior to theirs. Psychologically, this has a strong negative impact on children, which again contributes to their dropping out of school.

The ashram schools (residential schools for tribal boys and girls) started by the government in 1990–1991 are poorly maintained and sometimes lack even the basic facilities. The performance of the state in providing matching grant and maintenance of service and management of hostels is not encouraging. The pace of construction of hostels has been very slow and the basic amenities provided therein are substandard. Given the low levels of literacy among the ST population, several children from these communities happen to be 'first-generation learners'. In the absence of state support for helping them cope with studies, many children drop out of the schools. Therefore, very few are eligible to attend institutions of higher education, where the high rate of attrition continues. For example, members of agrarian tribes like the Gonds are often reluctant to send their children to school, because they need their children to work in the fields.

Another reason behind high dropout rates is the medium of instruction or language constraint where most of the tribal children do not understand the textbooks, which are generally in the regional language. The non-tribal teachers in tribal children's school are another problem where teachers do not know the children's language. This was also found in the study conducted by the Janshala Programme. Commission after commission have recommended that at least at the primary level students should be taught in their native language but recruitment of qualified teachers and determination of the appropriate language of instruction have always remained troublesome. From 2003, the state government has decided to ensure teaching in the mother tongue from Class 1 in tribal languages (Santhali, Mundari, Ho, Kurukh) and regional languages (Khortha, Kurmali) but the need is to develop teaching–learning material in these languages and to train/redeploy the teachers.

The issues and challenges in tribal education can be categorized as external, internal, socio-economic and psychological. The external constraints are related to issues at levels of policy, planning and implementation, while internal constraints are with respect to the education system, content, curriculum, pedagogy, and medium of instruction, etc. The third set of problems relate to the social, economic and cultural background of tribal and psychological aspects of first-generation learners.

STUDY OF AN ASHRAM SCHOOL IN JHARKHAND

The school is a primary residential school run by Naya Savera Vikas Kendra as shown in Figure 17.1. This residential school is located in Bagodar block of Giridih district surrounded by Birhor tribe

Figure 17.1 *Primary Residential School Run by Naya Savera Vikas Kendra*

habitation. Birhors are one of the most primitive tribal groups in Jharkhand. It has 50 students who belong to Asur, Birjia and Birhor tribes. It has three teachers. The name of the teachers are Mrs Sarita Kumari, Mr. Saryu Prasad and Mr Suresh Kr Murmu. The students come from Gumla and Latehar districts of Jharkhand which are mostly affected by left-wing Maoist extremism. Poverty and illiteracy are very high among these tribes in Jharkhand.

There are 50 students in the school. Gender-wise there are 34 boys and 16 girls staying in the hostel. Most of them are first-generation learners. As per teachers, parents of these children are not much interested in sending their children away from home for studying in residential school. Since poverty is very high in these districts, they want their children to work and contribute to the family income. So, bringing these children to residential school is a major challenge. Another problem is that when they come to the ashram school they go home after one year during summer vacation. Once they go home, they do not return to continue their studies. So, dropout rate is very high among the students. Next year a new set of students come to school. Due to this, the regularity of the students to their studies is not ensured and teachers complained that again they have to work hard with these first-generation learners. These students who get little oriented about studies drop out and discontinue next year and this cycle is continuing. So, retaining these children in school for further studies is a major challenge. Because of poverty, their parents want them to do child labour.

This school is located in the neighbourhood of Birhor tribe, one of the most primitive tribal groups in Jharkhand. But Birhors also do not send their children to ashram school. When teachers try to motivate them, they demand ₹200 in lieu of sending their children to school. This ₹200 is clearly the earning of the child by doing child labour.

EDUCATION OF TRIBAL CHILDREN AND MEDIUM OF INSTRUCTION

This is a primary residential school and they teach subjects such as Hindi, Santhali, English, Social Studies, Mathematics and Moral Science. The medium of instruction is in Hindi and Santhali. Books as well as uniforms are supplied to the students but the delivery of books is mostly irregular. Adequate infrastructure is not present in the school and so classrooms double up as dormitories during the night for these students. Complete boundary wall is also absent considering that this place is affected by left-wing extremism. This reflects a lack of commitment of authorities towards the education of these children. There is only one tribal teacher in the school who is Mr Suresh Kumar Murmu. Mr Murmu has studied up to intermediate in Santhali medium. So he teaches Santhali to these children and these children are taught Santhali in Ol Chiki script. One of the findings of this study is that on the ground of teaching children in tribal language they teach Santhali language along with Hindi and English. But the author did not find anything written in Santhali language on the school premises. All instructions were written in Hindi and English as shown in Figure 17.2.

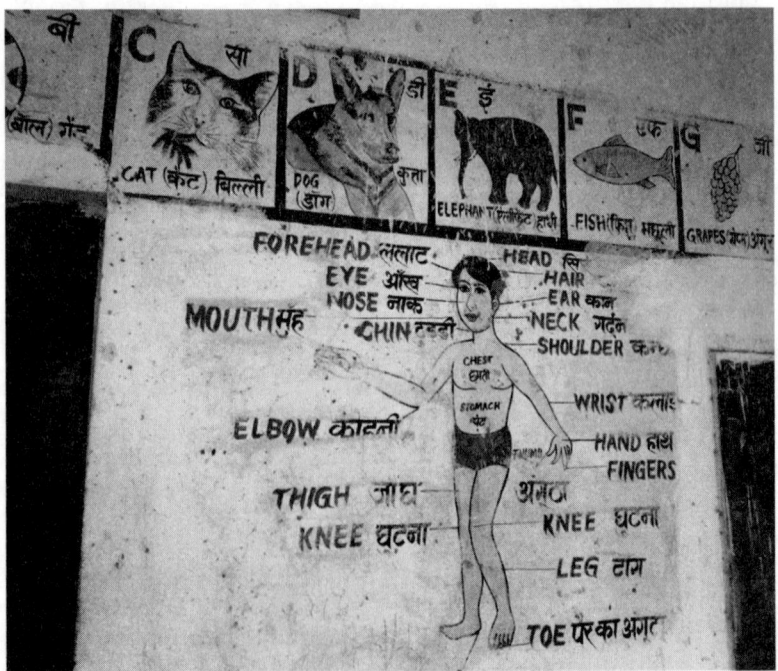

Figure 17.2 *School Premises Showing Santhali Not Being Used*

Another finding of this study is that in the name of teaching them in tribal language, they teach Santhali language but the mother tongue of these children is Nagpuri, which is different from Santhali. Therefore, Santhali does not come naturally to them, though some similarity is there. So these children are not taught in their mother tongue which is Nagpuri and Khortha.

The Santhali language which is taught to these children was included in the Eighth Schedule of the Constitution in 2003 because of the efforts of the All India Santhali Education Council, Jamshedpur. In this case also tribals themselves had to make effort to the Government of India and Ministry of Human Resource Development for recognition of their language so that students can study in Santhali medium and write exams in this language. Therefore, despite all the recommendations of Dhebar Commission, Education Policy and Right to Education, the government was found wanting in its pro-activeness in promoting the development of tribal languages and granting them recognition for the educational development of tribal children in their mother tongue. Another finding related to Santhali language is that it has 30 letters and it has capital and small letters like the English language. This script was written by Mr Raghunath Murmu in 1925 and most of the letters are similar to English alphabets. This also reflects the influence of Christian missionaries in developing tribal language.

Since the mother tongue of these children is Nagpuri, they are not interested in learning in Santhali. This is also one of the key reasons why they drop out. So, to retain these children for completing their studies, the medium of instruction should be in Nagpuri/Khortha and teaching-learning material should be developed in their language. This is emerging as a major lacuna in providing education and retaining these children in school for further studies.

The author did not find anything symbolic of tribal culture in school premises. They hardly celebrate tribal heroes such as Tilka Majhi, Birsa Munda, Sidhu Murmu and Kanho Murmu. There is a need to create an ambiance similar to their culture in schools. Celebrating tribal festivals, respecting tribal heroes and teaching them in their own language give a sense of pride and a sense of ownership which motivates children to study and continue their studies. In the absence of these measures by the authorities, students lose interest in their studies which they consider as something alien to them and which they do not want to continue. That is the reason for high attrition rates among students.

These children naturally excel in archery, but the author did not see any sports facility in the school. So good facilities for sports should also be provided which are similar to the native sports such as football and kabaddi.

Training of teachers should be done on a regular basis which does not happen. This also affects the motivation and enthusiasm of teachers to motivate the children and their parents to continue their studies. Majority of teachers in these schools should be tribal teachers which is not happening. There is only one tribal teacher in the school and so neither the children and nor the teachers are able to identify with each other.

The following figures of the school attest the findings of the study:

Figure 17.3: Name of the Teachers (Not All Teachers Are Tribal)
Figure 17.4: Food Menu That Is Not as per the Tribal Food Habits
Figure 17.5: Students Getting Food, Which Is Mostly Salted Rice with Water

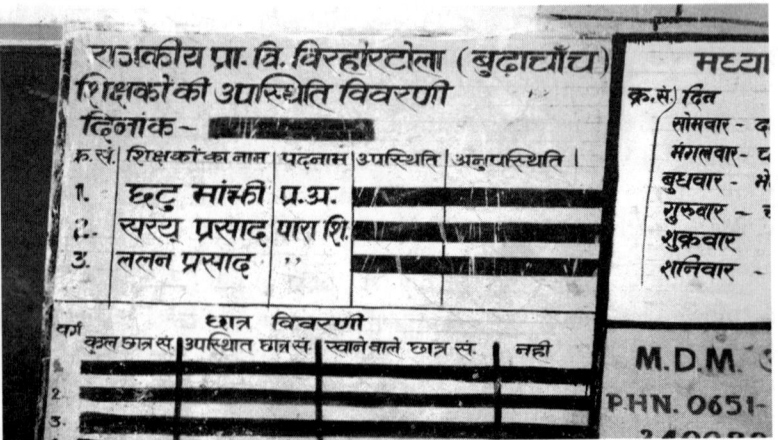

Figure 17.3 *Name of the Teachers (Not All Teachers Are Tribal)*

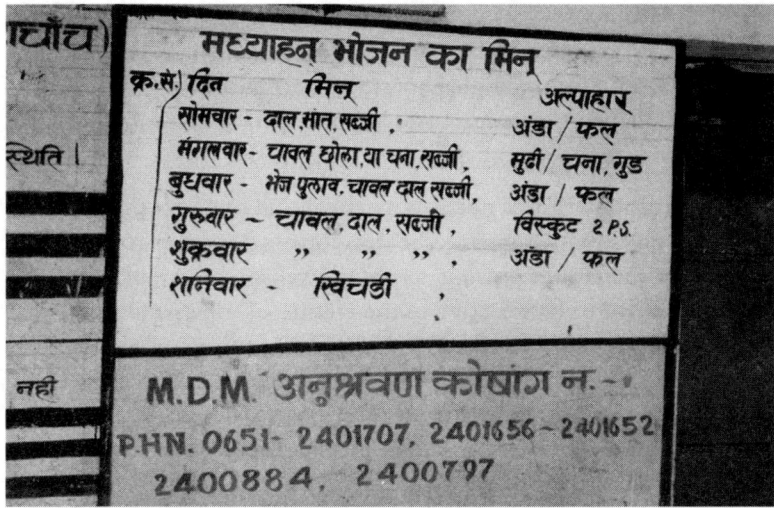

Figure 17.4 *Food Menu That Is Not as per the Tribal Food Habits*

Figure 17.5 *Students Getting Food, Which Is Mostly Salted Rice with Water*

CONCLUSION

Ashram schools were meant to use tribal mother tongues, employ tribal teachers and incorporate a lot of tribal culture into the curriculum. What happened is the opposite: Adivasi children are still being ridiculed and punished at school if they speak their own languages. One result is the rapid decline of hundreds of ancient languages, tied to nature-based economies that are sustainable in the long-term sense, that are simultaneously undermined by the large-scale boarding schools for tribal children.

Ashram schools should not remove tribal children from their culture and indigenous models need to be developed to teach tribal children in their mother tongue using more and more oral traditions. The education needs to be sensitive to the culture of tribals and pedagogy need to incorporate the tribal way of life in primary education and appoint teachers from tribal communities to remove the cultural gap between the teacher and the student. Ashram schools must promote respect for the local traditions of the tribals which enhances their self-esteem and empowers them.

MAJOR RECOMMENDATIONS OF THE STUDY

Some of the key recommendations of this study are as follows:

- Ashram schools should not be located very far away from the home of the students. Because students, as well as their parents, do not want to send their children away from home for a long time. This is also one of the reasons of their dropping out.
- Teachers appointed in the schools should be from tribal communities.
- Training of teachers should be done on a regular basis.
- The medium of instruction should be in the language of the tribal.
- There is a need to create an ambiance similar to their culture in schools. Celebrating tribal festivals, respecting tribal heroes and teaching them in their own language give a sense of pride and a sense of ownership which motivates children to study and continue their studies. In the absence of these measures by the authorities, students tend to lose interest in their studies, which they consider as something alien to them and which they do not want to continue. That is the reason for high attrition rates among students.
- The Government of India as well Government of Jharkhand should open research institutes for the development of the tribal languages and create teaching-learning materials in the tribal languages.

- Steps should be taken for starting a master's programme in tribal languages in Ranchi University and other universities in the state.
- Measures should be taken to provide employment to the parents of these children in employment and livelihood generation programmes of the government as well as non-governmental organizations (NGOs) so that they do not send their children for child labour.
- Indigenous models need to be developed to teach tribal children in their mother tongue, using more and more oral traditions.
- Ashram schools must promote respect for the local traditions of the tribals which enhances their self-esteem and empowers them.
- Efforts for assimilation of tribals into dominant culture by using either English or Hindi must stop. Authorities must promote respect for tribal language and culture so that they develop along their original genius.
- Child rights must be built into and remain integral to the entire educational process of tribal children.
- Schools should be opened for a cluster of panchayats so that the children are in touch with their parents.
- In places where they are not first-generation learners, the students can stay in residential schools in district headquarter also. Therefore, there should be flexibility in the approach towards the development of ashram schools based on need assessment and these should be region-specific programmes.
- There is a need to upscale and promote the communitization model developed in Nagaland where all the powers for welfare/development services from conceptualization to maintenance have been devolved to local communities.
- Research centres for the development of tribal languages should be opened in the universities.
- There is a greater need to involve civil society at both global and national levels for the promotion of education of tribal children. NGOs, both global and national, have ignored the education of tribal children.
- Education of tribal and other marginalized children for social justice must be highlighted as a key priority at the global and national level by both government and NGOs.

- The reason why ashram schools have not been very effective in providing education to tribal children is because of the heavy emphasis on formal education and formal pedagogy used to teach tribal first-generation learners whose culture is predominantly informal. Therefore, the teaching pedagogy used for tribal children should also be informal. There is an anomaly here in the sense that written traditions are emphasized in providing education to tribal children whose culture is predominantly based on oral tradition. Education should be provided in an informal manner using oral tradition for these first-generation learners and then vocational education should be provided to them.
- Community colleges should be opened in their localities.

REFERENCES

Government of India. 1991. *Census of India*. New Delhi: Ministry of Home Affairs.
———. 2011. *Census of India*. New Delhi: Ministry of Home Affairs.
Mishra, B. C., and A. Dhir. 2005. *Ashram School in India: Problems and Prospects*. New Delhi: Discovery Publishing House.
National Sample Survey. 2007–2008. 'Participation and Expenditure on Education'. NSSO 64th round. New Delhi: Ministry of Programme Implementation, Government of India.
NCPCR (National Commission for Protection of Child Rights). 2013. *A Report on the Status and Functioning of Ashram Shalas*, 5. District Kanker: State of Chhattisgarh.
Planning Commission. 1985. *Sixth Five Year Plan (1980–85)*. New Delhi: Government of India.

Chapter 18

Government Ashram School
Micro-Planning

D. K. Panmand

INTRODUCTION

The scheme called '*ashramshala* group' started in 1972–1973. There are 502 government *ashramshalas* under Tribal Development Department. In these *ashramshalas*, 206,163 tribal students are taking education in which 105,558 are boys and 105,605 are girls.

The scheme was started according to the local conditions. Initially, 20 ashram schools had been started, and step-by-step, there was an increase in the number of ashram schools, and now there are 552 ashram schools. Due to fewer number of students and some other reasons, some ashram schools have been merged and now there are as many as 502 government ashram schools that are in operation.

This is the only residential education centre providing education services to tribal residents in Tribal Sub-Plan/Scheduled Area, Modified Area Development Approach (MADA), Mini-MADA areas.

From every ashram school, the tribal students have taken education at least up to Classes 7, 10 and 12, and lakhs of students have attained higher education and graduation, post-graduation degrees.

Due to education services given to the tribal through government ashram school, the literacy rates of tribal men and women have certainly increased. As the government ashram schools are residential ashram schools, hence the facilities such as books, notebooks, uniform, snacks, food, and stationery are provided to the ashram school students free of cost.

Transformation is the rule of nature. During the transitional period, the numbers of Zila Parishad schools and private schools in tribal areas have increased. These schools are also providing free facilities. A great awareness has been built in the parents who studied in ashram schools. Through the scheme like "Sarva Shiksha Abhiyan, the schools are available in the adjoining areas and free facilities such as meals, books, stationery, and uniforms are being made available in such schools. Moreover, in the tribal areas or adjoining tribal areas, the facilities of education through English medium are available. Therefore, the attraction of the ashram school has started to decline. The attitude of the students and parents are changing. There has been a competitive environment for the ashram school that has been created. There is a need to maintain the ashram school in this competitive situation. The concept of academic quality started to be rooted in this competitive situation. Considering this situation, it is necessary to convert the ashram school like developed schools and colleges. Considering the migration of tribal people for employment, their economic conditions and such related matters, there is a need for resident government ashram schools. Considering this fact, residential ashram schools is the need of the time.

This necessity is not rejected by the tribal and social activists. But they expect that these ashram schools should be developed like renowned schools. Their expectation is acceptable. Due to continued education services provided to the tribal, today there are a lot of highly educated people in the tribal family. Their former outlook has changed. Therefore, running an ashram school in a traditional way is not acceptable anymore. It is mandatory to adopt modern educational technology in government ashram school. To create an attraction for ashram school among the tribal, special efforts need to be made. Due to a change in the attitude among the tribal parents, there should not be any shortage of facilities in the ashram schools. Action should be taken to fulfil or to provide all facilities in the ashram schools. The headmasters and the staff of the ashram schools are taking special efforts for this. Due to the efforts taken by the staff of ashram schools, many ashram schools got International Organization for Standardization (ISO) certificates. It is found that the parents are now interested to admit their child in such ISO-certified ashram schools. This work done by the concerned staff of ashram school is really appreciable and commendable. It is clear that our government ashram schools can be developed and might get the glory of earlier years again. A lesson should be taken from these ashram schools. We can change ourselves on our own. It has been proved that we are able to develop our ashram schools. We have the potential for innovation. There is a need for just words, inspiration, greatness, policy, persistence. However, it is not sustainable to bring any change by revolution. It is a good idea to adopt a system of evolution by applying the evolutionary method. Considering this criterion, to make 100 per cent of our government ashram schools more advanced than the developed schools, it is very necessary to prepare a micro-planning plan for each *ashramshala*.

According to this micro plan, a goal should be framed to provide minimum facilities in every ashram school in the next five years. Apart from this, the planning and execution of various innovative activities based on academic quality will also be helpful. It is necessary that the services of technical and educational service providers be made available, who will provide these services to the staff of ashram schools and supervisory officers, to make them capable. To develop a positive attitude towards their ashram schools, regular training and guidance should be given. It is necessary to take positive note of their work and make arrangement to provide services without their demand, so that time lapse in between providing the services will be saved and which will help in upliftment of ashram schools. It is necessary to reserve the financial provision for all these developmental processes.

For micro-planning of ashram schools, it will be better to review the self-estimated evaluation by each school. The staff of the school is well aware of its issue-wise problems and the remedy suggested by it will have to be implemented to solve the said problems. Therefore, it is intended that every ashram school has to take a self-review and do micro-planning on the school development plan. They will be more likely to implement the development plan which they have created not something which is not prepared by them, such a plan would not be effective. Hence, it will be appropriate to make them aware of the components of the plan and thereby motivate them to make a development plan and implement it.

ASHRAMSHALA CAMPUS AND MANAGEMENT INSPECTION

1. To fix minimum facilities for each ashram school.
2. To ensure the basic facilities required in the school.
3. To inspect the school as per 1 & 2 above, an inspection team having superintendent (G/L), senior secondary teacher, senior primary teacher, senior and junior college teacher, senior cook, senior Kamathi (senior multitask worker) and watchman will be constituted and inspect the ashram school by fixing the factor-wise lacunas and submit the report to the headmaster.
4. To fix the activities for the lacunas.
5. To determine the source of funds to implement this program by preparing write-up.
6. Proposal to be put forth in the budget as per the prescribed sources.
7. If there is a source besides budget, that is, corporate social responsibility (CSR), an expected write-up should be sent to them.

PURPOSE OF MICRO-PLANNING PLAN

Micro-planning plan aims at providing minimum facilities to all ashram schools to make them complaint-free. Some of the purposes of the plan are:

1. To complete the sanctioned strength of class-wise students in each ashram school, adopt programmes such as family visit in the school area, parents meeting, advertisement, promotion and publicity.
2. Provide teaching and non-teaching staff as per approved staff pattern to ashram school. For this, fill the vacant posts and make regular promotions every year. For the posts which are vacant due

to long-term leave, lack of recruitment/promotions, fill such posts and provide manpower by way of outsourcing.

3. Purchase or acquire enough land for each and every ashram–school building. For every school, there must be a basic infrastructure. Every school must have an independent school building, children's hostel, girl's hostel, *kothi gruh* (modern) well-equipped kitchen, multipurpose hall, dining hall, class-3/class-4 staff quarters, library, subject-matter laboratory, study room, updated sick room, computer room and so on.

4. To facilitate a water supply system for each ashram school. There must be free water supply scheme, overhead water-storage tank on each building, underground water-storage tank, bathroom, water-storage tank on toilets, hot water supply for bathing in bathroom, purified drinking water, water-storage tank for the kitchen, sewerage management and so on.

5. In every school building, there must be a class room for each class, library, laboratory, office, staff room, residential room in the hostel, bathroom, toilet, kitchen, lighthouse, multipurpose hall, dining room, study room, staff quarters and so on having necessary bulbs/tubes, fans arrangement. Similarly, there must be internal roads and electric facilities in the premises of ashram school buildings.

6. As an alternative to load shedding, there must be a provision of solar power plant, generators and similar electrical-power system.

7. To keep the smooth functioning of computers, generators, TVs, LED screens, projectors, solar power plants, sick room, laboratory machinery, electric motor, diesel engine, bore well and so on of ashram school, a relevant maintenance repairs contract must be made.

8. Half-yearly/annual maintenance repairs of all the above buildings.

9. A review of dangerous situation must be taken to protect the students and employees from an open well, open drains, broken windows/doors, open electric wires, gas cylinders and dangerous building.

10. The necessary furniture must be made available in the school building, library, study room, laboratory, sick room, residential rooms, dining hall, staff room, offices of headmaster and superintendent by making their regular maintenance repairs contract.

11. Provide English and semi-English medium facilities in ashram schools.
12. In each ashram school, a playground for kabaddi, cricket, volleyball, tennis, kho-kho games must be developed. Moreover, equipment to play indoor, outdoor games must be made available. For this, the services of a regular sports teacher, expert sports guide must be made available. School-level, project-level, division-level and state-level sports competitions must be organized. Services of science experts must be provided to create a scientific approach among students.
13. Provide expert guide services to solve the trials of mathematics, English, science studies. Implementation of expert institutions in this field or innovative projects should be undertaken by *ashramshala*.
14. To eliminate fear and create interest in the subjects such as maths, science, English, Hindi, and Sanskrit, the students must be enrolled in the competitive examinations conducted by the government/ semi-government private institutions. Students who get proficiency in these subjects must be awarded certificates on Teachers' Day/annual festivals/parent *melawa*/parent meetings and so on to encourage the rest of the students.
15. Students must be enrolled for national intelligence research and various scholarships examinations.
16. Regular review of teaching/study to remove the shortcomings from them and to keep the aim/goal for 100 per cent result for all class. Efforts should be taken so that a number of students will be in the A and B category in the result. Implementation of various initiatives for upgradation of C- and D-category class students.
17. To develop the attitude of students and to maintain the quality of the school, regular training must be given to teaching and non-teaching staff.
18. Develop the concept of teamwork in teaching and non-teaching staff. Considering their best contribution and by taking note of it, they should be awarded and honoured by giving them appreciation certificate in programmes such as Teachers' Day/school annual function and in state-level sports.
19. Annual function gathering should be organized in each ashram school. Ex-students should be invited to the function to present their thoughts to encourage the present students.

20. Take care of the health of students. Regular health check-up of students of ashram school should be undertaken and further arrangements made for treatment. Regular health check-ups and further treatment arrangements made for employees. Insurance cover made available to the students and employees.

21. Daily cleaning of bathroom, toilets, classrooms, students' residences, premises and so on at *ashramshala*. Make necessary arrangements for wastewater, regular pest control, drug spraying and providing mosquito nets to each student.

22. Create a record room in each ashram school.

23. Category-wise classification of useful and unwanted machinery, bedding material and so on by taking proper entry in the dead-stock register. Write off unwanted equipment. Make proper repairs of useful equipment.

24. Create subject-wise committees of all the staff of ashram school and give the responsibility to the concerned committee for monitoring concerned subject. The entire staff of the school should participate in the overall management of the school. The committees should encourage with their excellent performance by taking proper note.

25. The said committees should organize a study tour of other advanced schools and get their tour report. Implement the best/innovative initiatives undertaken by the said-advanced school in the ashram schools.

26. A Central Steering Committee should be constituted which consists of headmaster, assistant project officer (education), service provider and experts. The said committee will take the quarterly review of the work done by the ashram school subject-wise committees and will solve the problems for the smooth functioning of the schools.

27. The Central Steering Committee and ashram school subject-wise committees collectively study the Right to Education Act, ashram school code and all other guiding principles and prepare an annual micro-planning plan. Improve the school by making proper implementation of said annual micro-planning plan.

28. Each ashram school should publish an annual report regarding the special efforts taken by the staff of the school by using innovative and result-oriented programmes to complete the syllabus,

the contribution of students with regard to study, arts, sports and competition and the planning for next year.

29. Distribution (interchange) of the annual report in ashram schools. Implement the outstanding innovative projects in their respective *ashramshalas*.

30. During the year, there should be quarterly/half-yearly/yearly co-ordination with the best service providers such as the health department, construction department, education department, various service provider institutions, machinery assisted through CSR. The annual report should contain the best services provided by these service providers.

COMPONENT OF GOVERNMENT ASHRAM SCHOOLS, MICRO-PLANNING PLANS

Considering the above ideas, and to succeed in these ideas, it is expected to create a micro-planning plan. The general components of the micro-planning plan are as follows.

(Note: These examples are illustrated; each school's steering committee and the subject wise committee can determine the necessary components, sub-components of their ashram school).

The template can be prepared as per the Annexure enclosed.

Sr. No	Planning Component	Example of Sub-component
1.	Complete the student strength of each class	1. Survey of tribal families residing in ashram school areas to point out the eligible students.
		2. Publicity of admission process, facilities and benefits given to students.
		3. Arrange parents meeting in village areas by inviting local representatives, sarpanch, *gram sevak*, parents, for admission of students.
		4. Organize admission festival.

Sr. No	Planning Component	Example of Sub-component
2.	Appointment of employee staff, sanctioned posts and fix the services of each employee for each ashram school	1. Regular follow up to the project office to fulfill the sanctioned posts. 2. Make an arrangement to fill the post, which is vacant for a long time, by outsourcing. 3. Take the services of each staff as per post and hand over the charge accordingly.
3.	Ashram school complex with all buildings	1. Follow up to get enough land for the construction of buildings for the ashram school 2. Build the ashram school complex which includes a school building, a hostel for students, warehouse, kitchen room, dining room, multipurpose hall, staff quarters. 3. The necessary space should be made available for a playground in the center of ashram school complex. 4. A security wall compound should be constructed for ashram school complex having a main gate, so that third person or wild animals should not enter in the ashram school premises.
4.	Sports ground and sports material	1. Develop the sports ground in the place mentioned above to play the authorized games. 2. Make arrangements to develop indoor games also.
5.	Bathrooms and toilets as per criteria	1. As per criteria and sanctioned strength of students, toilets should be made available in boys and girls hostels. A separate toilet complex should be made available.

Sr. No	Planning Component	Example of Sub-component
		2. As per the number of students in boys/girls hostels, bathrooms should be made available with hot water facility.
		3. Set up a hand wash station outside the toilets. Make a hand wash bottle available there.
		4. Supply of water should be made available in the toilets.
		5. Set up a cloth-washing station near bathrooms.
		6. Make pipeline near bathroom to wash clothes. Take care that the sewage should not remain open and mosquitoes are not breeding. Also, regular spraying of Pesticides.
		7. Bathrooms and toilets should be cleaned daily.
6.	Arrangement of supply of water and separate supply of water system.	1. Considering the students and staff strength of ashram school, per person 55 liters of water should be made available.
		2. For this, make a separate water supply scheme.
		3. To store the water thus made available from this scheme, an underground tank, overhead tank should be made available at school building, boys/girls hostels, bathrooms and toilets, kitchen and dining hall with necessary pipeline.
		4. If there is a well in the school premises, it must be covered with iron grill.
		5. Make a borewell in the premises with an arrangement of motor and supply of water of said borewell to overhead tank. If there is a hand pump, manage wastewater.

Sr. No	Planning Component	Example of Sub-component
		6. Make an arrangement for water purification.
7.	Arrangement of electricity and alternate electricity.	1. Make sufficient arrangement of bulbs/tube lights, fans in ashram school building, classrooms, hostel residence, warehouse, kitchen, dining hall, etc.
		2. The arrangement of a streetlight at internal roads, playground, bathroom and toilets.
		3. As there is long-duration load shedding in ashram school area, make alternative arrangement like generator, solar power plant.
		4. Make proper repairs if electric wires are open.
		5. Make an arrangement of zero bulb in the Student's residence in the night.
		6. The ashram school premises must be shock free. Take care of it.
8.	Availability of furniture	1. Necessary furniture should be made available at school building, office, staff room, Computer room, library, laboratory, classrooms, hostel office, residential room, kitchen, dining, etc.
		2. Cupboard should be made available at residential room of students, so that they can keep their material safely.
		3. Follow up should be made with project office to get all the furniture.
		4. Routine repairs and maintenance of all furniture should be done.
9.	Availability of necessary educational material for each class to decorate classroom.	1. Make availability of separate class.
		2. Decorate the class and benches as per syllabus.

Sr. No	Planning Component	Example of Sub-component
		3. Encourage students and teachers to create subject-specific educational material for each class. Make necessary stationery available for this.
		4. Posters having messages, cartoons, etc., of food and nutrition should be pasted on dining-hall wall to guide students about nutrition.
		5. Similarly, posters, message board, slogans, etc., should be applied at the wall of library, study room, laboratory to give messages to students.
		6. Apply various posters, banners in the premises of ashram school.
10.	Necessary material and maintenance repairs contract	1. The necessary material should be made available at kitchen, dining hall, multipurpose hall, library, laboratory, sick room and others. For this, follow up should be made at higher office.
11	Updated laboratories	1. Build topic-wise laboratories.
		2. Make available necessary materials and equipment.
		3. Prepare a schedule for daily lab experiments for each class.
		4. Use the services of the lab assistant/ attendant in the laboratory.
12.	Updated Library	1. Books regarding entrance examination, scholarship examination, arts, culture, etc., should be made available.
		2. For this, the furniture such as cupboard, Table and chair should be made available.
		3. Make arrangement of parallel study room.

Sr. No	Planning Component	Example of Sub-component
		4. In the study room, the expert guidance for topics such as career guidance, entrance examination, competitive examination, scholarship examination should be made available.
13.	Updated sickroom	1. Make arrangement for sickroom in each School.
		2. Necessary furniture and equipment made available.
		3. Make arrangement to admit sick student in sick room.
		4. Make necessary seating arrangement for medical officer in the sick room and with their assistance, do the monthly, quarterly health check-up of students.
		5. Keep student health check-up register updated.
14.	Quality development innovative programmes.	1. Syllabus based, knowledge-based activities.
		2. Innovation based activities for hard subjects.
		3. Activities on students health and cleanliness.
		4. Activities on students' care, protection and rearing.
		5. Activities on central students' access.
		6. Student/parents counseling.
		7. Activities such as entrance examination, competitive examinations, scholarship examinations.
		8. Decorate class/premises.
		9. Self-study.
		10. Topic-wise science experiments.

Sr. No	Planning Component	Example of Sub-component

15.	Expert services	1. Determine the essential services of *ashramshala* component.
		
		2. For this, determine the expert person, organization, machinery. Formulating a panel of experts in such topics, component wise. Expert services are expected for the following topics.
		  1. Science experiments
		  2. Career guidance
		  3. Counseling
		  4. Guidance on hard subject
		  5. Activity/guidance on sports/arts/music.
		  6. Food, nutrition and health
		  7. Entrance examination/Scholarship examination.
		  8. Educational picnic
		  9. Writing, reading, essay writing, Answer sheet writing

16.	Student health	1. Health nutrient content habits for students
		
		2. Student health check-up and medication
		  1. Exercise
		  2. Yoga
		  3. Games

17.	Examination/ competitive examination/ scholarship examination	1. Guidance on writing half -yearly/yearly examination answer sheet. 2. Study of all types of entrance examination as per syllabus and writing of entrance examination answer sheet. 3. To enroll 100% students for all types of scholarship examinations. Practice of scholarship examination. 4. Honour successful students/teachers.

Sr. No	Planning Component	Example of Sub-component
18.	Student counselling/ counselor	1. Counseling on student behaviour 2. Guidance on health topic 3. Guidance examination 4. Guidance on security 5. Topic-wise/component-wise counselling panel should be formed for time bound counseling programme.
19.	Measures for student/staff performance review	1. Take a note of each class student for his/her performance in study, arts, sports, music, culture, etc. 2. For this performance, motivate the students, and accordingly activities to be implemented. 3. Take note of the remarkable performance done by teaching and non-teaching staff. Encourage staff for such a performance. 4. Honour students/staff publicly.
20.	Employee training and implementation of knowledge gained through training	1. To fix the topic of training related to school management, training related to duties. 2. Schedule a calendar to give such training. 3. Training machinery to give training; constitute experts' panel and accordingly take their services for training. 4. Do planning to implement the knowledge acquired through training.
21	Study tour and implementation	1. Organize study tours that will develop the attitude of students, employees. 2. Implementation of activities as per acquired knowledge during this tour.
22	Supervision (internal/ external supervision)	1. Internal school supervision through head master.

Sr. No	Planning Component	Example of Sub-component
		2. Hostel supervision through hostel superintendent.
		3. Supervision through extension officer.
		4. Supervision through assistant project officer.
		5. Fix supervision topic of each supervisor. By supervising these topics, determine the result. Troubleshoot the lacunas in that way.
23	Security	1. Guidance to students regarding security.
		2. Perform activities wherein the students should not face any risk.
		3. Building of security compound wall in the ashram school premises.
		4. Appointment of security guard.
24	Care and rearing of primary school student	1. Take the services of a female employee through outsourcing for the purpose of bathing the students from 1st to 4th standard, washing their cloths and to give them mental support.
		2. Fix the machinery to get such outsourcing services.
25	Diet and Nutrition	1. Fix the standard of diet through experts.
		2. Take the review of nutritional supplement as per standard diet.
		3. Make the changes in diet as per review.
		4. Use quality food grains and vegetables. Clean them properly before using them.
		5. Provide clean drinking water.

Sr. No	Planning Component	Example of Sub-component
26	Sports competition	1. Give training of authorized games along with school study syllabus.
		2. For this, appoint sports teacher, take services of sports experts.
		3. Organize school-level, project-level, Division-level and state-level sport competitions for better practice.
		4. The students/teachers should be honoured for their good performance in sports.
27	Science exhibition	1. Science experiment from student of each class.
		2. To present this art of students, science exhibition should be organized on Kendra shala, project and state level.
		3. The students/teachers should be honoured for their good performance in science exhibition.
28	Management of English and semi English	1. Create one semi English and English medium education management in one school from a complex of 10 ashram school.
		2. For this, necessary staff should be made available by giving them training.
29	Annual function	1. Arrange annual function of ex- and present students.
		2. Ex-student will share their experience.
		3. Organize arts and cultural programmes through this annual function.
		4. The students/teachers should be honoured for their better performance during the year.

Sr. No	Planning Component	Example of Sub-component
30	Coordination with service providers	1. Keep regular coordination with the service providers such as expert people, expert institutions, CSR machinery, health department, education department, construction department, malaria department, etc.
		2. These service providers should be honoured in annual function, Teacher's Day, in various manifest programmes.
31	Teacher's Day/ student/school award ceremony	1. In each school at project level, the teachers should be honoured on Teacher's Day.
		2. The students who scored excellent marks, should honoured in this programme.
		3. The school having excellent school management and school having all facilities should be honoured.
32	Survey of ashram school	1. *Ashramshala* is a centre providing education services to the nearby villages.
		2. Hence, an education survey should be done by concerned school in the villages near the school area.
		3. From this survey affectionate relationship with the tribal families of the village will be maintained.
		4. Invite each family to admit their student in ashram school.
		5. Complete the admission strength from 1st to 5th standard.
33	Cleanliness	1. Assure cleanliness in class rooms, residential rooms, kitchen, bathrooms, toilets, premises of ashram school.

Sr. No	Planning Component	Example of Sub-component
		2. For this, take the services of outsourcing.
		3. Clean food grains and vegetables, water used in the kitchen.
34	Maintenance and repairs	1. Fix the machinery for the maintenance and repairs of ashram school building.
		2. Fix the machinery for the maintenance and repairs of all equipment in the ashram school.
		3. Make an annual maintenance contract for maintenance and repairs.
35	Deadstock verification and write off	1. Constitute internal school verification cell, who will verify the dead stock register every year in a definite month.
		2. As per verification, classify the goods as proper for repairs and not proper for repairs.
		3. Make repairs of repairable goods.
		4. Do proper write off of goods which can not be repaired by following write off guidelines and disburse the said goods by adopting proper procedure.
36	Demand/supply/DBT	1. Place demand for funds for necessary items under direct benefit transfer (DBT).
		2. Other than these items, demand for the items like furniture, mattress should be made and get it by making follow up. Take the entry of these items in dead stock register.
		3. These registered items should be provided to students.

Sr. No	Planning Component	Example of Sub-component
		4. Other than this, also, place the demand for library and laboratory items and get them by making regular follow up.
37	Plantation, gardening/kitchen garden/sewage management	1. Develop the nursery in ashram school.
		2. Make the plantation near the security compound wall, surrounding play ground and other proper places.
		3. Place the flowering plants at proper place and maintain them properly.
		4. Develop kitchen garden on the premises.
		5. Use wastewater for gardening purposes.
38	Educational picnic	1. Organize educational picnic once in a year.
		2. Organize visits at developed school, award winning schools of near areas.
		3. The best activities of said school should be implemented in School.
39	Creation of record room	1. In every school, and every year, classify the records.
		2. To keep such classified record, create the record room.
		3. Appoint the record keeper who will maintain the record room.
40	The next developmental/ career guidance after the ashram school	1. Guidance for further education after completion of ashram school education.
		2. Career guidance.
		3. Institutions/colleges providing higher education.
		4. Facilities available for higher education.

Sr. No	Planning Component	Example of Sub-component
		5. The arrangement of accommodation at that place.
41	Topic-wise committees	1. Monitoring syllabus
		2. Teaching-study review
		3. Creation of Education Material
		4. e-Learning
		5. Topic -wise laboratory creation and monitoring
		6. All-round assessment
		7. Innovative activities
		8. Repairs, maintenance (building/machinery)
		9. Fixation of outsourcing
		10. Health and cleanliness
		11. Sports
		12. Arts/culture
		13. Scholarship
		14. Competitive examination/entrance examination
		15. Counseling
		16. Security
		17. Supervision
42	Steering committee	*Committee*
		1. Secondary headmaster–chairman
		2. Assistant project officer (education)-member
		3. Primary headmaster-vice chairman
		4. Concerned extension officer–member
		5. Senior high secondary teacher–member
		6. Senior secondary teacher–teacher
		7. Senior primary teacher–member

Sr. No	Planning Component	Example of Sub-component
		8. Lady superintendent–member
		9. Superintendent (male)–member secretary
		Terms of Reference
		1. Topic-wise review and monitoring
		2. Creation of micro-planning plan
		3. Time-bound implementation programme
		4. Preparation of annual assessment report

Chapter 19

Financing Tribal Education in India

Vetukuri P. S. Raju

INTRODUCTION

The concept of ashram schools is not relatively new to anyone. The term 'ashram school' was conceptualized in the late 1980s and can be defined as 'residential schools which impart education up to the secondary level to children belonging to Scheduled Tribes (STs)'. All the governments since the inception of this concept have taken several concrete steps to ensure that the ashram schools in India work and impart knowledge, wisdom and moral principles to all the deprived children in the society, and primarily the ones belonging to the STs section. This chapter focuses upon the financing of ashram schools in India since 1990–1991 and how successful this concept and scheme has been in uplifting the condition of STs in India and what has been the allocation status of funds so far by the central and state governments in this regard. The chapter intends to discuss the financial allocation and usage of the funds spent so far in developing and operating the various ashram schools in India.

This chapter is based on secondary data collected from different sources such as Government of India reports, Unified District Information System for Education (U-DISE) and commission reports.

SCHEME OF ASHRAM SCHOOLS

This centrally sponsored scheme was started in 1990–1991 to provide central assistance to the states and union territories (UTs) on 50 per cent and 100 per cent basis, respectively. During 1999–2000, funds were released for construction of 36 ashram schools. The primary motive of the government was to extend facilities such as establishment of residential schools for STs in an environment conducive to learning to increase the literacy rates among the tribal students and to bring them at par with other population of the country. The funding for the scheme to the state is done on matching (50:50) basis, while cent percent assistance is given to UTs.

The Standing Committee on Social Justice and Empowerment (Chairperson: Mr Hemanand Biswal) submitted its report on the working of ashram schools in tribal areas on 18 February 2014. Ashram schools are residential schools which impart education up to the secondary level to children belonging to STs. As per the definition and guidelines of the government, only the marginalized section and STs of the country are eligible for availing the benefits of these ashram schools and Mr Hemanand in his report submitted that the status of these schools seems more promising in the current scenario when compared to its sluggish growth in the early 1990s. The financing of these schools is carried under the direct supervision and instructions of Ministry of Human Resource Development (MHRD), Government of India along with a prior approval of the Ministry of Finance, Government of India.

GOVERNMENT'S INTEGRATED ACTION PLAN

While the literacy gap at the national level between STs and other groups has decreased to 14 per cent, there is a significant interstate variation with the literacy gap at 28 per cent in some states. The committee recommended collaborative effort by the Ministry of Tribal Affairs (MOTA), MHRD, state governments and non-governmental organizations to improve the literacy rate of STs.

IMPLEMENTATION OF THE ASHRAM SCHOOLS SCHEME

The MOTA has been implementing a central scheme which aims at establishing ashram schools in Tribal Sub-Plan (TSP) areas since 1990–1991. Under the TSP approach, a sub-plan specifically related to tribal welfare is formulated for areas that have been defined as having a high concentration of tribal population. The committee pointed that there is limited data on ashram schools. It also pointed out that only 862 Ashram Schools have been sanctioned till date. Of the 862 schools sanctioned, 246 have not been constructed as yet. The scheme has not been implemented in all TSP areas. No schools have been established in Tamil Nadu and West Bengal. Rajasthan and Jharkhand have established only nine and two schools respectively. Additionally, there has been significant delay in the construction of these schools.

FUNDING PATTERN AND FINANCING OF ASHRAM SCHOOLS

The scheme provides 100 per cent central financing for the construction of ashram schools for girls and boys in Naxal areas. The committee recommended providing 100 per cent central financing for all ashram schools. The committee expressed disapproval at the reduction of the budgetary allocation for the scheme from ₹75 crore to ₹61 crore at the revised estimate stage in 2012–2013.

ISSUES AND CHALLENGES IN IMPLEMENTATION OF THE SCHEME

The committee pointed out that substandard food is being provided at schools and hostels and schools are currently overcrowded. It recommended fixing norms for sharing of rooms and opening more schools where enrolment exceeds seat availability. The committee pointed out that 793 children died in ashram schools in Maharashtra between 2001–2002 and 2012–2013 as a result of scorpion or snake bites and minor illnesses. It recommended that the ministry should seek information from states regarding this issue and that schools must take steps to prevent the recurrence of these events. The committee recommended that ST youth should be encouraged to take up teaching in ashram schools and special training be provided to non-tribal teachers. A large number of ST children drop out of school, 55 per cent at the elementary level and 71 per cent at the secondary level. This is 22 per cent higher than the national average. The committee recommended developing local language textbooks and teaching children in their local language with a gradual shift to Hindi or English to address this.

FINANCING OF ASHRAM SCHOOLS

Financing, efficient allocation and judicious use of funds are some of the most important concerns and agenda for the government. It is certainly imperative for the government to analyse and study the performance of all the ashram schools in India on national as well as the state levels. The scheme 'setting up of ashram schools in TSP areas' is demand driven and implemented through the state governments/UTs. As per the provisions of the scheme, state governments are eligible for 100 per cent central share for construction of all-girls' ashram schools and also for construction of boys' ashram schools in Naxal affected areas. The funding pattern for the other boys' ashram schools is on 50:50 basis, while cent percent assistance is given to UTs for construction of both girls' and boys' ashram schools. The ashram schools are managed by the state concerned.

It has been proposed by the government to discontinue the scheme from 2018–2019 and subsume the intervention in the scheme 'special central assistance (SCA) to Tribal Sub-Scheme (TSS)'. The proposition has already been recommended by the Expenditure Finance Committee. Amount of funds allocated under the scheme 'setting up of ashram schools in TSP areas' during last five years is given below:

Table 19.1 *Year-wise Allocation of Funds*

Year	Allocation/Release of Funds (in Lakhs)
2013–2014	7,217
2014–2015	4,524
2015–2016	300
2016–2017	–
2017–2018	1,000

Source: http://pib.nic.in/PressReleseDetail.aspx?PRID=1513029

About 155 projects for construction of ashram schools in various states have been completed during the three years and current year period.

Table 19.2 *State-/UT-wise Number of Ashram Schools Supported by MOTA and State Government for Construction*

State/UT	Supported by MOTA	Supported by States/UTs	Total
Andaman & Nicobar Islands	Nil		
Andhra Pradesh	180	136	316
Arunachal Pradesh (non-TSP state/UT)	Not covered under scheme		
Assam	3	0	3
Bihar	Nil		
Chhattisgarh	157	1,058	1,215
Daman and Diu	Nil		
Dadra and Nagar Haveli (non-TSP state/UT)	Not covered		
Goa	1	0	1
Gujarat	164	0	164
Himachal Pradesh	Nil		
Jammu and Kashmir	Nil		
Jharkhand	11	83	94
Karnataka	28	5	33
Kerala	11	0	11
Lakshadweep (non-TSP state/UT)	Not covered		
Madhya Pradesh	405	784	1,189
Maharashtra	95	463	558
Manipur	Nil	5	5
Meghalaya (non-TSP state/UT)	Not covered		

(Table 19.2 Continued)

(Table 19.2 Continued)

State/UT	Supported by MOTA	Supported by States/UTs	Total
Mizoram (non-TSP state/UT)	Not covered		
Nagaland (non-TSP state/UT)	Not covered		
Odisha	97	684	781
Rajasthan	9	10	19
Sikkim	1	0	1
Tamil Nadu	Nil		
Tripura	24	29	53
Uttar Pradesh	7	5	12
Uttarakhand	12	10	22
West Bengal	Nil		
Total	**1,205**	**3,272**	**4,477**

Source: Ashram School State-wise Allocation Report, MOTA, Government of India.

The MOTA has sanctioned 13 ashram schools to be set up in different parts of Chhattisgarh including the pockets affected by the left-wing extremism. The 13 ashram schools sanctioned would accommodate 500 students. The state government officials said the proposal for opening the ashram schools was sent earlier. The ministry had responded to the request made by the Chhattisgarh Government and sanctioned the schools.

The places where the schools would be set up has not been disclosed. Many would come in the red zone. The Chhattisgarh Government has been taking a slew of measures to impart good education to the students in the Naxal–infested pockets so that it could help connecting the area with the mainstream of the society. The state-run Prayas centre had been taking care of children whose parents were killed in the Naxal violence in Bastar. The centre is located in Raipur and more than 100 students had qualified in the engineering and medical entrance examinations. The state government is mooting a plan to extend the branches of the institute in other parts of the state.

From the various discussions, and facts and figures observed so far in the write-up, one can conclude that the financing of ashram schools in India since 1991 has remained satisfactory, though initially sluggish in its development phase. All the states have performed fairly well and the financial grants have been distributed evenly among these states. The analysis of the various reports published by the MOTA, Government of India show that a few states have remained poor in their performance and several issues and concerns have been raised over the time period such as in Maharashtra. On the contrary, a few states have performed considerably well and all the financial grants and resources have been used judiciously in making the ashram schools better and efficient. The central and state governments have played an important role since the early 1990s in ensuring that the concept of ashram schools spreads across all the regions of India and uplifts the marginalized children of the society, primarily the STs. With time, the condition and functioning of ashram schools has improved and these schools have assisted in uplifting numerous children belonging to the STs group. In addition to that, the collaborative efforts of Ministry of Finance, MOTA and MHRD, Government of India have also played a massive role in laying down its foundation.

INTERSTATE ANALYSIS (2012–2013 TO 2016–2017)

Ashram Schools in Different States and UTs

Initially, the number of ashram schools in Andaman and Nicobar Islands stood at three and got reduced to one in the next four consecutive years. The total number of ashram schools for Andhra Pradesh stood at 270 in 2012–2013 and got reduced to 267 in 2016–2017. The total number of ashram schools for Arunachal Pradesh stood at 1,057 in 2012–2013 and got reduced to 577 in 2016–2017. The total number of ashram schools for Assam stood at 38 in 2012–2013 and got reduced to 27 in 2016–2017. The total number of ashram schools for Bihar stood at 319 in 2012–2013 and got increased to 333 in 2016–2017. The total number of ashram schools for Chandigarh stood at 3 in 2012–2013 and got reduced to 1 in 2016–2017. The total number of ashram schools for Chhattisgarh stood at 1,340 in 2012–2013 and got reduced to 1,301 in 2016–2017. The total number of ashram schools for Dadra and Nagar Haveli stood at 2 in 2012–2013 and got reduced to 1 in 2016–2017. The total number of ashram schools for Daman and Diu stood at 2 in 2012–2013 and remained the same till 2016–2017. The total number of ashram schools for Delhi stood at 2 in 2012–2013. The total number of ashram schools for Goa stood at 10 in 2012–2013 and got reduced to 3 in 2016–2017.

The total number of ashram schools for Gujarat stood at 844 in 2012–2013 and got increased to 1,001 in 2016–2017. The total number of ashram schools for Haryana stood at 28 in 2012–2013 and got reduced to 10 in 2016–2017. The total number of ashram schools for Himachal Pradesh stood at 27 in 2012–2013 and got increased to 57 in 2016–2017. The total number of ashram schools for Jammu and Kashmir stood at 21 in 2012–2013 and got increased to 27 in 2016–2017. The total number of ashram schools for Jharkhand stood at 131 in 2012–2013 and got reduced to 83 in 2016–2017. The total number of ashram schools for Karnataka stood at 638 in 2012–2013 and got reduced to 678 in 2016–2017. The total number of ashram schools for Kerala stood at 84 in 2012–2013 and got reduced to 48 in 2016–2017. The total number of ashram schools for Lakshadweep stood constant at 1 between 2012–2013 and 2016–2017. The total number of ashram schools for Madhya Pradesh stood at 2,376 in 2012–2013 and got reduced to 1,893 in 2016–2017. The total number of ashram schools for Maharashtra stood at 972 in 2012–2013 and got reduced to 960 in 2016–2017.

The total number of ashram schools for Manipur stood at 18 in 2012–2013 and got reduced to 13 in 2016–2017. The total number of ashram schools for Meghalaya stood at 45 in 2012–2013 and got reduced to 29 in 2016–2017. The total number of ashram schools for Mizoram stood at 9 in 2012–2013 and got reduced to 6 in 2016–2017. The total number of ashram schools for Nagaland stood at 4 in 2012–2013 and closed at the same figure in 2016–2017. The total number of ashram schools for Orissa stood at 2,121 in 2012–2013 and got increased to 2,402 in 2016–2017. The total number of ashram schools for Puducherry stood at 4 in 2012–2013 and closed at the same level in 2016–2017. The total number of ashram schools for Punjab stood at 16 in 2012–2013 and got increased to 17 in 2016–2017. The total number of ashram schools for Rajasthan stood at 128 in 2012–2013 and got reduced to 843 in 2016–2017. The total number of ashram schools for Sikkim stood at 10 in 2012–2013 and remained constant at 30 in 2016–2017. The total number of ashram schools for Tamil Nadu stood at 342 in 2012–2013 and got reduced to 255 in 2016–2017. The total number of ashram schools for Goa stood at 614 in 2014–2015 and got increased to 883 in 2016–2017. The total number of ashram schools for Tripura stood at 25 in 2012–2013 and got increased to 33 in 2016–2017.

The total number of ashram schools for Uttar Pradesh stood at 2,807 in 2012–2013 and got reduced to 1,887 in 2016–2017. The total number of ashram schools for Uttarakhand stood at 73 in 2012–2013 and got increased to 95 in 2016–2017. The total number of ashram schools for West Bengal stood at 511 in 2012–2013 and got increased to 598 in 2016–2017.

Enrolment in Ashram Schools

This section gives us the total enrolment of students between 2012–2013 and 2016–2017 in different states/UTs. The total enrolment of students in ashram schools for Andaman and Nicobar Islands stood at 780 in 2012–2013 and got reduced to 181 in 2016–2017. The total enrolment of students in ashram schools for Andhra Pradesh stood at 329,746 in 2012–2013 and got reduced to 171,840 in 2016–2017. The total enrolment of students in ashram schools for Arunachal Pradesh stood at 44,608 in 2012–2013 and got reduced to 31,254 in 2016–2017. The total enrolment of students in ashram schools for Assam stood at 9,611 in 2012–2013 and got reduced to 8,156 in 2016–2017. The total enrolment of students in ashram schools for Bihar stood at 133,836 in 2012–2013 and got reduced to 120,182 in 2016–2017. The total enrolment of students in ashram schools for Chandigarh stood at 1,991 in 2012–2013 and got reduced to 493 in 2016–2017. The total enrolment of students in ashram schools for Chhattisgarh stood at 115,020 in 2012–2013 and got increased to 131,575 in 2016–2017. The total enrolment of students in ashram schools for Dadra and Nagar Haveli stood at 820 in 2012–2013 and got reduced to 420 in 2016–2017. The total enrolment of students in ashram schools for Daman and Diu stood at 219 in 2012–2013 and got reduced to 162 in 2016–2017.

The total enrolment of students in ashram schools for Delhi stood at 993 in 2012–2013. The total enrolment of students in ashram schools for Goa stood at 852 in 2012–2013 and got reduced to 667 in 2016–2017.

The total enrolment of students in ashram schools for Gujarat stood at 131,196 in 2012–2013 and got increased to 160,497 in 2016–2017. The total enrolment of students in ashram schools for Himachal Pradesh stood at 7,058 in 2012–2013 and got increased to 9,700 in 2016–2017. The total enrolment of students in ashram schools for Jammu and Kashmir stood at 3,919 in 2012–2013 and got increased to 5,314 in 2016–2017. The total enrolment of students in ashram schools for Jharkhand stood at 25,609 in 2012–2013 and got reduced to 20,095 in 2016–2017. The total enrolment of students in ashram schools for Arunachal Pradesh stood at 44,608 in 2012–2013 and got reduced to 31,254 in 2016–2017. The total enrolment of students in ashram schools for Karnataka stood at 100,061 in 2012–2013 and got increased to 102,176 in 2016–2017. The total enrolment of students in ashram schools for Kerala stood at 25,408 in 2012–2013 and got reduced to 14,186 in 2016–2017. The total enrolment of students in ashram schools for Lakshadweep stood at 189 in 2012–2013 and got reduced to 126 in 2016–2017. The total enrolment of students in ashram schools for Madhya Pradesh stood at 264,346 in 2012–2013 and got reduced to 179,180 in 2016–2017. The total enrolment of students in ashram schools for Maharashtra stood at 288,710 in 2012–2013 and got reduced to 269,336 in 2016–2017.

The total enrolment of students in ashram schools for Manipur stood at 2,770 in 2012–2013 and got reduced to 1,883 in 2016–2017. The total enrolment of students in ashram schools for Meghalaya stood at 5,027 in 2012–2013 and got reduced to 4,710 in 2016–2017.

The total enrolment of students in ashram schools for Mizoram stood at 638 in 2012–2013 and got reduced to 421 in 2016–2017. The total enrolment of students in ashram schools for Nagaland stood at 925 in 2012–2013 and got reduced to 343 in 2016–2017. The total enrolment of students in ashram schools for Odisha stood at 519,348 in 2012–2013 and got increased to 617,239 in 2016–2017. The total enrolment of students in ashram schools for Puducherry stood at 838 in

2012–2013 and got reduced to 783 in 2016–2017. The total enrolment of students in ashram schools for Punjab stood at 5,600 in 2012–2013 and got increased to 9,139 in 2016–2017. The total enrolment of students in ashram schools for Rajasthan stood at 27,252 in 2012–2013 and got increased to 176,620 in 2016–2017. The total enrolment of students in ashram schools for Sikkim stood at 2,169 in 2012–2013 and got increased to 3,219 in 2016–2017. The total enrolment of students in ashram schools for Tamil Nadu stood at 55,156 in 2012–2013 and got reduced to 30,460 in 2016–2017.

The total enrolment of students in ashram schools for Telangana stood at 190,713 in 2012–2013 and got increased to 235,465 in 2016–2017. The total enrolment of students in ashram schools for Tripura stood at 5,060 in 2012–2013 and got increased to 6,397 in 2016–2017. The total enrolment of students in ashram schools for Uttar Pradesh stood at 591,086 in 2012–2013 and got reduced to 412,092 in 2016–2017.

The total enrolment of students in ashram schools for Uttarakhand stood at 9,746 in 2012–2013 and got increased to 14,078 in 2016–2017. The total enrolment of students in ashram schools for West Bengal stood at 212,524 in 2012–2013 and got increased to 287,419 in 2016–2017.

Availability of Teachers in Ashram Schools

This section gives us the total number of teachers present in the ashram schools from the year 2012–2013 to 2016–2017 for all the states. The total number of teachers present in ashram schools of Andaman and Nicobar Islands stood at 48 in 2012–2013 and got reduced to 12 in 2016–2017. The total number of teachers present in ashram schools of Andhra Pradesh stood at 10,423 in 2012–2013 and got reduced to 6,089 in 2016–2017. The total number of teachers present in ashram schools of Arunachal Pradesh stood at 2,065 in 2012–2013 and got reduced to 2,103 in 2016–2017. The total number of teachers present in ashram schools of Assam stood at 503 in 2012–2013 and got reduced to 465 in 2016–2017. The total number of teachers present in ashram schools of Bihar stood at 2014 in 2012–2013 and got increased to 3,199 in

2016–2017. The total number of teachers present in ashram schools of Chandigarh stood at 82 in 2012–2013 and got reduced to 28 in 2016–2017. The total number of teachers present in ashram schools of Chhattisgarh stood at 4,506 in 2012–2013 and got increased to 4,643 in 2016–2017. The total number of teachers present in ashram schools of Dadra and Nagar Haveli stood at 34 in 2012–2013 and got reduced to 23 in 2016–2017. The total number of teachers present in ashram schools of Daman and Diu stood at 9 in 2012–2013 and got increased to 16 in 2016–2017.

The total number of teachers present in ashram schools of Delhi stood at 50 in 2012–2013. The total number of teachers present in ashram schools of Goa stood at 48 in 2012–2013 and got reduced to 36 in 2016–2017.

The total number of teachers present in ashram schools of Gujarat stood at 4,268 in 2012–2013 and got increased to 4,942 in 2016–2017. The total number of teachers present in ashram schools of Haryana stood at 364 in 2012–2013 and got reduced to 159 in 2016–2017. The total number of teachers present in ashram schools of Himachal Pradesh stood at 359 in 2012–2013 and got reduced to 605 in 2016–2017. The total number of teachers present in ashram schools of Jammu and Kashmir stood at 237 in 2012–2013 and got reduced to 391 in 2016–2017. The total number of teachers present in ashram schools of Jharkhand stood at 752 in 2012–2013 and got reduced to 678 in 2016–2017. The total number of teachers present in ashram schools of Karnataka stood at 4,325 in 2012–2013 and got reduced to 4,302 in 2016–2017.

The total number of teachers present in ashram schools of Kerala stood at 1,536 in 2012–2013 and got reduced to 857 in 2016–2017. The total number of teachers present in ashram schools of Lakshadweep stood at 10 in 2012–2013 and got increased to 19 in 2016–2017. The total number of teachers present in ashram schools of Madhya Pradesh stood at 6,724 in 2012–2013 and got reduced to 6,437 in 2016–2017. The total number of teachers present in ashram schools of Maharashtra stood at 8,644 in 2012–2013 and got reduced to 8,452 in 2016–2017.

The total number of teachers present in ashram schools of Manipur stood at 166 in 2012–2013 and got increased to 168 in 2016–2017.

The total number of teachers present in ashram schools of Andhra Pradesh stood at 10,423 in 2012–2013 and got reduced to 6,089 in 2016–2017. The total number of teachers present in ashram schools of Meghalaya stood at 239 in 2012–2013 and got increased to 238 in 2016–2017. The total number of teachers present in ashram schools of Mizoram stood at 64 in 2012–2013 and got reduced to 41 in 2016–2017. The total number of teachers present in ashram schools of Nagaland stood at 74 in 2012–2013 and got reduced to 62 in 2016–2017. The total number of teachers present in ashram schools of Odisha stood at 12,892 in 2012–2013 and got increased to 16,334 in 2016–2017. The total number of teachers present in ashram schools of Puducherry stood at 65 in 2012–2013 and got reduced to 62 in 2016–2017. The total number of teachers present in ashram schools of Punjab stood at 222 in 2012–2013 and got reduced to 419 in 2016–2017. The total number of teachers present in ashram schools of Rajasthan stood at 828 in 2012–2013 and got increased to 7,170 in 2016–2017. The total number of teachers present in ashram schools of Sikkim stood at 110 in 2012–2013 and got reduced to 204 in 2016–2017. The total number of teachers present in ashram schools of Tamil Nadu stood at 2,018 in 2012–2013 and got reduced to 1,321 in 2016–2017.

The total number of teachers present in ashram schools of Telangana stood at 6,494 in 2012–2013 and got increased to 8,604 in 2016–2017. The total number of teachers present in ashram schools of Tripura stood at 298 in 2012–2013 and got increased to 389 in 2016–2017. The total number of teachers present in ashram schools of Uttar Pradesh stood at 8,226 in 2012–2013 and got increased to 8,292 in 2016–2017. The total number of teachers present in ashram schools of Uttarakhand stood at 456 in 2012–2013 and got increased to 759 in 2016–2017. The total number of teachers present in ashram schools of West Bengal stood at 5,599 in 2012–2013 and got increased to 7,907 in 2016–2017.

CONCLUSION

From this comprehensive article covering all aspects relating to the financing of ashram schools in India along with the status of ashram schools in different states/UTs, one can make a valid conclusion that the budget of the government (MOTA) has grown rapidly since the early 1990s and continues to expand in the present scenario as well. The government's budget of ₹1.5 crore of opening ashram schools in Madhya Pradesh has grown rapidly with the latest figures of MOTA and Ministry of Finance giving the figures as ₹97.5 Crores for 398 ashram schools in the country for the year 2016–2017. This certainly shows a positive sign for the upliftment and betterment of the marginalized sections of the society and at the same time gives a positive indication regarding the channelling of funds by both the ministries.

Further Readings

Ananda, G. 2000. *Educating Tribal: Ashram School Approach*. New Delhi: Commonwealth Publishers.

Ball, J. 2010. *Enhancing Learning of Children from Diverse Language Backgrounds: Mother Tongue-based Bilingual or Multilingual Education in Early Childhood and Early Primary School Years*. Victoria: Early Childhood Development Intercultural Partnerships, University of Victoria.

Baxter, P., and S. Jack. 2008. 'Qualitative Case Study Methodology Study Design and Implementation for Novice Researchers'. *The Qualitative Report* 13 (4): 544–549.

Bilthare, D. P. 1954. *Adimjatiyon Ka Sikshan*. Report of the Second Conference for Tribes & Tribal (Scheduled) Areas, 166–176. Lohardaga, 11, 12 and 13 November 1953. Delhi: Bharatiya Adimjati Sevak Sangh.

Biswal, G. C. 1991. *Needs and Problems of Tribal Community in Odisha with Regard to Education: An In-depth Study*. PhD (Edu). Baroda: Case.

Biswas, Parthasarathy. 2014. 'Of 382 Ashram Schools Okayed for Tribal, Only 66 Come Up in 10 Years'. *Indian Express*, 21 May.

Brown, Emma. 2015. 'Washington is Taking Notice of Crumbling Native American Schools'. *Washington Post*, 19 May.

———. 2017. 'US Government Has Dismally Failed to Educate Naïve American Children, Law Suit Alleges'. *Washington Post*, 12 January.

Bureau of Education. 1944. *Post-war Educational Development in India*. Report of the Central Advisory Board of Education. Delhi: Bureau of Education.

Castagna, Angelina. 2014. *Teach for America*. Available at https://www.teachforamerica.org/stories/why-are-native-students-being-left-behind (accessed on 3 April 2020).

Census of India. 1961–2011. *Census 1961 to 2011*. New Delhi: Census of India.

Chopra, R., and P. Jeffery, eds. 2005. *Educational Regimes in Contemporary India*. New Delhi: SAGE Publications.

Department of School Education and Literacy Development. 2018 *Annual Report*, 2017–18, Government of Jharkhand: Ranchi

Department of Welfare. 2018. *Annual Report, 2017–18*. Government of Jharkhand: Ranchi.

Desai, B., and A. Patel. 1981. *Ashram Schools of Gujrat: An Evaluative Study*. Ahmedabad: Tribal Research and Training Centre, Gujrat Vidyapeeth.

Desai, I. P. 1953. *High School Students in Poona*. Pune: Poona Deccan College.

Dewey, J. 1959. *School and Society*. Ruiru: Phoenix Publishers.

District Information System in Education. New Delhi: National Institute of Educational Planning and Administration.

Durkheim, E. 1959. *Education and Sociology*. New York, NY: Free Press at Glencoe.

General, R. 2001. *Census of India 2001*. New Delhi: Ministry of Home Affairs, Government of India.

Government of India. 1961. *Report of the Scheduled Areas and Scheduled Tribes Commission*. Vol. I 1960–61. Delhi: Government of India.

Government of Kerala. 2016. *Tribes*. Available at https://www.wayanadu.com/pages/tribes-in-wayanadu (accessed on 3 April 2020).

Government of Maharashtra. 2010. *Guidelines for Eklavya Model Schools*. Maharashtra: Tribal Development Department.

———. 2010. *Guidelines for Navodaya Vidyalaya*. Maharashtra: School Education Department.

———. 2012–2013. *Guidelines for Kasturba Gandhi Balika Vidyalaya (Margdarshak Suchana)* 201–13,

Sarva Shiksha Abhiyan. Maharashtra: Government of Maharashtra.

Government of Odisha. 1994. *Tribal Education in Orissa in the Context of Education for All by 2000AD—A Status Paper*. Odisha: Tribal Welfare Department.

———. 2004. *Odisha Human Development Report*. Bhubaneswar: NCDS.

———. 2014. *School and Hostel Management Guidelines*. Odisha: Tribal Welfare Department.

Hasnain, N. 2004. *Indian Society and Culture: Continuity and Change*. New Delhi: Jawahar Publishers & Distributors.

Heredia, Rudolf C. 1995. 'Tribal Education for Development: Need for a Liberative Pedagogy for Social Transformation'. *Economic & Political Weekly* 30 (16): 891.

Johari, Aarefa. 2016. *By Introducing Bilingual Education, Maharashtra Hopes to Keep Adivasi Children in School*. Available at https://scroll.in/article/819962/by-introducing-bilingual-education-maharashtra-hopes-to-keep-adivasi-children-in-school (accessed on 3 April 2020).

Jojo, B. 2011. 'Government Ashram Schools for Tribals: An Outcome Budget'. *Indian Journal of Social Work* 72 (4): 605–616.

Koilash. 1993. *Tribal Education and Occupation*. New Delhi: Kanak Publications.

Mackenzie, P. J., and Jo Walker. 2013. *Mother-Tongue Education: Policy Lessons for Quality and Inclusion*. Policy brief. Johannesburg: Global Campaign for Education. Available at http://www.campaignforeducation.org/docs/reports/GCE%20Mother%20Tongue_EN.pdf (accessed on 3 April 2020).

Mannheim, K. 2001. 'An Introduction to Sociology'. In *Sociology as Political Education*, edited and translated by D. Kettler and C. Loader, 1–78. New Brunswick, NJ: Transaction Publishers.

MHRD. 1992. *National Policy on Education 1986, Plan of Action, 1992*. New Delhi: Government of India.

———. 2007. *Sarva Shiksha Abhiyan—Tribal Development Plan*. New Delhi: Government of India.

MHRD. 2009. *The Right of Children to Free and Compulsory Education Act, (RTE) 2009*. New Delhi: Government of India.

———. 2012. *Recommendations on the Guidelines for Implementation of Programmes and Schemes under Scheduled Castes Sub Plan (SCSP) and Tribal Sub Plan (TSP) in the Ministry of Human Resource Development*. New Delhi: Government of India.

Mishra, B. B. 1996. *Education of Tribal Children*. New Delhi: Discovery Publishing House.

Ministry of Tribal Affairs. 1974. *Tribal Sub-plan*. New Delhi: Government of India.

National Commission for Protection of Child Rights. 2013. *A Report on the Status and Functioning of Ashram Shalas, State of Chhattisgarh, District Kanker*, 5. New Delhi: National Commission for Protection of Child Rights.

National Council of Educational Research and Training. 1970. *Education and National Development: Report of the Education Commission 1964–66*, 245–246. New Delhi: NCERT.

———. 1978. *Fourth All India School Education Survey*. New Delhi: NCERT.

Nettle, D., and S. Romaine. 2000. *Vanishing Voices: The Extinction of the World's Languages*. Oxford: Oxford University Press.

Norwich, B. 2002. 'Education, Inclusion and Individual Differences: Recognising and Resolving Dilemmas'. *British Journal of Educational Studies* 50 (4): 482–502.

Ota, A. B., and R. P. Mohanty. 2009. *Education of the Tribal Girl Child: Problems and Prospects*. Bhubaneswar: Scheduled Castes & Scheduled Tribes Research and Training Institute.

Padma, Velaskar. 2005. 'Educational Stratification, Dominant Ideology and the Reproduction of Disadvantage in India'. In *Understanding Indian Society: The Non- Brahaminic Perspective*, edited by S. M. Dahiwale. Jaipur: Rawat Publication.

Panda, S.C. 1983. 'An Empirical Study of Education of Tribal in Orissa'. In *Fourth Survey of Research in Education*. Vol. II, 1983–88, edited by M. B. Buch, 1448. New Delhi: NCERT.

———. 1998. *An Empirical Study of Education of Tribal*. New Delhi: Radha Publications.

Parsons, T., and A. H. Halsey. 1959. 'The School Class as a Social System'. *Schools and Society: A Sociological Approach to Education*: 32–40.

Parth, M. N. 2017a. 'Tribal Schools of Maharashtra: Students Live and Study in Abysmal Conditions. *Firstpost*, 22 January. Available at https://www.firstpost.com/india/tribal-schools-of-maharashtra-students-live-and-study-in-abysmal-conditions-3213706.html (accessed on 3 April 2020).

———. 2017b. Tribal Schools in Maharashtra Part 3: Abysmal Security, Sexual Assault Cases Remain an Alarming Concern. Available at https://www.firstpost.com/india/tribal-schools-of-maharashtra-part-3-abysmal-security-sexual-assault-cases-remain-an-alarming-concern-3209148.html (accessed on 3 April 2020).

Patel, S. 1991. *Tribal Education in India: A Case Study of Orissa*. New Delhi: Mittal Publications.

Pati, S., and S. Panda. 2010. 'Regional Disparities, Inclusive Growth and Displacement in Odisha'. *Mainstream* 48 (6).

Planning Commission. 1969–2017. 4th, 7th, 12th Five-Year Plan Documents. New Delhi: Planning Commission.

Pradhan, P., and J. Pattanaik. 2012. 'Challenges in Education of Schedules Caste and Scheduled Tribe Children; Case Study of Ashram School'. *The Raveshaw Journal of Educational Studies*: 23–32.

Pratap, D. R., and C. C. Raju. 1973. *Study of Aided Elementary Schools of Srikakulam, Visakhapatnam, East Godavari and West Godavari Districts of A. P.* Hyderabad: Tribal Cultural Research and Training Institute.

Rani, Midatala. 2000. 'Tribal Languages and Tribal Education'. *Social Action* 50: 414–419. Available at http://el.doccentre.info/eldoc/n00_/01oct00SOA7.pdf (accessed on 3 April 2020).

Roy Burman, B. K. 1986. 'Tribal Development: Meaning and Scope'. In *Tribal Development in India (Problems and Prospects)*, edited by B. Choudhry. New Delhi: Inter-India Publication.

Salunke, S. 2016. *In Search of Hope: Report of Technical Committee for Prevention of Deaths of Students in Ashram Schools*. Maharashtra: Tribal Development Department.

Saraswathy, H. 2016. 'Impact of Residential School and Current Challenging Issues of Tribal Education in Odisha'. *Scholarly Research Journal for Humanities Science and English Language* 3 (15): 3573–3581.

Sarda, Meenal, Rekha Sharma Sen, Shailaja Menon, Suman Sachdeva, Sunita Singh, and Venita Kaul. 2016. *Early Language and Literacy in India: A Position Paper*. New Delhi: U.S. Agency for International Development (USAID) and CARE India.

Sharma, R. C. 1984. *Effect of Incentive Schemes on Scheduled Castes and Scheduled Tribes Girls*. Rajasthan: SIERT.

Sharma, Sugan. 1996. *Education Opportunities and Tribal Children*. Udaipur: Shiva Publishers and Distributors.

Shukla, S., and Krishna Kumar. 1985. *Sociological Perspective in Education: A Reader*. New Delhi: Chanakya Publications.

Singh, S., and S. Saxena. 1987. 'Achievement Difference and School Effects'. *Indian Tribal Educational Review* 30 (1): 20–24.

ST & SC Development, Minorities & Backward Classes Welfare Department, Government of Odisha. 2017–2018. *Annual Report, 2017–18*. Odisha: ST & SC Development, Minorities & Backward Classes Welfare Department, Government of Odisha.

Sujata, K. 1993. *Education in Ashram Schools: A Case Study of Adilabad District*. New Delhi: NIEPA.

———. 1999. *Education of India Scheduled Tribes: A Study of Community Schools in the Districts of Vishakhapatnam, Andhra Pradesh*. Paris: International Institute for Educational Planning, UNESCO.

Suresh, P. R. 2013. *Social Structural Determinants of Education among Tribal in India*, 78–80. Thesis submitted to the Cochin University of Science and Technology. Kochi: Department of Applied Economics, Cochin University of Science and Technology.

Tata Institute of Social Sciences. 2015. *Status of Government and Aided Ashram Schools in Maharashtra*. Mumbai: TISS.

Tellis, W. 1997. *Introduction to Case Study*. The Qualitative Report. Fort Lauderdale, FL: NSUWorks.

Tilak, J. B. G. 1992. 'Education, Health, Nutrition and Demographic Changes: A Review of Evidence'. *Indian Journal of Labour Economics* 25 (2): 113–122.

Times of India. 'Maharashtra Government Says No Funds to Compensate for Ashram School Deaths, Draws HC Ire'. *Times of India*, 13 January.

Tribal Development Department. 2017. *Report on Deaths in Ashram Schools*. Maharashtra: Tribal Development Department.

———. 2018. *Annual Report, 2017–18*. Gujarat: Tribal Development Department.

UNESCO. 2009. *Overcoming Inequality: Why Governance Matters Education for All*. Paris: UNESCO.

———. 2016. Global Education Monitoring Report. Paris: UNESCO.

UNICEF. 2016. *Status of Education in Tribal Areas of Maharashtra*. New York, NY: UNICEF.

———. 2017. *Input Note Based on Secondary Review of Literature for Revision of Ashram School Codebook*. Mumbai: UNICEF.

Velaskar, Padma. 1998. 'Ideology, Education and the Political Struggle for Liberation: Change and Challenge among the Dalits of Maharashtra'. In *Education, Development and Underdevelopment*, edited by Sureshchandra Shukla and Rekha Kaul, 210–240. New Delhi: SAGE Publications.

Von Fürer-Haimendorf, C., and F. H. C. Von. 1982. *Tribes of India: The Struggle for Survival*. Oakland, CA: University of California.

WEBSITES

http://aptwgurukulam.ap.gov.in/ (accessed on 18 November 2018).
http://pib.nic.in/PressReleseDetail.aspx?PRID=1513029 (accessed on 3 April 2020).
http://suprativa.org/jp.htm (accessed on 18 November 2018).
http://www.tgtwgurukulam.telangana.gov.in/ (accessed on 18 November 2018).

About the Editor and Contributors

EDITOR

R. R. Patil is presently a Professor in the Department of Social Work, Jamia Millia Islamia; a central university, New Delhi. He has been teaching graduate, postgraduate and doctoral students since October 2000 and has completed 19 years in the university. Apart from teaching, he has been continuously involved in research and publications. So far, he has 2 major research projects and more than 25 publications (national and international) including research articles, policy papers and books to his credit. He has authored/edited two books, namely *Dalit Christians in India* and *Empowering Dalits: Non-Governmental Organizations in Western India*. He has been regularly presenting papers and delivering lectures in national and international seminars and conferences. Recently, he has submitted a research project titled 'Mapping of Residential Schools in Tribal Areas', sponsored by ICSSR, New Delhi, in 2017.

Apart from academic contributions, Professor Patil has been serving universities in different administrative capacities. He has served as the head of the Department of Social Work and dean of the School of Social Sciences, Central University of Rajasthan, in the year 2012–2014. His research interest areas include development studies, marginalization, social exclusion and civil society, and all his research and publications contribute towards enriching literature and documentation of the above research areas. Apart from this, he has been organizing seminars, conferences and workshops on different themes in the above areas.

CONTRIBUTORS

Pradyumna Bag is an Assistant Professor in the Department of Sociology, JMI, New Delhi. His areas of expertise are rural and agrarian society, caste, tribe and gender, and social inequality and social exclusion. Some of his publications in journals include 'Myth and Reality of Sustainable Development: View from a Village'; 'Bartan System: Socio-legal Dimensions of Unclean Occupation in Odisha'; 'Ambedkar's Quest for Social and Economic Democracy'; 'Culinary Diversity and Food Security: Exploring Diverse Dimensions of Food Security'; and 'Denial of Dignity: Work, Identity and Impurity'.

Dhaneswar Bhoi holds a PhD degree from the Centre for Social Justice and Governance, School of Social Sciences, Tata Institute of Social Sciences, Mumbai. Currently, he is pursuing his post doctorate from National Institute of Educational Planning and Administration (NIEPA), New Delhi and is consultant to the Department of Higher Education, Ministry of Human Resource Development (MHRD), New Delhi. He has published 15 articles in different journals and edited books and presented 20 papers in different national and international seminars within the country. He is also an associate editor and reviewer for different national and international journals.

Muhammed Shafi C. T. is a Research Scholar/UGC-JRF-NET Fellow in the Department of Social Work, (JMI), New Delhi. He completed his graduation in economics and master's in Sociology from IGNOU, New Delhi. Presently, he is pursuing PhD on the title 'Alternative Schooling for Tribal Children: Case Study of Tamil Nadu and Karnataka'. His areas of research are tribal studies, development and Islamic microfinance.

Saumya Deol is a Research Scholar/UGC-JRF Fellow at the Department of Social Work, JMI, New Delhi. She received her master's in social work with specialization in social development from the same institution. She is also a graduate in economics (honours) from the University of Delhi. She is currently pursuing her MPhil on homelessness in Delhi. Her areas of research work include homelessness, social and educational development of Scheduled Tribes and community-based care for the elderly.

Alkha Dileep is an Assistant Professor in the Department of Social Work at Wayanad Muslim Orphanage Arts and Science College, affiliated to University of Calicut, Wayanad, Kerala. She is specialized in medical and psychiatric social work. She is presently researching on life skill and tribal mental health.

Gomati Bodra Hembrom is an Associate Professor at the Department of Sociology, JMI. She has been teaching in the department since 2005. She has completed her MA, MPhil and PhD degrees in sociology from the Centre for Study of Social Systems, Jawaharlal Nehru University (JNU), New Delhi. Her area of specialization and research interests include gender studies, tribal studies, social stratification, research methodology, media studies, ecology and society. She has published in many journals and edited volumes. She has also presented papers in many national and international conferences and seminars.

Prakash Chandra Jena works as an Associate Professor and Head of Department, School of Education, K. R. Mangalam University, Delhi-NCR. He is the recipient of Best Researcher Award by Division of Research and Development (DRD), Lovely Professional University, Punjab, and also Adarsh Vidya Saraswati Rashtriya Puraskar, in 2017, by Global Management Council, Ahmedabad. He is the author of 5 books and has published 34 chapters in edited books.

Bipin Jojo is a Professor at the Centre for Social Justice and Governance, TISS, Mumbai. He also holds a PhD from TISS. He has been involved in teaching, research and training in the areas of tribal issues—governance, land, forest, education and social work with tribal perspective. He has written several academic articles and reports for government and non-government organizations in these areas. He has also been associated with several academic and development organizations nationally and internationally.

Noorjahan Kannanjeri is an Assistant Professor and Head of the Department of Social Work at Wayanad Muslim Orphanage Arts and Science College, affiliated to University of Calicut, Wayanad, Kerala. After completing MPhil in psychiatric social work from Central Institute of Psychiatry (CIP), Ranchi, she has been working in child and adolescent's mental health. Her other focus areas are skill development of children and adolescents in tribal community as well as in institutions. She is pursuing her PhD from TISS.

Saurabh Katiyar is an Indian Administrative Service (IAS) officer of 2016 batch. He completed BTech and MTech in electrical engineering from IIT Kanpur. He is currently posted as a Sub-Divisional Magistrate SDM and Project Officer in the Tribal Development Department, Government of Maharashtra at Palghar district of Maharashtra.

Naresh Kumar is working as an Assistant Professor in the Department of Educational Policy at NIEPA, New Delhi. He completed doctorate and postdoctorate from JNU in the discipline of sociology. He specializes and contributed research papers in the areas of educational policy, political economy of education and occupational mobility of the marginalized communities.

R. Vasundhara Mohan is presently a Programme Director at the Institute of Indian Culture, Mumbai. She holds a PhD degree in political science from Rajasthan University, Jaipur and advance diploma in Russian language. She was an Associate Professor and Director of Centre of Eurasian Studies, University of Mumbai. She has 8 books to her credit and published over 50 research papers in the national and international journals of repute.

Bibekananda Nayak is working as an Assistant Professor cum Assistant Director in the Centre for the Study of Social Exclusion Inclusive Policy, Babasaheb Bhimrao Ambedkar University, Lucknow, Uttar Pradesh. He obtained MA, MPhil, PhD degrees from the Centre for the Study of Social Systems, JNU. He has more than 12 years of teaching and research experience. He has completed more than five research projects sponsored by different organizations. He has contributed many research papers and book chapters on social exclusion of Dalits and tribals, rural development, public policy and environmental health.

D. K. Panmand holds BA in economics and a master's degree in social work. He has retired as a Joint Commissioner, Tribal Development Department, Government of Maharashtra. During a long period of administrative career with the department, he served as an Assistant Project Officer, Child Development Project Officer, Chief Officer Children-Aid Society, District Women and Child Development

Officer, Assistant Commissioner, Deputy Commissioner, Deputy Director Central Vigilance Commission, Nashik district, Government of Maharashtra.

Vetukuri P. S. Raju is an Assistant Professor at the Department of Educational Finance, NIEPA. He holds a PhD degree in education. He has published a book and a number of research papers on equity issues in elementary education, centrally sponsored scholarships/incentive schemes, vocational skills, development of education in Sri Lanka, teacher management, information and communications technology (ICT) and ethics in educational administration, etc. He has also conducted several research and evaluation studies for the Department of School Education and Literacy and the Department of Higher Education, MHRD, Government of India.

Chipemmi Awung Shang is a PhD scholar at the Department of Social Work, JMI. He holds a master's degree in social work from Dibrugarh University, Assam. He has also worked with a non-governmental organization for few years. Currently, he is pursuing PhD in social work on the topic titled 'Dropout in Secondary Education: A Study of Scheduled Tribes in Selected Districts of Manipur'.

Sonal Shivagunde holds a PhD degree in tribal education and master's degree in social work. She has been engaged by state and central governments, World Bank, Asian Development Bank (ADB), Department for International Development (DFID), UNICEF, United Nations Development Programme (UNDP), etc. for state and pan-India project management, research, developing strategy and vision documents, designing and providing technical support on school transformation programmes and advisory. She has a book on tribal education and has published several papers on tribal education. Currently, she is working with Tribal Development Department, Government of Maharashtra, for reforms in tribal education.

Mrityunjay K. Singh is working as an Assistant Professor in the Department of Social Work, Assam University, Silchar, Assam. He holds PhD in social work from the Department of Social Work, JMI. He was an editor of *Social Work Journal* (biannual journal), Assam

University. He writes on issues of social development, globalization, governance, rural development rights and livelihoods, public policy and social research.

Buveneswari Suriyan is an IAS officer of 2015 batch. She is BE in computer science and engineering. In IAS, she worked as an Assistant Secretary in Ministry of Petroleum and Natural Gas, Government of India, for three months. She also worked as an SDM and Project Officer for Integrated Tribal Development Project in Pandharkawada, Yavatmal district, Maharashtra. At present, she is posted as a Chief Executive Officer, Zila Parishad in Nashik, Maharashtra.

Rajashri Tikhe holds a master's degree in social work from TISS. At present, she is a consultant to United Nations Children's Fund (UNICEF) as well as Tribal Research and Training Institute, Pune, to design advocacy and policy framing for the education of children from tribal, rural and seasonal migrant communities. She regularly writes on education of tribal children in magazines and newspapers. Her article titled 'Strokes Unfolding Unexplored World: Drawing an Instrument to Know the World of Adivasi Children' was published in *Indigenous Knowledge* (June 2017).

S. N. Tripathy is a retired professor from Gokhale Institute of Politics and Economics, Pune, Maharashtra. He holds LLB, PhD and DLitt. degrees in economics from Berhampur University, Odisha. He has authored, co-authored and edited 55 books, comprehensively on rural and tribal development and labour problems, and published 200 research papers. He has also served as a Professor of Economics at Mahatma Gandhi Labour Institute (MGLI), Ahmedabad, Gujarat.

Index